MW00339065

THE INTERNATIONAL
WARMBLOOD
HORSE

THE INTERNATIONAL
WARMBLOOD
HORSE

A Worldwide Guide to Breeding and Bloodlines

DEBBIE WALLIN, JANE KIDD & CELIA CLARKE

SECOND EDITION

KENILWORTH PRESS

Published in Great Britain by
The Kenilworth Press Ltd
Addington
Buckingham
MK18 2JR

© Debbie Wallin, Jane Kidd and Celia Clarke 1991 and 1995

First published 1991
Reprinted 1992
Second edition 1995

British Library Cataloguing in Publication Data
A CIP record for this book is available from the British Library

ISBN 1-872082-71-8

Typeset in 11/12.5 Goudy by The Kenilworth Press Ltd
Printed and bound in Great Britain by
WBC Book Manufacturers, Bridgend

Contents

Foreword
by
Dr HANFRIED HARING

Managing Director of the Breeding
Department of the German Equestrian Federation, and Managing
Director of the German Olympic Committee

IN THE LAST DECADE the Warmblood horse has triumphed around the world as a sport horse. It has ousted other breeds which were the traditional winners in the three Olympic equestrian disciplines. The reason is a breeding policy focused on performance in these disciplines and taking into account temperament and character. With approximately 120,000 broodmares in the European Community there is a large base for Warmblood breeding.

Especially in recent years there has been a growth in the exchange of breeding animals between the individual breeding areas, but despite this the breeding areas have not lost their independence. On the contrary, it has been established that breeding areas could increase their importance if they were able to adjust their breeding programme to the requirements of equestrian sport. The combination of the traditionally acquired knowledge with the modern findings of science has been crowned with success.

As we are on the threshold of the realisation of the European market, it is of particular importance that the Commission of the European Community clearly defines horse breeding as a branch of agriculture. With a ban on trade barriers the exchange of breeding horses will be encouraged and unlimited regional use of horses in sport will be guaranteed. The competition this generates will once again lead to an increase in performance, as long as the breeding areas orientate their breeding programmes even more towards the findings of modern science, and the obligation to harmonise programmes does not level the quality towards the inferior.

Faced with these new conditions, this book about Warmblood breeding in the world, divided according to individual breeding areas, must be appreciated. The prevailing bloodlines are explained in detail. Compiled with special care the facts are effectively completed by a historical description of the development of horse utilisation, whose viewpoint differs agreeably from previous publications.

Abbreviations and Conventions

ABBREVIATIONS

The following abbreviations, which are in fairly common usage in Warmblood breeding, are used throughout this book:

AHSA	American Horse Shows Association
AI	Artificial insemination
AQPS	Autre Que Pure-sang (French x TB)
ATA	American Trakehner Association
Aust	Australian Warmblood
AWHA	Australian Warmblood Horse Association
AWSHA	Australian Warmblood Sport Horse Association
Bav	Bavarian Warmblood
BLUP	Best linear unbiased predictor
BWB	British Warmblood
BWBS	British Warm-Blood Society
BSH	British Sports Horse
BSHR	British Sports Horse Register
DH	Danish Head Stud Book
DLG	Deutsche Landwirtschafts-Gesellschaft (German Ministry of Agriculture)
DS	Danish Main Stud Book
DSA	Dansk Sport Heste Avlsforbund (Danish Sports-horse Breed Society)
DV	Danish Warmblood
FN	Deutsche Reiterliche Vereinigung eV (FN) (German National Equestrian Federation)
FT	French Trotter
Gldt	Gelderlander
Gron	Groningen
Hesse	Hessen Warmblood

Hann	Hannoverian
HIS	National Light Horse Breeding Society (HIS)
Hg	Hungarian
Holst	Holstein
HPH	British High Performance Horse Sales
ID	Irish Draught
Jg	Yugoslavian Warmblood
KWPN	Koninklijke Vereinigung Warmbloed Paardenstamboek in Nederland
Mlpk	Malopolski Polish Warmblood
NFWP	Belgian Warmblood
NTR	Weatherbys' Non-Thoroughbred Register
NWP	North Netherlands Warmblood Stud Book
NXX	NTR graded into BWBS Stud Book
NZ	New Zealand Warmblood
Old	Oldenburg
Ostpr	East Prussian
OX	Arab graded into a Warmblood stud book
PB	Privately owned stallions in most German breeding districts
PSI	Performance Horse International Sales
Rhld	Rheinland
Rhpfs	Rheinland-Pfalz-Saar Warmblood
S	Stud book mare
SF	Selle Français
SIRE	Système d'Identification Reportoriant les Equidés
StPr	State premium award
SV	Swedish Warmblood
TB	Thoroughbred
Trak	Trakehner
TBF	Trakehner Breeders' Fraternity of Great Britain
U	Ungraded Warmblood
Ukr	Ukrainian Riding Horse
Unreg	Unregistered Warmblood
USET	United States Equestrian Team
Westf	Westphalian
Wlkp	Wielkopolski Polish Warmblood
WPN	Dutch Warmblood
Wurt	Baden-Württemburg
X	Anglo-Arab graded into a Warmblood stud book
x	Cross- or part-bred
XX	Thoroughbred

CONVENTIONS

Because of the large number of different breeds, sources, organisations and breeding districts discussed in this book, the information on individual horses cannot always be supplied in a standardised format. However, insofar as possible the following conventions have been used throughout, regardless of the breed or geographic origin of the horse being discussed. We hope that this will help readers to be able not only to compare and contrast the different approaches used by the various breeding areas, but also to recognise the overall similarities and related bloodlines.

BLOODLINES

In most chapters sire lines only are cited. In other words, if an animal is described as: Drabant (Kokard/Pergamon), this means that Drabant was by Kokard, and out of a mare by Pergamon. However, in the chapters on the Trakehner, France, and the Dutch Warmblood, the name of the dam is usually given in the form: Drabant, by Kokard out of Tomona by Pergamon.

In addition, significant members of important bloodlines are emphasised in bold in the relevant section of each chapter.

BREED ABBREVIATIONS

In each chapter the breed of those horses imported into the breeding district or stud books concerned is indicated using the standard breed abbreviation (see above). Those horses who are not identified in this way at some point in the chapter invariably originate in the breeding district or stud books being discussed. All horses cited in the index are accompanied by the appropriate breed abbreviation.

DATES

Where possible the date of birth of every animal is given; for example: Drabant (1946).

SPELLING

Although we have tried to standardise spelling as far as possible, there may be some inconsistencies from breeding district to breeding district, for example in the use of 'oe' and 'ö' etc., particularly when stud books have been computerised and the 'ö' use has become impractical.

Introduction

by
JANE KIDD

WARMBLOODS HAVE BEEN IMPORTANT for many years in Continental Europe but have only been used in any numbers by the English-speaking nations during the last twenty years. They have enjoyed a meteoric rise in popularity, and today nearly every top American, Canadian and British show jumper and dressage rider can be seen mounted on a Warmblood. Over the last decade the Olympic and World titles in jumping, dressage and driving have fallen to Warmbloods. It is only in eventing that the Thoroughbred or three-quarter cross-bred has held its own, and even in this sphere the increasing use of Thoroughbred in Warmblood breeding has led to better and better performances. The 1992 Olympic Champion Kibah-Tic-Toc was a Warmblood, most of the German gold medal three-day event team in Seoul were Warmbloods, the 1980 Alternative Olympic champion Monaco was a Warmblood, and so was Oran, the 1981 European event champion.

In all important equestrian orientated countries the Warmblood is one if not *the* fastest-growing group of horses, but there still is plenty of confusion as to what is a Warmblood.

The only uncontested definition is that the Warmblood is neither a hot blood (Arabs and Thoroughbreds) nor a cold blood (heavy horses). These curious terms do not refer to body temperatures but to temperament. The origins appear to be German, whose term *Kaltblut* confusingly translates directly as cold blood, when it really means phlegmatic. *Warmblut* means a manageable temperament, which is what is needed for a general riding and driving horse that is neither intended for racing nor agricultural or industrial work.

There has been a certain amount of discussion as to whether the Cleveland Bay and Irish Draught should be included as

10

Warmbloods, but for the purposes of this book we shall accept that the distinguishing feature of Warmbloods is that they are specifically bred by selective methods to produce an athletic, sound horse with a good temperament; the breeding stock used is registered, has pedigrees and is graded to ensure that it is likely to improve the quality of the next generation of Warmbloods.

The breeders' aim is to produce the best possible riding horse for their area or country, and to this end they have used restricted numbers of specially selected Thoroughbreds, Arabs, Anglo-Arabs and Warmbloods from outside their area if they thought these would inject beneficial qualities into the stock. The Warmblood has never been a pure bred – it has always been defined by area, e.g. Swedish, Dutch, Holstein, Westphalian, etc. – and a foal is usually registered where it is born. The Dressage World Cup-winning stallion Gauguin de Lully is by and out of Swedish Warmbloods but was born in Switzerland, and is claimed as both a Swedish and a Swiss Warmblood.

This means that the Warmblood is more correctly referred to as a breed population rather than a breed, and today the Trakehner is the closest any Warmblood can get to being called a pure bred. Prior to the end of the last war they were defined by area, but they were forced to evacuate their breeding grounds around the Trakehnen stud, which is now in Russia but was originally in East Prussia, at the end of the war. The administrators could not define registration by area, and therefore restricted stock to Trakehners and the occasional specially selected Thoroughbred or Arab, but not other Warmbloods.

Although some English-speaking countries are running their own Continental-style breeding organisations, like the American Trakehners Association and the British Hannoverians, apart from the exceptional case of the Trakehner, the Warmblood is by definition a regional breed population, not a pure bred, and the important aim is to produce the best possible performance horse. A Warmblood is not directly comparable with pure-breds like Britain's mountain and moorland breeds, or America's Morgan, horses that are bred to conform to a breed definition.

With the various Warmblood societies being very competitive to produce the best possible performance horse, they have been quick to use outside blood whenever this would help them achieve their objectives. This has led to an extraordinary degree of internationalisation in Warmblood breeding. Breed administrators eager to improve their country's or area's Warmblood buy in Warmblood stallions and sometimes mares with fashionable blood. The result is that the influence of the 'great' Warmblood sires has not been confined to their native area; their names are found in the pedigrees of Warmbloods around the world.

The following gives an indication of some of the most famous sires. France can boast of some of the best, and foremost amongst them is the Selle Français stallion Almé by Ibrahim who in the 1970s and 1980s stood in three different countries – The Netherlands, Belgium and France, and has sons in many more, including Denmark, Sweden, Germany and the USA. The other important French sire is Furioso XX, a Thoroughbred whose sons included Furioso II, who stood in Germany producing more than fifty-five graded sons, his full brother Mexico, who sired the great Dutch stallion Le Mexico, and Futuro who helped produce top-class Oldenburgs.

German Warmbloods, particularly the Hannoverian, Holstein and Trakehner, have been instrumental in helping to establish the newer Warmbloods – Danish, Dutch, Belgium, Swiss and British strengthening such established ones as the Swedish, and upgrading their own country's other regional breeds like the Westphalian, Bavarian, etc.

Tke Trakehner, along with the Thoroughbred and Anglo-Arab, has been used to refine breeds all over the world. The most famous Trakehner sires certainly include Donauwind by Pregel, who left licensed sons like Dolomit in Denmark before going to America and producing the great World Cup show-jumping winner Abdullah. Another is Abglanz by Termit, who was graded into the Hannoverian stud book; and his famous son Absatz, who produced one of Denmark's best sires, Allegro, and high-class Westphalians as well as the top Hannoverian stallion Argentan and show-jumping World Cup winner Aramis. In Holland, Marco Polo was imported as a Trakehner, although he was by the Thoroughbred Poet XX, and he had a big influence. Amor was even more important to the development of the Dutch Warmblood and is yet another example of plenty of mixing, being by the Trakehner Herscherr, but registered as a Holstein as he was born in Schleswig-Holstein but was then exported to Holland to become one of the patriarchs of the Dutch Warmblood.

An influential Westphalian is Roemer by Pilatus, and he, like so many, did not stay where he was born but was exported to become the top producer of dressage horses in Holland before going to the USA.

Hannoverians have had more influence on Warmbloods than any breed other than the Thoroughbred. It is only the Dutch and the French who have not used them extensively. The top sires must include the best of the D-line, Duellant by Dolman, who is in the pedigree of so many leading horses; Goldfisch, an originator of the G-line with such relations as Gotthard, Grande and Garibaldi; Wendekreis by Ferdinand, with such popular sons as Wagner and Werther; Wöhler by Flügeladjutant has representatives around the world and is not far back in the pedigree of today's top Hannoverian stallion Weltmeyer by World Cup I. Bolero by the Thoroughbred Black Sky XX is another with sons in many countries, and a Bolero broodmare won the first European Breed Championships in 1990 and another of his daughters was third.

The Holstein stallions have been important in the development of the Dutch and Danish Warmbloods. Their best known Thoroughbred, Ladykiller XX by Sailing Light, is the sire of Landgraf, Locarno (in Denmark), Laredo (in the USA), Lord who sired the great Livius, and Ladalco, an international eventer who sired British graded stallion Lenard. Ramzes, the Anglo-Arab from Poland, was used to breed Holsteins and has such top stallion sons as Rigoletto (in Holland), Roland and Raimond, sire of the highly international Ramiro who is a graded Holstein, Westphalian and now Dutch Warmblood standing in Holland. The most influential of the traditional, heavier Holsteins is probably Farn whose sons include the great Dutch stallion Nimmerdor.

The Swedes' most famous horse must be Gaspari by Parad, whose sons include top dressage stallion Herkules, and grandchildren the Dressage World Cup winner Gauguin de Lully. In neighbouring Denmark the best known is May Sherif with his four Olympic performers at the Seoul Olympics, one of whom was the top stallion Matador. With the use of artificial insemination May Sherif has had progeny born around the world, and for a few seasons he stood in Finland.

Far from complete, this gives a picture of how international Warmblood breeding has evolved. It must not be overlooked that more and more countries are developing their own Warmbloods, including Switzerland, Austria, South Africa and South America, but with as yet relatively small numbers of breeding stock, they have not been covered in this book.

Warmblood breeding is taking off, fired by the great demand for performance horses. Pure-breds like the Thoroughbred, Arab and Cleveland Bay might produce representatives that meet the requirements of some of today's competition riders, but this is more by accident. In the case of the Warmblood, chance is reduced to the smallest possible proportions through rigorous selection of breeding stock to produce the best possible performer.

The Warmblood Approach to Breeding

An historical introduction using the German Warmblood
as an illustration

by

JOHN CLARKE

Chairman of the British Warmblood Society from 1982 to 1992

OVER THE CENTURIES there have been two main ways in which man has tried to maximise the potential of the horse. The first has been through the invention or improvement of mechanical aids – bits, bridles, saddles and harnesses. The second has been through the selective breeding of horses to produce animals specially suited to particular kinds of work. Since breeding is the main concern of this book, my task is to explain the origins and philosophy of the 'Warmblood approach to breeding', details of which form the substance of the chapters which follow.

To a greater or lesser extent, all societies involved with horses have produced philosophies of breeding, and it is important to appreciate that there have been many such philosophies rather than one. For the historian, an examination of these various philosophies provides a fascinating angle of insight into the nature of the societies that have produced them. For our purposes, it is important to give a clear geographical location to the Warmblood philosophy. It originated on the Continent rather than in the English-speaking world and its true homeland has been in North Germany. In Anglo-Saxon countries, the very phrase 'Warmblood horse' is of recent origin and some people remain puzzled by it. The philosophy that lies behind Warmblood breeding is even less understood. Common sense suggests that Warmblood owners and breeders in Britain and in the world beyond Europe should be willing to learn from the accumulated experience of Germany, Scandinavia and the Low Countries.

It is one thing to recognise the existence of a diversity of traditions and quite another to understand them. This has proved a particularly intractable problem with Warmbloods. Many new Warmblood owners have learned the meaning of certain technical terms – such as the difference between 'registration' and 'grading' and between 'Haupt' and 'Select' – yet are still left with the feeling that they do not understand why things are done in a particular way nor what end is in view. Anglo-Saxon attitudes can be equally puzzling to most Europeans. In fact, a considerable intellectual and imaginative effort is required for those brought up in one tradition to comprehend the other. The crucial thing is to appreciate that both attitudes have deep roots in the past.

When it comes to summarising what most Continental horsemen think of the breeding policies in Anglo-Saxon countries and *vice versa*, the essential point is that Anglo-Saxons tend to think that there is too much regulation on the Continent, and that Continentals think that there is too little in Britain and America. We have to appreciate that attitudes to horses, like most other things, represent a mixture of a rational response to current conditions and instinctive loyalty to traditions many centuries old.

In Britain horses have not played such a vital role in defence as they have in Europe. With the accession of James I in 1603 and the disappearance of the Scottish frontier, Britain's political and geographical boundaries became co-extensive. It followed that Britain was less vulnerable to attack than her land-locked Continental neighbours, and if invasion did come, it would be by sea, not in the shape of men on horseback. Sea-borne invaders could be best deterred by other ships. In terms of national defence, horses were of relatively modest importance.

With the country united and fairly prosperous and safe behind wooden walls, the state could afford to relax and a fairly substantial amount of liberty could be conceded. There was no need for a large standing army in peace time and the absence of such an army allowed a parliamentary system to flourish. In the eighteenth century, and a good deal later, armies meant horses. In the case of England, however, the small size of the land forces meant that the state had a correspondingly modest interest in breeding horses for military purposes. In such an environment, it is hardly surprising that the emphasis of horse breeding was largely diverted towards leisure activities. Thus, in eighteenth-century England, wealthy, self-confident and politically dominant aristocrats took the lead in breeding Thoroughbreds for racing. Here there was a specific end in view and rigorous standards were applied.

In the nineteenth century the Industrial Revolution in England inevitably diminished the relative importance of agriculture to the national economy. The interests of industry and commerce were now paramount and any surviving sectional agricultural interests were less influential. The State's sole purpose was to further the interests of its individual members, an aim largely achieved by letting them get on with their own affairs in the way each considered best. State initiatives affecting horses were rare and of relatively small importance, like a scheme to produce better Welsh ponies to serve in coal mines. There was no room for state studs in a world like this.

If there is some connection between this brief sketch of British history and British attitudes to horse breeding, then what of the Continent?

By definition, all Continental countries shared at least one land frontier with another state. They were vulnerable to invasion over land – as Britain was not. Their governments had to be more alert to the dangers of invasion and hence were forced to devote more attention to the production of horses for military purposes. Such was their vulnerability that they were compelled to maintain standing armies in peace time, both as a deterrent to potential aggressors and to provide an immediate and effective defence if an invasion actually materialised. In other words, the breeding of suitable horses for the cavalry and to pull guns and baggage trains *was* a matter of vital national interest. It is quite understandable that Continental states should concern themselves with horse breeding. It is essential for the British and Americans to appreciate that contemporary Continental attitudes spring directly from the military considerations of earlier generations.

But the differences go deeper than that. With a standing army at his disposal, a Continental ruler had a ready instrument to enforce the collection of taxes. He was thus dispensed from the need to consult Parliamentary bodies or to obtain their consent to taxation. Although Parliaments had been almost universal in Europe in the Middle Ages, they tended to decline or disappear from the sixteenth century – precisely the time when the English Parliament was becoming more powerful. For most of Continental Europe, the seventeenth and eighteenth centuries saw the golden age of absolute monarchy. There was an absolutist regime in Denmark, and Gustav III of Sweden seemed to be following the European trend when, in 1772, he organised a *coup d'état* against the Swedish Parliament. Louis XIV's boast, *'L'état, c'est moi'*, represented the aspiration if not the reality of most European kings and princes. There were exceptions, notably in Poland. But the fate of Poland – which was finally wiped off the map by absolutist, better organised and predatory neighbours – only pointed to the folly of continuing with weak states. The difference between Britain and the Continent produced one strange anomaly. In recent years, the Hannoverian horse has become one of the best known Warmblood breeds. Despite the long-standing political and cultural links between Britain and Hannover, the Hannoverian Verband follows a Continental rather than a British philosophy of breeding. While the Hannoverian monarchs were constitutional monarchs in Britain, they were absolute rulers in their German homeland.

Before 1871, Germany was a geographical expression, or at best an aspiration towards a political entity rather than an actual one. In the eighteenth century, there were as many German states as there are days in the year and even after 1815 there were still over thirty. In the flat plains of Northern Germany, there could be no natural frontiers and many states possessed little obvious *raison d'être*. It was clear that some of these states would be swallowed by others; the crucial question was which ones would be swallowed and which ones would do the swallowing. In the end, it was Prussia that emerged as the victor in this protracted contest.

The difficulties encountered in trying to weld this motley collection of territories into a major state were enormous. Only by superhuman efforts of discipline, self-sacrifice, planning and obedience could Prussia hope to stand comparison with more 'natural' states. In Britain, the ideas of *laissez faire* might have made good sense; in Prussia they would have resulted in the country falling apart. As a Great Power, Prussia was a planned and artificial creation from the start. (In the course of the next few pages we shall have much to say of Prussia. In many ways, it represents the most extreme example of the *dirigiste* approach to Warmblood breeding, yet we shall best understand the difference between the Anglo-Saxon world and Continental traditions if we concentrate on Prussia – the model which Continental breed societies (except France) follow to a greater or lesser extent.) The first Prussian requirement was to create a common identity – so that Rheinlanders, for example, could learn to think of themselves as Prussians. One way of doing this was through the discovery, if necessary through the invention, of a glorious past with which all subjects could identify. There can be no doubt of the importance of the horse in the history/mythology of Prussia. Eighteenth- and nineteenth-century Prussia was portrayed as the heir of the Teutonic Knights of the Middle Ages. The Knights had recruited members from all over Germany and beyond – the future Henry IV of England served with the Order in a 'Crusade' against Lithuania in 1390. The Knights were presented as heroes who had formed the medieval spearhead of the age-old German mission, the *Drang nach Osten*, the 'drive to the East', to bring German *Kultur* to lands hitherto occupied by primitive Slavs.

East Prussia, known as the *Kreuzritterstaat*, 'the State of the Knights of the Cross', and its successor, the Duchy of Prussia (founded in 1525) were essentially warrior states engaged in frequent battles with their neighbours. There was an early recognition of the military necessity of a supply of good horses. Such things were too important to leave to chance and the Teutonic Order founded the first 'state' stud farm in the world, at Georgenburg in 1264.

But 'scientific' horse breeding involves more than 'state' stallions; there is also the question of mares. Here again the *Kreuzritterstaat* was of crucial importance. In order to make the areas they conquered irreversibly German, the Knights had to attract 'civilian' settlers. Large numbers of peasants were moved all the way across Germany to set up farms, villages and even towns. To ensure the scheme's success, the Knights and their associates assisted the emigrants by organising transport, housing and tools, and they laid out the new farms on a standard pattern. In effect what took place was a planned migration and some historians believe that German addiction to planning actually dates from this experience. Although there were sometimes conflicts of interest between the peasant farmers and the Prussian state, there was an underlying affinity – each needed the other. The basic relationship was support in return for obedience. In terms of horse breeding the scene was set for the 'classic' German pattern of peasant farmers sending their mares to the state stud, keeping the foals for a few years and then selling some of them back to the state – either for military purposes or for stallions. In effect, both parties to the arrangement had an interest in maintaining high standards, standards which gradually became enshrined in tradition.

Although the basic pattern was established in the Middle Ages, some of the details had to wait until more recent times. We return to the eighteenth century, the great age of Prussian state building. Even more than the manipulation of history, the way to make Prussians feel Prussian was to bring a sense of union in the face of an enemy, if necessary by deliberately provoking war, as in the attack on Austrian Silesia in 1740. A sense of union could be forged in the Army of Frederick the Great. The development of the right kind of horses, seen by many as the key to victory, was a matter of national priority.

Warfare and the consequent need for cavalry and other types of horse was only one aspect of state involvement in breeding. Identification with the state was to be fostered by display and ceremony; military parades and reviews became an important part of state propaganda. The Kings of Prussia were themselves part of this propaganda. They were usually seen by their subjects not only riding on horseback, but also wearing military uniform. Eighteenth-century rulers were not just concerned about impressing their own subjects; they wanted to create a powerful impression on other rulers as well. The chief criterion was the grandeur, polish and magnificence of courts and palaces. Again, horses played a crucial role; enormous sums were spent on building stables and riding schools (virtual palaces in their own right) and the art of dressage was regarded as one of the most essential accomplishments of the courtier. Here, perhaps, the best example is not in Prussia but in her great rival Austria, where we can still see the Spanish Riding School next door to the Hofburg Palace in Vienna. Most of the smaller German rulers were eager imitators.

It appears therefore that horse breeding was intimately associated with statecraft. The selective and deliberate creation of distinctive breeds as a long-term policy and associated with particular states was part and parcel of the growth of state consciousness. As states became increasingly distinct, so greater uniformity was required among the subjects within each – and so with each breed. Ultimately each state wanted its 'own' horse.

The unification of Germany was not achieved peacefully but by a series of wars. Yet the Germany formed in 1871 was not an entirely centralised state; the old rulers retained their titles, state governments continued to function and to control aspects of agricultural policy. In theory at least, Bavaria actually possessed a separate army. Thus separate breeds continued. Although in reality Germany had been conquered by Prussia it suited the politicians to disguise this. Unification may have been welcomed by liberals and intellectuals but not all horse owners come into either of these categories.

But there was another important dimension. The industrialisation of Germany had scarcely begun before 1871. Germany was still an overwhelmingly agricultural society. When industrialisation did come it took a course radically different to that experienced in Britain. In Britain, industrialisation was associated with the acceleration of Enclosure and the disappearance of 'the English peasantry', if indeed such a body had ever existed. Thus, the proportion of the population connected with agriculture suffered both a relative and an absolute decline. In Germany, no such absolute decline took place. There was no enclosure movement and peasant farming remained the norm over much of the Reich. Thus the 'agricultural lobby' was much more influential in German politics than in Britain; it was able to secure agricultural protection and state support against cheap imports of grain from Russia or the United States. There was one problem here; those who derived their main income from horses had an obvious interest in cheap grain and hence might have been attracted to free trade ideas. In order to persuade horse breeders to support general agricultural protection, the state had to offer other incentives – to expand the military purchases, to provide direct or indirect help to enable them to find customers, not only in Germany but also elsewhere. The German breeders had a strong incentive to produce the best quality 'product'. As railways spread over Continental Europe, exports of German horses rose sharply. Indeed, at least in part, it was the growth of these exports that persuaded other countries to introduce German methods, if only to protect their own markets. Although horse breeding clearly involves an interest in and love of horses, the element of economic calculation, the idea of horse-raising as an industry was also present. In Britain, except among the racing fraternity, such considerations may seem mutually exclusive; on the Continent few breeders would have seen any inherent contradiction between the two.

The great thing about the Germans was that they knew what they wanted from their horses. The military *desiderata* were expressed most succinctly in the official German army veterinary report produced in the aftermath of World War I:

The East Prussian horse should be the best war horse available. It has been found to be hard, full of endurance and demanding little. During the mobile war it has willingly participated in long marches and shown great endurance of all hardships and privations. Aside from a few flaws in temperament and the fact that after excessive stress some animals refused their feed, there were no complaints from anyone of the faults in the East Prussian horse…Hoof diseases, illness and lameness were rare. The regular to slightly narrow hoof of solid, finely fibered substance of the East Prussian horse enables it in an excellent manner to endure any kind of footing for extended periods of time without damage and assures dependable movement everywhere.

The defeat of Germany in World War I and what were regarded as the unfair terms of the Treaty of Versailles had major implications for German horse breeders. East Prussia, one of the most important horse breeding areas, was now separated from the rest of Germany by the 'Polish Corridor'. Restrictions on the size of the German army meant that one major market contracted enormously compared to the days before 1914 or during the war itself. Political instability in Eastern Europe, coupled with a European trend towards higher and higher tariffs curbed export markets. Economic catastrophe in Germany meant that there were fewer horses wanted for leisure purposes. The development of motor transport in towns was yet another blow.

Faced with such adverse circumstances, radical re-thinking was imperative. Of course, there were ways of easing the problem. The military clauses of Versailles could be evaded especially after the signature of the Treaty of Rapallo of 1922, which allowed the German army to hold manoeuvres in Russia, well away from the prying eyes of the Allies. Further, the 'horse lobby' was still strong enough to influence economic policy. In particular, Germany was in a position to insist that primary producers, especially in Eastern Europe, could only send their products to Germany if they agreed to take German products, including horses, in return.

Here we need to consider one of the most important aspects of the German breeding philosophy. It is crucial to appreciate that, while there may have been clearly defined breeding goals for Hannoverians, Trakehners and the rest, these goals did not remain constant. Because of the large number of mare owners, there was a large genetic pool. Also, it was always possible to bring in stallions from other breeds, often Thoroughbreds. The breeds were essentially flexible and were made heavier or lighter as customer taste and demand required.

In the inter-war period, the use of tractors was virtually unknown on the Continent. It seemed that whatever the vagaries of other sectors of the market, farm work would continue to provide a basis for the continuance of a breed. In Fritz Schilke's *Trakehner Horses: Then and Now* we learn just how *useful* and *cost effective* a Warmblood mare was expected to be:

The East Prussian broodmare so-to-speak had to pass a daily performance test on her breeder's farm. The farmer could not afford to keep mares merely to produce foals. His broodmares had to be fully usable on his farm. Mares which could not meet the requirements of farm operations were eliminated sooner or later...The endeavour of the East Prussian Warmblood breeders was the attainment of equal performance in several fields of use. With this objective in mind, new tests were developed. East Prussia instituted a three-part exam:
A. Performance test with a plough, team of two, single share plough, time required 4 hours, pulling resistance per horse 120 kg, width of furrow 30.35 cm. Minimum area to be ploughed 2.2. morgen (app. 1.4 acres).
B. Performance test in heavy harness: pulling a load, team of two, on hard road for 25 km with a load of 2.5 t including wagon, excluding driver. The first 21 km walk and trot as desired with a maximum time of 6 minutes per km. The last 4 km walk, maximum time 11 minutes per km.

C. Final test under a rider, free walk, free trot without minimum performance. Gallop 2 km in a total maximum time of 5 minutes, 30 seconds.

Although the German breeds were generally designed to be capable of 'equal performance in several fields use' the emphasis changed. Thus horses probably became heavier in the 1920s when agricultural functions predominated, to lighten again in the 1930s as German rearmament accelerated under the Third Reich. Yet perhaps the greatest testimony to the versatility of the Warmblood horse came at the end of World War II when, as the Russian armies poured in to East Prussia, the peasant farmers harnessed their horses to wagons and drove westwards, over rivers with no bridges and without adequate food for weeks on end. Of course, many perished in the attempt but an astonishing number survived.

The crucial thing about Warmbloods is careful breeding, using knowledge of bloodlines on both sides, to aim at a specific objective. The calculation may not always succeed but the *probability* of success will be greater than if pedigrees are unknown. The irony of the situation is that in recent years when the long-standing military, agricultural and transportational importance of the horse has become a thing of the past, the significance of these attitudes and systems has become more crucial than ever. The horse is now largely a 'leisure' animal. Yet leisure industries are notoriously exacting in their standards; more than ever horses are required to be outstanding in particular activities – dressage, eventing or show jumping and still be capable of all-round excellence, even if they may be excused plough-ing duties. The infinite variety and adaptability of Warmblood families means that breeds can develop in any way that is required yet still maintain their distinctive identity.

The Germans, and Continentals generally, have used their skill and knowledge to maximise this potential, whereas the AngloSaxon *laissez faire* background has led to a more random approach to breeding which has not covered Warmbloods. Increasing integration with the Continentals and the huge successes of Warmbloods in competitions have changed attitudes, and Warmblood breeding, although at an early stage in Anglo-Saxon nations, is becoming a major part of their horse industry.

The Structure of Warmblood Breeding in Germany

by

JANE KIDD

MOST WARMBLOODS ARE DEFINED by country. The exception is Germany. It produces the largest number of Warmbloods – 39,000 foals per year – and although they are sometimes described as German Riding Horses they are better known under the names of their regionally based associations, like the Hannoverian and Holstein. The only exception to this division into regionally based breeds is the Trakehner, which was developed and established in East Prussia, but when large numbers of them migrated to the West after the Second World War the Trakehner was accepted as a national breed in the area then known as West Germany. Of all the Warmbloods it is the closest to pure bred, as only Arab and Thoroughbred are used as outside blood.

The breeds from the fifteen breeding areas of West Germany are accepted for their stud book, partly on pedigree, but also according to where they were born. Hence it is possible for a Hannoverian dam and sire to produce a Westphalian foal if it is born in Westphalia. However, the result of a mating between a Westphalian bred and graded mare and a Hannoverian-graded stallion is likely to result in a Westphalian-registered foal as in this case the dam's status decides the kind of papers issued.

There is a common breeding aim for the German Warmbloods which was established in 1975 as:

Breeding is aimed at producing a noble, large-framed and correct horse with dynamic, spacious and elastic motions – well-suited to any riding purpose because of its temperament, its character and its ability to provide an easy ride.

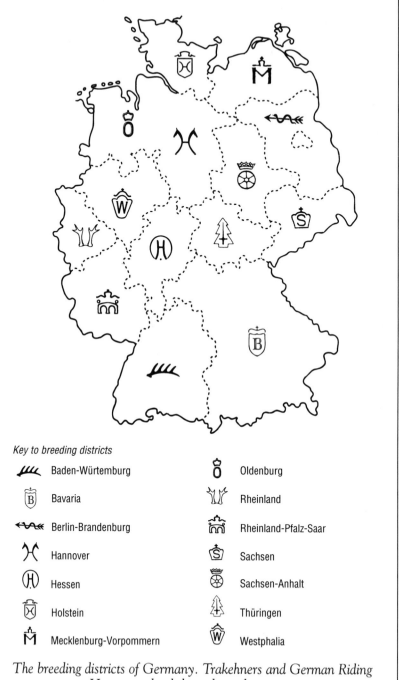

Key to breeding districts

Baden-Würtemburg		Oldenburg	
Bavaria		Rheinland	
Berlin-Brandenburg		Rheinland-Pfalz-Saar	
Hannover		Sachsen	
Hessen		Sachsen-Anhalt	
Holstein		Thüringen	
Mecklenburg-Vorpommern		Westphalia	

The breeding districts of Germany. Trakehners and German Riding Horses are bred throughout the country.

The breeds are organised regionally by breeders' associations and nationally by a breeders' federation made up of representatives from the area breeds whose numbers are in proportion to the numerical strength of the breed they represent. The breeders are closely connected to the competitors as it was the German breeders who were responsible for establishing the National Federation for the disciplines. At the beginning of this century the breeders found their traditional market for their horses – the army – reducing its demand, and they took the logical step of creating their own demand by promoting equestrian sports and with them the need for an athletic horse. Today co-ordinating all national and international activities of the breeders is the responsibility of the Breeding Department of the Deutsche Reiterliche Vereinigung, which is based at Warendorf alongside the headquarters for the German Olympic Committee and other divisions of the German National Federation.

The former East Germany was divided into five breeding associations – the federal states of Mecklenburg, Brandenburg, Sachsen-Anhalt, Sachsen and Thuringen and each of these has the same rights as the breeding associations that made up the original Breeding Department of the German National Federation.

By far the most important German breed is the Hannoverian, which in 1993 had 18,763 broodmares registered, the next in numerical strength is the Westphalian with 9575, then the Oldenburg – 7568, the Baden Wurttemburg – 5924, the Bavarian – 5577, the Holstein – 5532, the Rheinland – 3381, the Hessen – 2912, the Mecklenborg – 2504, the Rheinland-Pfalz-Saar – 2355, the Sachsen-Anhalt – 2212, Berlin – 1868, Sachsen 1785 and the smallest of all, Thuringen with 933. The Trakehner, which is bred nationally, has 4639 registered mares, placing it next in numerical importance to the Holstein.

Chapter 1

The Trakehner

by

CELIA CLARKE

THE STORY OF the development of the present-day 'Warmblood horse of Trakehner origin' is both long and complex. It begins with the Schweiken horse of the Middle Ages and goes on to the high-class all-round East Prussian horse bred at the Trakehnen Stud (the origin of the name) for the household of King Friedrich Wilhelm II of Prussia. It is a fascinating saga, virtually the history of Europe in microcosm. The very fact that it is now known as the Trakehner breed, rather than as the East Prussian (which was often the case until the end of the Second World War) signifies that the numerical strength of the breed, and its original homeland in East Prussia, were both major casualties of the Soviet advance westwards in the final years of the war. Probably as a result of this, the development of the modern Trakehner in the post-war years, using considerable amounts of Thoroughbred blood on old East Prussian bloodlines, has caused some European breeders to view the lighter, more elegant Trakehner of today as a substantially different type from its somewhat heavier and less flighty East Prussian ancestor. Indeed, some Warmblood breeders go to considerable pains to ensure that the Trakehners they now use on their Warmblood mares are as similar as possible to the pre-war model in type, temperament and blood-lines – even, in some cases in Scandinavia, using the old breed name 'East Prussian' rather than 'Trakehner' to denote their preference. Sadly, however, since 1945 the amount of East Prussian blood available to Warmblood breeders has been severely limited, although the influence of the East Prussian remains strong in Poland, where it has been an important element in the development of Polish Warmbloods, particularly the Wielkopolski, and in the Russian Republic, within whose boundaries the remains of the estate at Trakehnen now lies.

The reasons for all the different influences, and their effects upon the Trakehner breeder, are discussed in the historical introduction of this book, so it is necessary to repeat them here only briefly. Readers wishing to delve even further into the history of the Trakehner should consult *Trakehner Horses: Then and Now* by Fritz Schilke, *The Trakehner* by Eberhard von Velsen and Erhard Schulte, and *The Flight of the East Prussian Horses* by Daphne Machin-Goodall.

Although the foundation of horse breeding in East Prussia was laid in 1232, when the Teutonic knights colonised the land and discovered the merits of the small and handy Schweiken horse, the first key date in the history of the Trakehner breed proper is 1732, when the central stud at Trakehnen was formed for royal use only by order of Friedrich Wilhelm II. It combined the bloodlines of the existing stud farms at Sperling, Beatricken, Insterburg, Budupoenen, Guddien, Ragnit and Schreitlaken. However, even though Trakehnen was created by royal edict, in its very early years its stock was not particularly impressive and it was not until Graf Lindenau (the first Chief Stud Administrator to reside at Trakehnen) was appointed in 1787, that a serious assessment of stock took place. Graf Lindenau culled 25 of the 38 stallions in residence, and 144 of the 381 broodmares, declaring that they were 'not lean and strong boned enough, moved too narrow in the hindquarters and there were too many curbs; some horses were eliminated because they were suspected of having spavins and some had boxy hooves'.

This drastic culling and Graf Lindenau's decision that 'from now on only pure gold must be used for the sires at Trakehnen, be they Thoroughbreds, Arabians or other breeds', at once expanded the role of the stud from that of a royal stables to a centre for producing breeding stallions for the whole of Prussia. Native mares owned by farmers could now be mated with stallions standing at Trakehnen, and the system of collaboration between farmers and state stud officials that was to prove so efficient in producing lightweight, quality horses for the army for the next 150 years began to develop. In fact, right from the very beginning large numbers of mares were approved for breeding each year – for instance 7324 in 1796 alone (although interestingly these mares were obviously much smaller than those of today as only 2679 were 15.3hh or above, and some were as little as 14hh).

During the nineteenth century the stringent standards initiated by Graf Lindenau continued to be enforced and the East Prussian horse improved in quality and type, carrying an increasing amount of Thoroughbred and Arab blood as time went on. By 1860 a total of 15,559 mares were being bred to the Trakehner stallions (of whom 64.8% were Thoroughbred), and by 1912 the figure had risen to 48,467 mares, with the number of Thoroughbred stallions at stud rising to

84%. A correspondingly high proportion of the progeny were destined for light cavalry use, so the East Prussian breed therefore suffered a marketing problem even more acute than those of the other German Warmblood breeds when the Treaty of Versailles limited the German army to 100,000 men in 1919.

By the early 1920s the future of the East Prussian horse therefore appeared to be as a dual-purpose farm horse and in the 1920s and 1930s – when Graf Lehndorff was the Director of Trakehnen – stronger part-Thoroughbred stallions (known as 'reinforcement stallions') were often used. Administratively, during this period the chief role of Trakehnen was to produce breeding stallions and to this end it maintained on average 350 mares and 18 stallions in an estate of 2441 acres. The animals owned by the stud were split up according to age and sex and the broodmare herds were also divided around the estate according to colour. Four other state studs at Georgenburg, Rastenburg, Braunsberg and Marienwerder also produced high-quality East Prussian stock, mainly sired by stallions born at Trakehnen, and some privately owned stallions were also available, chiefly around Danzig (now Gdansk).

Performance testing was firmly established by this time, with a stallion testing station being established at Zwion in 1926. Here, the emphasis was on a three-day cross-country test held in the autumn of the stallion's three-year-old year, in which strict criteria relating to way of going, temperament, health, feed utilisation and stamina were set and the famous Trakehnen hunts across the formidable fences on the estate were found to be an admirable preparation. Such was the careful selection process that operated in the months prior to the stallion testing that on average only 10% of the candidates failed. Broodmare performance tests under saddle were attempted in East Prussia in the early 1920s, but these were not entirely successful, chiefly because of the differing abilities of the riders involved, and also because many farmers were unwilling to submit their mares to be tested as they had already proved themselves in farm work. A broodmare test biased more towards harness work was then introduced, and this proved more popular, but by 1936 it had been decided that an all-round test of work – both under rider and in harness – should be instigated, and this extremely tough test, involving such things as ploughing at a specified speed, pulling a heavy load a set distance in a maximum time, and work at all paces under rider proved invaluable to farmers and breeders in evaluating the worth of their mares.

These performance tests ensured that the East Prussian horses were selectively bred to be sound, tough and efficient utilisers of food, qualities that were to prove invaluable to them in the troubled days of the last war. The Trakehnen stock fell victim to the vicissitudes of war in the autumn of 1944, when the advancing Russian troops forced the Trakehnen stud to abandon its estate. Stallions, broodmares and youngstock were loaded on to westbound trains, and East Prussian farmers had to harness their broodmares to carts and undertake an appalling journey to safety in the same direction, travelling under almost impossible conditions across a frozen landscape of land and sea.

This catastrophic flight of the East Prussian horses ahead of the advancing Russian troops is one of the great sagas of equine and human history and the most recent of the many external pressures to act on the breed. Much of the flight from their homelands in the most easterly parts of Prussia, through what is now Poland and what became East Germany, took place in the bitterly cold months of December 1944 and January and February 1945, with many of the mares in foal and practically every adult horse harnessed to the now famous 'trek wagons', in which were carried any possessions that the fleeing owners were able to rescue. The loss of stock left behind in Russian-occupied territory and in Poland, and the harsh conditions encountered on the journey meant that only about 1600 horses out of an original stud book numbering nearly 27,000 survived to settle in West Germany in 1945. In addition, the refugee status of their owners, plus the very difficult economic conditions in West Germany during the following two years, decreased the breed's numbers still further, until only about 700 mares and 60 stallions survived, and no foals were being born.

In 1947, in a determined bid to save the breed from extinction, Siegfried Freiherr von Schrocten and Dr Fritz Schilke (respectively chairman and secretary of the original East Prussian stud book society, the Ostpreussische Stutbuchgesellschaft) collected and identified the horses and founded the Verband der Züchter und Freunde des Ostpreussischen Warmblutpferdes Trakehner Abstammung eV (the Association of Breeders and Friends of the Warmblood Horse of Trakehner Origin, or Trakehner Verband as it is usually known). This organisation took over the administration of records and created a regional breeding structure for Trakehner breeding in West Germany, with studs and stallions in each breeding area. From being a homeless breed, the Trakehner at once became the only national West German breed, with a structure that would influence all aspects of Warmblood breeding throughout the country.

The period since 1950 has seen an astonishing revival in the fortunes of the Trakehner breed. No longer the homeless refugees, the top lines of the breed have spread their influence far outside the realms of the pure Trakehner breeder into the competitive world of Warmblood breeding, where its improving qualities are valued worldwide. The geographical dispersion of the breed throughout West Germany, and its consequent appearance in the pedigrees of many non-Trakehner competition horses throughout Europe and North America, have helped to spread the Trakehner gospel until by the beginning of the 1990s, not only were about 1400 foals per year being registered in West Germany with the Trakehner Verband, but a number of the most popular stallions such as Caprimond (1985) by Karon cover over sixty mares a year in their districts, when standing against other locally based Warmblood stallions. In addition, with the outstanding success of such horses as the World Cup and Olympic show-jumping winner Abdullah (1970) by Donauwind, and the top international dressage horses Edinburg (by Elever) and Biotop (by Blesk), the market for Trakehners with proven competition bloodlines has increased worldwide. Top prices at auction can now reach as much as £86,000 ($129,000) for a riding horse, and the champion and reserve two-year-old approved stallions sold at Neumünster in 1994 cost their new owners £86,000 ($129,000) and £70,000 ($105,000) respectively with a broodmare offered for sale at the same time fetching a record price of £44,000 ($66,000).

Donauwind (1965) by Pregel, sire of the Olympic gold medallist Abdullah, and a graded stallion in Germany, Denmark and the United States.

BREEDING POLICY

It is important, when studying Warmblood breeding, to bear in mind
that before German unification in 1871, Germany was made up of a
number of different states and the locally organised breeding areas
under the control of a local breed society reflected this structure. As a
result, horses bred in the Hannover area therefore became known as
Hannoverians, those bred in the Schleswig-Holstein area became
known as Holsteins, those bred in Westphalia became known as
Westphalians and so on. This structure is still being maintained
today by the controlling national organisation, the Deutsche
Landwirtschafts-Gesellschaft or DLG (the German Ministry of
Agriculture, which also organises the annual DLG Show at which each
German breed society presents an elite group of breeding stock every
year to compete in an inter-breed championship). However, although
the Trakehner Verband is under the overall control of the DLG,
members of the Trakehner breed are an honourable exception to this
breed-naming rule, as they are still known as Trakehners wherever they
are foaled. However, although the generally accepted definition of a
Warmblood as being a performance horse developed by upgrading
native mares through the use of infusions of selected and performance-
tested outside blood applies to the Trakehner, over the last two
centuries the breed has developed into a very different type from those
originating from the other German breeding areas, such as Oldenburg,
Hannover and Westphalia. These have become very similar to each
other and are often impossible to differentiate without examining each
individual horse's brand but the Trakehner is distinguishable because it
is the only 'pure' breed of Warmblood type. Unlike the other regional
breed societies who have used many of the same sires, regardless of
breed (with popular stallions being graded into two, three or even four
different stud books) the Trakehner breeding authorities allow
up-grading only through the limited use of high-quality Thoroughbred,
Anglo-Arab and Arab stallions, who are graded into the breeding stud
books alongside stallions with Trakehner blood. However, once such
stallions are graded into the breeding stud book their progeny
are treated as 'pure-bred' Trakehners despite their mixed origins.
Trakehner stallions and mares are, of course, frequently graded
into other Warmblood stud books to improve the quality and
conformation of more old-fashioned stock, and have proved invaluable
in doing this.

An important aspect of the breeding policy of the Trakehner Verband, as with all well-organised Warmblood breeding organisations, is
the stallion licensing and grading process. Following a pre-selection in

August, an annual stallion licensing show for two and-a-half-year-old colts is held every October in Neumünster, where the potential stallions are subjected to a rigorous examination. Only those colts that are likely to enhance and improve the breed are chosen and the unlicensed stallions are put forward for sale at the auction held in conjunction with the licensing, along with some successfully licensed stallions. In the summer following the licensing, the three-year-old stallions have to undergo the normal West German 100-day performance test at Adelheidsdorf (near Celle), Klosterhof Mendigen (Lower Saxony) or Marbach (Baden-Württemburg) alongside stallions of other breeds, and only if they meet the points requirement of both the state and the breed are they considered fully graded and accepted as stallions. Some particularly outstanding stallions of merit are designated premium stallions to indicate their superior qualities.

Mares are graded into the Verband stud books based on an inspection by qualified judges and approval of their bloodlines. Graded mares are branded on the neck and their progeny by graded Trakehner stallions are eligible for branding and registration following inspection. However, the top mares cannot be state premium mares because of the national status of the breed and are therefore described simply as premium mares. The stringent performance testing of Trakehner mares, which came into force during the inter-war years fell into disuse after the 'flight', but in 1985 an optional four-week-long mare testing at two stations in Handorf and Medingen was introduced, in addition to the already established optional one-day field test regularly held at Traventhal. The long-term effects of this mare-testing policy cannot yet be fully analysed, but the tests are already proving popular with mare owners.

GENERAL DESCRIPTION OF THE TRAKEHNER

The Trakehner horse is an elegant middleweight horse with a great deal of quality. It is usually chestnut, bay, dark brown, black or grey in colour according to the mare family from which it originates. It can vary in height from 15.2hh (157.5 cm) to 17hh (173 cm) but about 16hh (162.5 cm) is the norm. It is noted for its beautiful head with large eyes and a small muzzle, and often the face has a pronounced dish. It should have an elegant, tapering neck, a good shoulder, and a well-rounded croup (although some of the mare lines do have a tendency to pass on a flat croup which is very hard to eradicate). It generally has a good middle piece, although again some mares can be a little long, and its legs are hard, with short cannons and excellent sound feet. It is prized for its action, which although not always as powerful as some Warmblood breeds, is straight, true, full of impulsion and often extravagant in trot. Under saddle, whilst some families (such as the progeny of Donauwind) are noted as being very rideable, the breed as a whole – although thought of as kind – has the reputation of being brilliant but flighty, and a rather difficult ride at times. However, it does have tremendous stamina and endurance and is valued for its thriftiness in keeping.

IMPORTANT BLOODLINES

As with all Warmblood breeds a number of important sire lines have developed over the years, and these will be discussed later in this section. However, one of the many things that makes Trakehner breeders different from other Warmblood breeders is the importance they place on broodmare lines. The foals are given the same initial as their dam – a practice almost unique in Warmblood breeding – and elaborate charts of broodmare families are a regular feature of Trakehner literature.

In pre-war days many high-class mare herds existed throughout East Prussia and the main stud at Trakehnen had five distinct mare herds based on colour running on the estate and outlying studs. As with many aspects of the Trakehner, the 'flight' decimated the old established broodmare lines, so the ones most frequently found in the present day are founded in the following mares (the vast majority of whom were survivors of the trek), the descriptions used being based on those of Fritz Schilke:

• **Alwina** by Hyperion, out of Liebling by Pilger. Dark chestnut Trakehner (1946). This mare belongs to a line from the main stud at Trakehnen. Members of her family represent a good breed type; they have a good frame of desirable, medium size and a good skeleton. Graded stallions from this broodmare line include Albross (1964) by Pergamos and Arminius (1971) by Kurfürst.

• **Amika** by St Szirgupöner, out of Kuratesse by Baccarat. Bay Trakehner (1940). Also her full sister **Arkade**, a dark brown Trakehner (1932). These full sisters founded a family of good deep size, with a powerful deep-chested build with a good to very good way of moving. Graded stallions of note from this line are the above-average mover Amagun (1968) by Gunnar and the Swedish-graded Unikum (1962) by Traumgeist XX.

•**Blitzrot** by Hirtensang, out of Blitzmädel by Kupferhammer. Chestnut Trakehner (1942). All the mares of this family are large, long-lined and stand over a lot of ground. They have short and sturdy legs, are of good breed type and are ground-covering movers. Their temperament is pleasing and their character uncomplicated. This family is quite narrowly based, but even so it has produced such important stallions as Carajan II (1961) by Carajan and Bernstein (1964) by Gunnar.

•**Corrida** by Bussard, out of Corinna by Ararad. Black Trakehner (1941). Corrida was a noble, large daughter of Bussard, and all members of this family are clean and clear in type, with sharply defined outlines. They have good overall behaviour, are full of impulsion when moving, are easily ridden and have a pleasing temperament. Bay is the dominant colour of this family and the graded stallions Celestin (1971) by Hessenstein and Coktail (1971) by Habicht carry on this tradition.

•**Donna** by Cancara, out of Dongola OX by Jasir OX. Grey Trakehner (1938). Donna was an excellent broodmare out of a pure-bred Arab dam. Both large- and medium-sized models are produced by this family, who are noted for their pleasing temperament and dependable character. The famous mare Donaulied von Schimmelhof (1960) by Boris, the dam of the well-known stallions Donauwind (1965) by Pregel and Muschamp Danube (1969) by Isenstein, comes from this family, which has also produced such influential sires as Tsherkess (1955) by Tropenwald, an early Trakehner in Canada, and Donauschimmer (1969) by Valentin, who spent time at stud in the United States as well as in West Germany.

•**Dankeschön III** by Löwenritt, out of Dankeschön by Clan. Chestnut Trakehner (1944). This family hails from one of the few mares to go back to the Löwe/Markeur line on the sire's side. A good foundation and a lot of impulsion are noted in members of this family, and in recent years the line has distinguished itself by producing several excellent breeding stallions, all with good overlines and conformation; examples include Tausendassa (1967) by Keith, Tannenberg (1966) by Sterndeuter and Schöne Abend (1958) by Abendstern. The mares are of a good, motherly type, of the best medium size with a pleasing exterior and an agreeable disposition; descendents of the mares Schönbrunn (1951) by Bento, the full sisters Schönfliess (1965) and Schönwalde (1967) by Anteil, and Tannenmeise (1967) by Sterndeuter are particularly highly valued.

• **Elfe** by Adamas OX, out of Edda by Illyrier. Grey Trakehner (1940). Elfe was a mare with Arab blood on both sides of her pedigree, and was very productive, producing foals until the age of twenty-four. The family have a gracious disposition and an uncomplicated character and the mares are noble, lean, beautiful, easy keepers and of good medium size. Important members are the DLG show winner Esra (1953) by Herbstwind, her Neumünster champion son Erzsand (1967) by Flugsand, the highly graded stallion Elfenglanz (1971) by Magnet and their descendants.

• **Feodora** by Canino, out of Fee by Nordwest. Grey Trakehner (1942). A medium-sized noble, expressive family who are good keepers with an outgoing disposition, good musculature and good impulsion. Important stallions produced include Fedor (1960) by Reichsfurst and Ferlin (1969) by Maharadscha.

• **Fischhausen** by Ali, out of Falle by Forstrat Wenzel. Bay Trakehner (1950). This family has good overall volume and lean lines and is easy to handle both under saddle and in hand. Harnisch (1963) by Handelsherr is probably the best-known stallion member.

• **Gitarre** by Keith, out of Gitta by Alarich. Trakehner (1949). Gitarre was very fertile and dependable and the family she gave rise to have a good overall impression, large frame and good rideability. The DLG winner of 1972, the mare Griseldis (1966) by Pindar XX, and the graded stallion Grimsel (1970) by Kassio, are particularly well known.

• **Goldelse** by Polarstern, out of Gondel by Waldjunker. Black Trakehner (1938). One of the best families to hail from the main stud at Trakehnen, members are medium-sized, have solid bodies and legs, a clear breed type and are likely to be dark in colour. The graded stallions Goldregen (1943) by Creon and Goldlack (1968) by Hortus show that this line has produced consistently well over the years.

• **Halensee** by Hannibal, out of Halma by Dampfross. Black Trakehner (1942). This is a line of particularly high reputation because of its quality, harmoniousness, beauty and good overall frame. Halali (1960) by Gabriel, who was a noted riding horse sire and Hartung (1962) by Ilmengrund, who was extensively used at stud – first in the Rheinland and then in Sweden – are examples of the stallions that have been produced.

• **Handelsherrin** by Moet XX, out of Handelsschule by Greif XX.

Black Trakehner (1918). Based on Handelsherrin's two granddaughters Handschelle (1940) by Polarstern and Handschrift (1940) by Hirtensang, this family produces a good frame, strong bones and particularly good riding characteristics. A number of stallions from the line were sold abroad, but Habicht (1967) by Burnus is probably its most famous member so far.

•**Herbstzeit** by Bussard, out of Herbstzeitlose by Ararad. Chestnut Trakehner (1942). This family produces many top mares and stallions with good character, above-average action and good rideability. Hirtentraum (1967) by Traumgeist XX is a typical member.

•**Isola Longa** by Tyrann, out of Isola Bella by Marduck XX. Dark brown Trakehner (1938). An outstanding mare family tracing to the main stud at Trakehnen, nobility, a large frame and clear overall impression are its characteristics. It is a top mare line and has also produced such stallions as the much-travelled Ibikus (1967) by Hertilas.

•**Kassette** by Harun al Raschid OX, out of Kasematte by Flieder. Grey Trakehner (1937). Another mare with an Arab parent, she founded a significant and extensive family of above-average individuals with good temperament. Kassio (1963) by Abglanz was a particularly important stallion from this line.

•**Kokette** by Cancara, out of Kokarde by Ararad. Bay Trakehner (1938). Kokette was closely related to Kassette, and produced many colts at stud, four of whom were graded, the chief amongst them being the important stallion Komet (1952) by Goldregen.

•**Korralle VI** by Jubel. Black Trakehner (1922). This family comes from a line dedicated to producing horses for the army before the 'flight'. Almost all members of the family are bay or brown, and are of very good quality with a good frame and an overall impression that is harmonious and noble. A large family, it has produced many significant breeding stallions, of whom Kurfürst (1966) by Pregel and Prince Condé (1967) by Prince Rouge XX are particularly notable.

•**Massliebchen** by Exzar, out of Malve by Mameluck. Grey Trakehner (1928). One of the most beautiful and harmonious mares of East Prussia, she has passed on to her descendants beauty, nobility, good rideability, excellent action and good temperament. A number of good stallions have been produced by this family, and Malachit

A famous representative of the Kokette mare family, the stallion Komet (1952), whose bloodlines can be found throughout Europe and North America.

(1964) by Major and Magnet (1964) by Pregel appear in many pedigrees.

•**Marke** by Marktvogt, out of Feldrose by Hexenschuss. Chestnut Trakehner (1941). A long-lived mare, one of her most important sons was Maharadscha (1957) by Famulus, an outstanding producer of riding horses and broodmares, as well as being the sire of Flaneur (1965).

•**Peraea** by Hirstensang, out of Per Adresse by Fetysz OX. Grey Trakehner (1943). Also **Pelargonie** by Lowelas OX, out of Perina by Fetysz OX. Grey Trakehner (1942). These closely related mares founded a family of medium size, with a good frame, good action and true Trakehner type. The outstanding stallion Pregel (1958) by Tropenwald, who was the sire of Donauwind, comes from this family and a number of graded breeding stock were exported to Argentina and Canada.

•**Polarfahrt** by Bussard, out of Polarluft by Astor. Black Trakehner (1940). A double winner at the DLG show, her family have good type, a good frame and very good action; many members are dark in colour. The broodmares are of particularly high quality, including those tracing their descent from Polaria (1962) by Schöne Abend and her daughter Polarnacht (1971) by Habicht.

- **Suska** by Hellespont, out of Susanne by Preator. Bay Trakehner (1941). Female members of this large family tend to be strongly influenced by the stallion used upon them and are therefore apt to vary considerably in size and characteristics, although most tend to move very well.

- **Saaleck** by Erhabener, out of Sava by Bachus. Black Trakehner (1940). This large and expanding family has very good breed type and a harmonious overall impression. The graded stallions Schwarm (1966) by Traumgeist XX and Schwalbenflug (1968) by Impuls are typical of the notable breeding stock produced by this line.

- **Schwindlerin** by Alibaba, out of Schwinge by Paradox XX. Dark brown Trakehner (1940). A family known for the many top mares it produces and for its fertility, good feed utilisation, harmonious conformation, suppleness and willingness to perform. The graded stallions Sleipnir (1967) by Herbsturm and Seeadler (1971) by Habicht should be noted in particular.

- **Tapete** by Pythagoras, out of Tapferkeit by Gauss. Dark brown Trakehner (1938). This expanding family of medium-sized horses with good breed type, fertility and movement seem to have shed their earlier reputation for flighty temper. A number of good stallions have been produced by this family, with the half-brothers Trajan (1964) by Carajan and Tschad (1971) by Prince Rouge XX being particularly favoured.

- **Velegue** by Hirtensang, out of Wiborg by Bulgarenzar. Chestnut Trakehner (1936). This 'typey' family has good riding-horse characteristics, a medium frame, good temperament and good rideability. The stallion Valentin (1965) by Abglanz was successful in eventing as well as being a proven sire of stallions.

- **Wally** by Gebhard, out of Wienerin by Neander. Black Trakehner (1942). This family has a good frame, a pleasant character and a willingness to perform. The well-known stallion Waldzauber (1971) by Kassio comes from this family.

STALLION LINES

In the halcyon days before the Second World War many strong stallion lines were established in East Prussia, both at Trakehnen and elsewhere. The chief ones amongst them were:

- The **Perfectionist** line, based on Perfectionist XX (1899) by Persimmon and Persimmon's three sons, **Tempelhüter** (1905), **Jagheld** (1906) and **Irrleher.**
- The **Dingo** line, based on **Dampfross** (1916) by Dingo and **Diebitsch** (1908) by Dingo.
- The **Obelisk** line, based on **Charm** (1902) by Obelisk and **Lichtenstein** (1906) by Obelisk.
- The **Padorus** line, based chiefly on **Markeur** (1901) by Padorus.
- The **Parsival** line, based on **Parsival** (1912) by Morgenstrahl.
- The **Astor** line, based on **Astor** (1922) by Walkenflug.
- The **Waldjunker** line, based on **Waldjunker** (1919) by Vasco.
- The **Habakuk** line, based chiefly on **Bulgarenzar** (1915) by Habakuk.
- The **Paradox XX** line, based on **Paradox XX** (1919) by Christian de Wet XX.
- The **Lehnsherr XX** line, based on **Lehnsherr XX** (1927) by Caligula XX.
- The **Fetysz OX** line, based on **Fetysz OX** (1924) by Bakszysz OX.

The catastrophic effect of the 'flight', which resulted in the loss of such stallions as Fetysz OX, Hyperion, Pythagoras and Creon, and the gelding of a number of high-class stallions such as Sulieman by Pythagoras, even after they had safely arrived in the West, drastically restructured the emphasis of these lines, and the most important bloodlines of today, although similar in outline, have significant changes in emphasis. These modern lines are therefore discussed below:

- The **Dampfross** line from the Dingo son Dampfross. This is certainly the most important stallion line in the Trakehner breed today. It has many members and it is really only possible to highlight a very small percentage of the modern representatives of the line. It is the line of Abglanz (1943) by Termit, and of all Abglanz's many descendants, such as Donauschimmer (1969) by Valentin. It is the line of Pregel (1958) by Tropenwald, and of his outstanding son Donauwind (1965) with his twenty-plus graded sons including the outstanding American show jumper Abdullah and the important sire Matador (1974). It is the line of Komet (1952) and, through him, of

Hessenstein (1958) by Komet, a Trakehner stallion graded with numerous other breed societies including the Hannoverian Verband and the Holsteiner Verband.

Hessenstein (1958), Isenstein (1964) and the British-based Muschamp Danube (1969). Gunnar (1960) by Komet also comes from this line, as does his son Amagun. Herbsturm by Sansturm represents yet another branch, and Marduc (1977) by Halali and his son Anduc (1981), Tausendassa by Keith, and the Totilas grandson

PEDIGREE OF **DONAUWIND** – BAY TRAKEHNER, 1965			
Donauwind DH 252 (Trak)	Pregel	Tropenwald	Termit
			Tropenglut
		Peraea 832	Hirtensang
			Per Adresse
	Donaulied von Schimmelhof 2319	Boris	Gabriel
			Bea 101
		Donau von Schim-melhof 1571	Hanskapitän
			Donna 831

Harnisch (1963) by Handelsherr are yet more branches. Finally, Dampfross is also represented in Hannoverian bloodlines by his son Semper Idem, who through his son Senator founded one of the most important sire lines in show jumping. In pure-bred Trakehner breeding Semper Idem is better known as a founder of an important new broodmare line through his daughter Wachau.

•The **Perfectionist XX** line, based on Poseidon, is most obviously represented by Schöne Abend's son Schabernack (1962) and grandson Rondo (1970).

•The **Perfectionist XX** line, based on the Jagheld/Ararad/Hutten line, has the outstanding stallion Impuls (1953) by Humboldt as its best-known representative, with Tenor (1978) by Tümmler, the two Schwalbenflug offspring Insterruf (1972) and Kassius (1970) and the Hartung son Symbol (1970) all being proven stock-getters. The Templehüter branch of this family now exists mainly in the broodmare herd.

The old Trakehner lines that are mentioned in the earlier list but which do not appear in the list above have not ceased to exist. They have, however, failed to fulfil the expectations held of them before 1945 and are now less significant in the breed.

Some new lines have also come to the fore in recent years and any record of the present Trakehner breed is incomplete without them:

•The **Famulus** line has Maharadscha (1967) by Famulus and his son Flaneur (1965) as its most noteworthy members. Flaneur has proved himself to be one of the most consistent stallion producers of the 1970s and 1980s, with his son Arogno and grandson Caprimond (by Karon) being in very high demand amongst mare owners.

•New Thoroughbred lines include those of Stern XX, Maigraf XX, Traumgeist XX (the sire of the outstanding dressage horse Hirtentraum, and the graded stallion Unikum who was leased to Sweden), Pindar XX (the line responsible for Ibikus by Hertilas), Prince Rouge XX and Pasteur XX, whose son Mahagoni (1974) and grandson Bartholdy (1980) were very influential in the latter part of the 1980s.

•New Anglo-Arab bloodlines include those of Burnus (1948) by Lapis X, which has already produced the eventing stallion Habicht, and Marsuk X (1963) by Paladin, an established sire of broodmares.

INFLUENCE OF THE TRAKEHNER

Because of the dispersal of Trakehner stallions and studs throughout West Germany after the 'flight', the Trakehner breed found itself in a unique position to act as an improver to some of the major Warmblood breeds in the world. From as early as 1948 Trakehner stallions were being used enthusiastically by non-Trakehner Warmblood breeders throughout West Germany for what the breed is especially suited – helping to produce a modern Warmblood competition horse. Of course, it has always been the concern of Trakehner breeders over the last fifty years to preserve the irreplaceable gene bank of pure-bred blood from which the breed acquires its elegance, movement and thriftiness, but they have also not been slow to capitalise on the opportunities given to them to extend the type and numbers of mares their stallions can cover. Practically every major breeding district in Germany has a group of Trakehner stallions graded into the district breeding organisation, and the same applies to other European countries, where the Trakehner has had a profound impact, not only on established stud books, like that of Sweden, but also on the newer ones such as the KWPN in the Netherlands, Dansk Varmblod in Denmark and the British Warm-Blood Society in Great Britain. It is therefore primarily in this role – as an improver rather than as a

A number of show jumpers, including the British high jump record holder, Everest Lastic, were sired by Lateran (1942) by Helikon.

PEDIGREE OF **HESSENSTEIN** – BAY TRAKEHNER, 1958			
Hessenstein (Trak)	Komet	Goldregen	Creon
			Goldelse 683
		Kokette 691	Cancara
			Kokarde
	Sonett 1652	Famulus	Fetysz OX
			Faschingsnacht
		Sonja 1334	Wilder Jäger
			Soldanelle 80

pure-bred horse – that we will discuss the influence of the Trakehner.

In the largest breeding district of Germany, Lower Saxony which is the home of the Hannoverian – Trakehners have been used on local Warmblood mares with outstanding success since pre-war days. Probably the most famous Trakehner stallion to stand in Hannover was Abglanz (1943) by Termit, who founded the very popular modern-type A line of the Hannoverian breed, so profound was his influence. The grey Lateran (1942) by Helikon, Hansakapitän, Altan, Cyklon, Humbolt and the Celle-based stallions Hessenstein (1958) by Komet and Inselkönig (1966) by Kapitän also made their mark on the Hannoverian breed, as did the Semper Idem son Senator.

In Baden-Württemberg the Trakehner was the chief breed used to upgrade the farm horse to the competition horse and the principal actors in this change were (amongst others) Julmond (1938) by Julianus, who did not take up stud duties there until the advanced age of twenty-two, Ilmengrund (1958) by Humboldt, Amor (1970) by Maharadscha, Kufstein (1972) by Maerchenstein and Donauwind's outstanding sire Pregel (1958) by Tropenwald.

In Hessen, the influence of the Trakehner has been particularly strong in lightening the heavier type of Oldenburg-related mares, with Kosmos (1956) by Hansakapitän, Thor (1959) by Humboldt and Thor's son Mandant (1964) making a particularly strong mark. Such important stallions as Schöne Abend (1958) by Abendstern and Isenstein (1964) by Hessenstein fulfilled the same roles in the now combined districts of Rheinland-Pfalz and the Saarland.

In the Westphalian state stud at Warendorf, Bernstein (1964) by Gunnar and Garamond (1964) by Gabriel were highly valued in the 1970s, and Hannoverian stallions carrying the blood of Abglanz, Semper Idem and Lateran are also popular. The Warmblood breed developed in the Rheinland shows even more Trakehner influence, however. Many Trakehners already licensed not only with the Trakehner Verband, but also with other Warmblood breeding areas – such as Garamond and Bernstein – have been introduced into the stud book, and with many of the studs being in private hands, the brood-mare band is of good quality and also contains many Trakehner mares, as well as carefully selected modern-type mares of other breeds.

The original broodmare band of the Oldenburg district was of a heavier type and the great strides made in modernising the breed are to a considerable degree due to the improving qualities of Trakehner bloodlines, either through the direct influence of such high quality stallions as the DLG exhibit Herbsturm (1962) by Komet and Magister (1964) by Major, or through the judicious use of top class Hannoverian stallions with Abglanz, Semper Idem and Lateran blood.

Finally amongst the German breeds, in Bavaria the blood of Komet (1952) by Goldregen, who stood there in the 1960s and Kassio (1963) by Abglanz is particularly highly valued for use on non-Trakehner mares.

In the Netherlands the blood of Marco Polo (1965) by Poet XX is very highly prized. He was an outstanding sire of show jumpers, particularly from rather solid old-fashioned mares, and his most famous progeny are probably the late Caroline Bradley's show jumper Marius

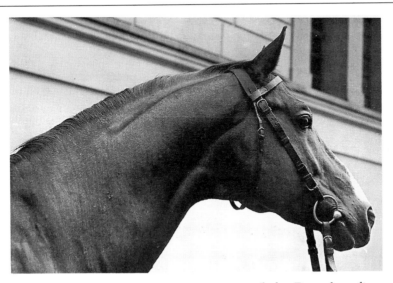

The most famous post-war representative of the Dampfross line, Abglanz (1943) by Termit, who founded the A-line in the modern Hannoverian breed and is a sire of international importance.

and the speed horse Vivaldi, ridden by Melanie Smith. As well as producing competition horses, he also sired some sons who themselves became graded in the Netherlands. These included Legaat, Adios and Irco Polo, all of whom – like his competition horses – were out of native Dutch mares with little or no Trakehner blood.

Some breeding of pure Trakehners does take place in Denmark, but it is principally because of its value as an improver of Warmbloods that Denmark has become the home of a number of famous Trakehner stallions over the past twenty-five years, including such influential stock-getters as Donauwind (1965) by Pregel, Ibikus (1967) by Hertilas and Gunnar (1960) by Komet. This outcross has not only produced some notable competition horses, but also a number of influential stallions including Dolomit (1979) by Donauwind and Ibi-Bell (1978) and Midt West Ibi-Light (1985) both by Ibikus. Donauwind's well-known daughter Diana also achieved immediate success at stud as she became the first-ever gold-medal mare in Denmark and produced two graded stallion sons in Denmark, Domino (1983) by the Hannoverian Luxemburg, and Diamond (1982) by the Hannoverian Allegro, who was supreme champion at his grading, as well as Diadem (1984) by Weltstar (Hann), a graded British Sports Horse stallion. Donauwind also sired the successful British-based Danish Trakehner show jumping stallion, Cannabis (1977).

Swedish breeders have also used a significant percentage of old East Prussian blood over the past hundred years, and even in the immediate post-war years, when the future of the Trakehner breed as a whole was in such a parlous state, such stallions as Heristal (1939) by Hyperion, Polarstern (1946) by Portwein and Unikum (1962) by Traumgeist XX found their way to the Swedish State Stud at Flyinge

PEDIGREE OF **IBIKUS** – BAY TRAKEHNER, 1967			
Ibikus DH 261 (Trak)	Hertilas	Loretto	Pindar XX
			Lorica 1514
		Herbstgold 2025	Totilas
			Herbstzeit 687
	Isolda 2481	Impuls	Humboldt
			Italia 54
		Isolda Madre 929	Pythagoras
			Isola Longa 688

and made a permanent impact on the Swedish breed. The blood of Marco Polo can also be found in Sweden through the two Irco Polo sons, Irco Marco and Irco Mena, who are proving popular sires of show jumpers.

In Britain, both pure-bred Trakehners and part-Trakehner Warmbloods are bred. Ever since 1960, when the graded stallion Korsar (by Hanskapitan out of Kordel by Indra) and two mares (Teri and Guntramis) were imported, followed by Donauwind's half brother Muschamp Danube (by Isenstein), interest in the Trakehner breed has grown steadily, and the Trakehner Breeders Fraternity of Great Britain (or TBF), is the sole official body concerned with Trakehner breeding in Great Britain.

Under the watchful eye of official Trakehner Verband judges, the TBF now grades its own stock, brands them with their own adapted version of the Trakehner brand, and issues the necessary registration documents. The TBF also pioneered the British Performance Test which takes the form of a qualification period with assessment followed by a final assessment session which normally runs over a number of days. This British Performance Test has now been taken over by the National Stallion Association (NASTA), the body which supervises stallion licensing procedures in the UK and is accepted by the Trakehner Verband. This performance test is compulsory for stallions and optional for mares.

Many British-based Trakehners are also used extensively for Warmblood breeding purposes. Most of the Trakehner mares and stallions used at stud in Great Britain are therefore also graded into the appropriate breeding studbooks of the British Warm-Blood Society (the BWBS) and a substantial number of their part-bred Trakehner foals can therefore be registered with and receive papers from other Warmblood organisations.

A number of significant Trakehner stallions were imported into Britain during the 1980s. These included Istanbul, now returned to Germany and Illuster (by Osterglanz XX). Both of these stallions were already proven producers in West Germany, where Istanbul had already sired a number of noted broodmares and Illuster's daughter Corna had become Riding Horse Champion of all breeds in West Germany in 1985. A number of high-class mares have also been imported including StPrSt Schlobitten (by Malachit) who is the dam of the 1976 Neumünster champion Schiwago (by Tannenberg), StPrSt Cordula (by Schiwago) and StPrSt Marcella (by Postmeister), herself already the dam of a champion foal in Britain. Since being imported Schlobitten has produced a British-born colt Holme Grove Solomon (by Fernando), who was approved by the TBF in 1988 and graded by the BWBS in 1989.

Other outstanding mares in Britain include StPrSt Roma II (by Ferlin) who was a Verden prize winner, StPrSt Fleuron (by Patron), StPrSt Copelia (by Bartholdy), StPrSt Godrington Tessa III by Acajou and StPrSt Godrington Havel V by Maifeuer, all of whom have contributed greatly to the quality of the TBF stud books.

At present, a number of Trakehners foaled in Great Britain have been accepted as graded by the TBF. There are two sons of the Russian mare Opushka (by Oplot), namely Fleetwater Olympus (by Downlands Hasardeur) and Fleetwater Opposition (by Muschamp Danube), who was Junior European Three-Day-Event Champion before retiring to stud. These join two older stallions graded and performance tested some time ago, namely Roland by Arminius and Downlands Cancara by Indigo II. Cancara is now famous in Britain as the Lloyds Bank 'Black Horse', and Roland has produced Sharolla Rainmaker (who was shortlisted for the Junior National Dressage Team) and Muschamp Fipps (who jumped Nations Cup for Annette Lewis). Muschamp Korsakoff (by Muschamp Danube) also looks like following in his sire's footsteps as a top competition horse sire.

Heuriger by Herzbube, a member of the Dutch silver medal-winning dressage team at the 1994 World Equestrian Games at The Hague.

More recent stallion importations include Beatos (by Kosmos), Handstreich (by Memeleruf), the top money winning Grand Prix Dressage Horse Va-Tout (by Wie Ibikus), Inspekteur (by Mahagoni) the American Olympic Dressage Horse and Muschamp Maestro (by Matador), the *Dressage Magazine* Young Dressage Stallion of the Year in 1994. However the earlier import Downlands Isolan (by Donauwind) has so far mainly concentrated on his competition career as a dressage horse.

Downlands Isolan's three-quarter brother the Danish-bred Trakehner Cannabis (by Donauwind out of Catya by Herzbube) is the only other direct representative of the Donauwind male line in Britain. but his career as a show jumper – and the fact that although graded with the BWBS he was unsuccessful at the TBF grading – means that he has not been used for Trakehner breeding, although he is growing in popularity amongst Warmblood mare owners because of his competition record.

As yet it is not possible to assess the long-term impact of Trakehner breeding on the British competition horse scene. Both Trakehner and Warmblood breeding in Great Britain are still in their early years, with only a limited number of home-bred sires at stud, and few horses old enough to compete under saddle. However, with the quality of stock so far imported and a number of studs already building on established foundations, continued growth in the numbers of owners, breeders and foals registered looks to be the future of the Trakehner in Great Britain.

In Eastern Europe, the influence of both the modern Trakehner and the heavier East Prussian horse has been significant not only in the development of the Polish Warmblood, but also in a number of the riding horse breeds of the former USSR since the Second World War. By reason of the geographical location of the original stud at Trakehnen, which lay so far in the east of Prussia that it is now part of the Russian Republic, large numbers of East Prussian horses were claimed as war booty and found themselves in Poland and behind the Soviet border once fighting ceased. These animals were therefore lost to Trakehner breeding in western Europe, and until very recently 'pure-bred Trakehners' bred in considerable numbers in Poland and Russia, were considered as very suspect by the Trakehner Verband and were not accepted into the Verband's stud books – or those of any of the Trakehner breeding organisations that it recognises outside Germany.

The rise and fall of the popularity of Trakehners in North America is dealt with more fully in the chapter on Warmbloods in North America, but even so it is important here to point out that, as is the case in many parts of the Trakehner and Warmblood breeding world, the influence of Donauwind is paramount: not only did he end his long and successful stud career at Yancey Farms, but also he was the most sought-after Trakehner sire of the later 1980s. His son, the Olympic gold medallist and World Cup winner in show jumping, Abdullah (1970) was imported into America *in utero* and his semen is not surprisingly in demand all over the world.

The Neumünster champion Morgenglanz (1965) by Abglanz sired a considerable number of top-class competition horses in America, as well as founding his own sire line with his son Traum and his grandson Troy.

Other top-graded stallions to be exported to North America include the Olympic dressage horse Azurit by My Lunaria XX, Elgius (1979) by Mackensen who was reserve champion at Neumünster in 1982, Donauschimmer (1969) by Valentin who was champion of his performance testing, and Zauberklang (1974) by Prince Condé who was reserve champion in his performance test and is already the sire of proven dressage horses in the USA.

Unfortunately, it is not possible to assess accurately how influential the Trakehner has been or will be in helping to produce a North American Warmblood horse, because of the lack of an overall authoritative Warmblood breeding organisation on the North American continent, but perhaps Trakehner breeding stock will find its true value as both a pure breed and an out-cross for other Warmbloods – when comprehensive statistics become available.

As a competition horse, the record of the Trakehner has perhaps been a little hampered by problems of temperament. Although they have often scored well in national competitions, particularly in Young Horse classes in Germany and in dressage competitions in North America, only limited numbers have represented their countries. Apart from the show-jumping stallion Abdullah, for the United States, and the eventing stallion Habicht for West Germany, the most notable Trakehners in the competition field in recent years have been the 1994 World Championships team silver medal winner Heuringer by Herzbube, the Olympic dressage horses Pentagon (1970) by Condus and Azurit by My Lunaria XX and the show jumpers Livius (1971) and Pezewever (1971). However, the number of international competition horses with at least some percentage of Trakehner blood must be almost countless. It is the Trakehner spirit that helps them to make top competition horses (witness the A-line Hannoverian for dressage horses) and it is this quality that should be prized above all in the Trakehner. It is essential for successful Warmblood breeding.

Chapter 2

The Hannoverian

by

DEBBIE WALLIN

THE HANNOVERIAN STATE STUD (Landgestüt) was founded in 1735, but it was not until the German Royal Agricultural Society created the Hannoverian Warmblood Stud Book in 1888 that all the original pedigrees and breeding records from the Landgestüt were brought together to form an official stud book. In 1922 the Verband Hannoverscher Warmblutzüchter (the Society of Hannoverian Warmblood Breeders) came into existence, and this organisation is still the governing body of the Hannoverian breeding area today. It is a private corporation while the State Stud at Celle is state-owned.

Initially, the main uses of the Hannoverian were as a cavalry and artillery horse, and also as an all-round farm animal. In the 1950s, as its purpose changed, a more modern, dual-purpose animal was sought that would be able to do lighter farm work whilst also being suitable as a carriage horse and riding horse combined. A large number of Thoroughbreds and good Trakehners were brought in to help modernise and consolidate the breed type. As the Hannoverian breeders increased in numbers, private breeders also took to standing stallions, all of which had to go through the inspection and licensing process alongside the state-owned sires. In the 1980s and 1990s the competition amongst privately owned, talented, high-class stallions was fierce, and many of the most successful sires date from this time.

The Hannoverian Verband rapidly expanded its role and offered help and incentives to breeders. In 1939 up-dated rules for the mare grading shows were established. These ran in conjunction with mare performance tests, and state premiums were awarded to exceptional mares. In addition, auctions were started for riding horses and breeding stock and, in the 1980s, for yearlings.

The Hannoverian breeding area thus soon became one of the best and largest breeding areas in Germany. Other countries, and other breeding societies within Germany, attended the shows there, and purchased stallions and mares as reliable foundation stock for their own breeding programmes. In the last twenty years Denmark, Belgium, Great Britain, the United States and Austria, and to a lesser extent the Netherlands and Sweden, have all benefited from Hannoverian bloodlines, and certainly one can find Hannoverian pedigrees amongst almost all of the established Warmblood breeds today.

BREEDING POLICY

As Hannoverians have been bred for a great many years, it is extremely interesting to note the results of changing policies adopted over the years. As the market demanded a different type of horse, the Verband had to review and change its judging criteria, and re-educate its breeders (mainly local farmers) to a newer type of medium-weight animal bred for riding and high-level competition work, rather than for farming or hunting pursuits. The grading and show classes were therefore the obvious means of consolidating a new breed type.

The mares' stud book inspection is divided into four sections as follows:

• *Main Stud Book (H symbol)* To be eligible for this a mare must have four generations of recognised pedigree. The dam of the mare must be graded in the Main Stud Book or Stud Book. She must also have a final score of 6.0 points in conformation and movement and no score lower than 5.0 in the other grading criteria. Mares graded into the Main Stud Book receive an Hannoverian H brand on the left side of the neck.

• *Stud Book (S symbol)* To be eligible for this a mare must have three generations of recognised pedigree and the dam must be in the Main Stud Book, the Stud Book or the Pre-Stud Book. She must have a final score of no lower than 5.0 points and no score lower than 4.0 in any of the grading criteria. Mares graded into the Stud Book receive an Hannoverian H brand on the left side of the neck.

• *Pre-Stud Book I (S symbol) and Pre-Stud Book II (A symbol)* These books are only open to mares living within the main Hannoverian breeding area that do not fulfil the requirements necessary for entry into the Main Stud Book or the Stud Book. They are branded with a Hannoverian horse's head brand.

Mares from outside the Hannoverian breeding area that are entered for grading with the Hannoverian Verband are only eligible for the Main Stud Book or the Stud Book as their bloodlines dictate.

State premium awards are given to outstanding mares (the top 10-15%) by the Lower Saxony State Government to encourage breeders to retain certain bloodlines and quality for breeding within the area. To qualify, a mare must be three years old, be covered by a graded sire and be a winner of a 1A prize at an official Verband show. She must also then successfully complete a ridden test for basic gaits, rideability and jumping. The owner of the mare agrees to retain her for breeding during the next three years and her colt foals must be offered to the state stud at Celle. She must also be shown at the grading show for the next three years, and during this time she cannot be sold without the permission of the state Chamber of Agriculture. If the mare fulfils all these requirements to the necessary standard she is then confirmed as a State Premium Stute (StPrSt).

Foals sired by Hannoverian-graded sires currently in the breeding stud book are branded on the left thigh with the same brand that its dam carries on her neck, and those foaled in the Hannoverian breeding area also receive a number on the left side of the neck.

To qualify for entry into the breeding stud book stallions must have a full pedigree with both dam and granddam graded into the Main Stud Book. It is also preferable for the dam to have passed the ridden performance test.

Many foals are purchased by private 'stallion rearers', and the state-owned stallion-rearing stud at Hunnesrück also purchases numerous potential stallions as foals and runs them on in groups until as two-and-a-half-year-olds they are ready to attend licensing in November.

The stallion licensing is held at the society's indoor school in Verden. The licensing starts with a veterinary inspection, which has become much stricter. As of 1994, due to the high instance of hereditary wind problems a veterinary examination for Laryngeal hemiplegia (more commonly referred to as roaring or whistling) is required for potential stallions and State Premium candidates. The colts are then loose-jumped and shown in hand. An interesting condition of entry requires that the state stud has first choice of purchasing a number of the best newly licensed colts. This makes certain that the top quality breeding sires remain in Germany.

Following licensing, privately owned colts must pass a 100-day ridden performance test with marks of at least 90, while the state-owned sires must complete eleven months of testing. The first crop of foals are also inspected, and if they do not reach the required standard, the sire may still be removed from the breeding stud book.

Regional mare shows and riding horse classes abound, possibly the most interesting being the National Agricultural Show, usually called the DLG Show, where the best mares and stallions from each breeding district compete against one another for the supreme championship. International judges are invited from other leading breeding societies abroad. The late summer Ratje-Niebuhr Show, which was initially known as the Louis Wiegels Show, is the largest and most prestigious show for Hannoverians. It has classes for all ages of breeding mares, as well as classes for the families of foundation mares, which enables the public to see two or three generations of exceptional mares together.

GENERAL DESCRIPTION OF THE HANNOVERIAN

The member's guide of the Hannoverian Verband describes the breed as follows: 'A correctly built, noble, versatile Warmblood horse, capable of superior performance under saddle, with big ground-covering, yet light and elastic gaits, good temperament and an honest character.'

Today the preferred height is between 16hh (162cm) and 16.2hh (168cm) (neither too big nor too small), with good, flat bone, short cannons and hard, neat, (but not upright) good hooves. A much better shoulder and wither have appeared since the late 1980s, with a longer, more elegant front and much more attention has been given to a good free walk. The rather old-fashioned flatish croup and high-set tail is disappearing in favour of a longer, squarer, more muscular croup. Heads are more refined than in the past, and the quality is leaning more towards a blood type of animal yet with plenty of substance.

IMPORTANT BLOODLINES

All progeny entering the breeding stud book of the Hannoverian Verband are required to take a name starting with the first letter of the sire's own name. Although not foolproof as so many sire lines are available, one can have a fair guess at an animal's lineage if one knows the first letters of each name in its pedigree. Due to the large numbers involved, it would be beyond the scope of this book to discuss every sire line. We have decided to cover those that have made the largest impact on the modern Hannoverian and made our selection accordingly, with a bit of guess work on the future.

THE D-LINE

Probably the most famous and successful line is the D-line, founded by the English Thoroughbred Devils Own XX (1887). The most important modern representative of this line is generally thought to be Duellant (1943), by Dolman, a rather heavy stallion with enormously powerful action. His descendants are to be found within almost every breeding country in the world, both in sport and at stud. He sired no fewer than forty-two licensed stallions and numerous highly graded mares which won at the DLG Show. His stock were equally at home in show jumping and dressage, and his relatives, like Deister (1971), by Diskant, one of the world's top show jumpers of the 1980s ridden by Paul Schockemöhle, continue to prove the worth of this important foundation line. Duellant's best-known descendants are probably the Celle stallions Duft II (1958), whose son Darling (1971) was a prolific sire of high-quality broodmares, and Duft I (1957), a high money earner in terms of competition winning progeny and sire of the graded stallions Diplomat (1967) and Duktus (1968).

Gotthard (1949) by Goldfisch II, world-famous sire of international competition horses, mainly in show jumping. Shown here at twenty-eight years of age, his blood is sought by riders and breeders alike.

Duellant's sire Dolman (1933), by Detektiv, also produced Dollart (1938) who founded another branch of the D-line, mainly in jumping, through Domspatz (1952) and Don Carlos (1962). The D-line is a very large family, successful and highly thought of in breeding terms. Thomas Füch's Dollar Girl by Dynamo is rated as one of the 1990s best show jumpers. She originally competed for Switzerland, and was purchased at the Verden Auction, but now is ridden by Nick Skelton for Great Britain.

THE G-LINE

Founded by Goldammer II (1919) by Goldschläger I, the prime source of today's G-line is really Goldammer's son Goldfisch II (1935), the sire and grandsire respectively of Gotthard and Grande, the names everyone automatically associates with show jumping, but interestingly enough, many international dressage horses are now coming to the fore, specifically from the Grande side of the pedigree line. Very muscular horses, and often rather plain in looks, their athletic ability was outstanding. Both Gotthard and Grande have numerous graded sons at Celle today (e.g. the Gotthard son, Garduelan), and the G-line brings in exceptionally good prices at auction. Everest G-Line (jumped by Britain's Nick Skelton), Gaylord by Gralsitter (rider Hanke Luther), Grunox by Grunewald (ridden by Monica Theodorescu), Gigolo FRH by Graditz (rider Isabell Werth) and Gifted by Garibaldi II, a Grand Prix dressage horse in the United States for Carol Lavell, are just a few names that carry on the tradition. The FRH has been formed by the retired president Herwart v. d. Decken to promote Hannoverian horses and stands for the Association for the Advance-

PEDIGREE OF **GARDEULAN** – LIGHT BAY HANNOVERIAN, 1975			
Gardeulan I 311324075 (Hann)	Gotthard 3838	Goldfisch II 3137	Goldammer II
			Flugamme
		Ampa H 40287	Amateur I
			Ameline
	Waldrun H 72377	Waidmannsdank (XX) 4085	Neckar
			Waldrun
		St Pr St Felsengräfin H 66443	Ferdinand
			Faschingswerk

ment of Riding in competition on Hannoverian Horses.

The Hannoverian verband is also trying actively to encourage the breeding of horses destined for the showjumping circuit. They have instigated a new program called the Program der Hannoveraner Springpferdezücht which selects mares for their 'above average ability of producing show jumpers'.

The system for entry to this program relies on data recorded under Breeding Values as well as the mares own record either in competition or in the evaluation of her Mare Performance Test results. A list of recommended sires is selected each year and sent to the owners of mares in this new program.

THE F/W-LINE

Ferrara (1935), by Feinschnitt, sired Feuerland (1940) and Ferdinand (1941) who can certainly lay claim to a prolific and successful line of their own, albeit not quite as famous as the modern G-line. Confusingly, this line changed into the W-line between the mid-1940s and 1990, when it again returned to the F-line for the naming of its stallions. Because of this, Feuerland's son born in 1948 was named Weiler, and this line can be traced to the World Cup show jumper Waltzerkönig (ridden by Franke Sloothaak).

Ferdinand was Ferrara's best-known son. Out of a Helgoland mare, he not only sired international competition and Olympic team horses like Ferdl (a gold medal winner for Alwin Schockemöhle) and Mehmed (for Reiner Klimke), but his sons founded an important and still extremely prolific sire line. Best known is probably Wendekreis (1967) followed closely by Wedekind (1966) and Winnetou (1964). This line is remarkable as the jumping abilities continue through each generation from the Wendekreis son Wagner (1975), a grey stallion with Gotthard on his dam's side, to his talented Celle-based grandson Wanderer (1980). Bred from the best jumping blood available, Wendekreis's eldest son Werther (1973) is one of the most sought-after sires at Celle. Ferdinand himself was no beauty, being rather short of rib and possessing a steep sloping croup, but his talent for producing performance horses cannot be questioned.

The other branch of the F-line is the Flick-Fling line, which like the Ferrara line changed to W in the 1940s, but did not revert to F in 1990, retaining W as its distinguishing feature. Flügeladjutant (1938), by Flügelmann I, sired two outstanding sons Wöhler (1950) and Florentiner II (1953). Both were extraordinary movers and were used as 'action trotters' at the stallion displays at Celle. Wöhler had enormous success with his high-priced youngsters at Verden auctions, and though he was barely 15.3hh in height, his stock were renowned for their muscular build, correct legs, workable temperament and powerful action. His son Woermann (1971), out of a half Thoroughbred mare, was the main sire of the W-line foaled in the 1980s. Florentiner II's progeny became known for their jumping ability through Widerhall (1964), the sire of Caroline Bradley's International show jumper Tigre, and his son Wienerwald (1971) who is also highly regarded as a show jumping sire.

OTHER IMPORTANT BLOODLINES

A number of lighter-weight Trakehners and Thoroughbreds were introduced to help modernise the heavier mares, thereby producing a more rideable model for the future. Mention must therefore be made here of three lines: those of Abglanz and Senator, both descendants of the famous foundation sire Dampfross (1916), by Dingo, and the Thoroughbred line of Der Löwe XX (1944), by Wahnfried XX.

•**Abglanz**'s most famous son, Absatz (1960), was a stallion of great beauty, with a lovely head and light, free action. This A-line produced excellent state premium broodmare families as well as highly graded stallions, and combined very successfully with the Grande line, adding elegance to the plainer G-line mares.

•**Senator**'s (1951) best sons were Sesam I (1955) and Sender (1955). Sesam's famous son Servus (1961) is an all-round sire of competition horses, being responsible for the Grand Prix dressage horse Slibovitz and becoming one of the top ten money-earning sires of 1989. He is also the sire of Herr Rubens' Grand Prix dressage horse Schiwago, and in the United States his son Spartan has also competed at Grand Prix level for Sascha Himmelmeyer. Another Himmelmeyer owned Servus son, San Antonio (purchased at the 1986 Verden auction), has commenced his jumping career well. Tric Tac expanded Servus's reputation as a sire of show jumpers by competing for Egypt in the Seoul Olympics. Outside Germany the Senator line also prospers. One of the best mare lines in Denmark was founded on the black stallion Solist by the Sender son Seelöwe (1961) out of a Der Löwe XX mare. This line is often rather small in height, but with very harmonious conformation and big, elegant, elastic movements.

•**Der Löwe XX** (1944) himself was only just over 15.2hh (157.5cm) and was light of bone, but his progeny excelled in sport. Probably the best known are Der Lord and Liostro. Although he sired only five graded sons, they went on to found a line through Lugano I (1954) and Lugano II (1958). Not particularly large horses, their blood was a consolidating influence in the 1970s and was still active in the early 1990s through Lanthan (1978), Lysander (1981), and Legat (1983), all owned by Celle. Der Löwe reappears again as the dam's sire of the privately owned stallion, Ritual (1985) by Ramiro (Holst.). Ritual's first progeny are often topping the Verden Foal Auctions, and he has also been graded for use within the Holstein Society.

The following modern stallions are also of particular note:

• **Bolero** by Black Sky XX. Chestnut Hannoverian (1975). Bolero was a three-quarter Thoroughbred stallion who unfortunately died at the all-too-early age of twelve years. He had a profound impact in the Hannoverian breeding area in the 1980s. A new B-line has been founded, and his sons have been exported to numerous countries around the world: Bonsoir (1986), Bohème (1985) and Belucci (1983) went to Denmark, and a Bolero son has also been purchased by Belgium. Bruderherz (1981) and Barter (1984) stand in the United

Bolero (1975) by Black Sky XX. Founding sire of a new B-line in the 1990s with his many highly graded sons and daughters, Bolero also produced winners at the German National Riding Horse Championships, and highly priced stock sold at the Verden Auctions.

States. Used mainly on Grande, Argus and Duellant mares, Bolero continually produced horses with good shoulders and withers, modern toplines and an elastic action. His daughters consistently win at major shows and were awarded state premiums. From his first group of five sons selected to attend the licensing show at Verden in 1982, no fewer than four were licensed, and his sons have regularly continued to excel at licensing in the 1980s. in 1984 the German National Riding Horse Championship went to Boruschkin (later sold at the Verden auction for 110,000DM to a dressage rider) by Bolero out of an Argus mare. Understandably in West Germany, breeders began referring to the 'Bolero boom'. This success continued with further record prices at various auctions, and the 1986 DLG championship was won by the three-year-old Bolero daughter Batumi. In the United States, Bosky by Bolero out of a Wendekreis mare became the best dressage horse at second level, and in the 1987 auctions another daughter, Bino Bo, sold for a record price whilst the highest priced foal at auction was the Bolero son, Ben Gurion, who made 32,000DM. Luckily, despite Bolero's early demise, frozen semen had already been collected before his death but he has left many sons and daughters within the Hannoverian breed to continue his strong influence for a number of years.

PEDIGREE OF **BOLERO** – CHESTNUT HANNOVERIAN, 1975			
Bolero 310111275 (Hann)	Black Sky (XX) 666 PB	Blast	Djébé
			Gale Warning
		Madrilene	Court Martial
			Marmite
	Baronesse H 76050 (Hann)	Bleep (XX) 615 PB	Pinza
			The Satelite
		Atlastaube H 54614 (Hann)	Athos
			Fliegerheil

•**Matcho X** by Pancho II X. Black French Anglo-Arab (1978). Matcho X is a small stallion of exceptional beauty owned by Celle. His progeny, like those of Bolero, have gained considerable success in both the mare and stallion grading shows. His daughters are sought after and always in the state premium awards. His licensed sons are muscular with very good croups and clean limbs. During the 1980s and 1990s his sons were in the top rank of licensed and performance-tested youngsters. Celle has purchased a number of his graded sons, and, like Bolero before him, Matcho X has shown extremely good results when crossed with G-line mares, particularly those sired by Goldstein (by Gotthard). For a number of years colts with this blood combination have been attending the licensing with excellent results – Anne-Grethe Törnblad (Denmark) has chosen the black graded stallion Supermax Macho (1986) (Matcho X/Goldstein) as a potential Grand Prix dressage horse.

- **Argentan** by Absatz. Bay Hannoverian (1967). Out of a Wohlan dam, and one of the last sons of Absatz to stand at stud. His own line is well established, with Airport (1982), Aircraft (1984), Al Capone (1985) and Archipel (1985) representing him in Germany, Agent (1984) and Aspirant (1979) in Denmark, and Ansas (1980) and Aktuell (1973) for a time, in the United States. Argentan is noted for both his dressage horses and his show jumpers, particularly as he sired Aramis, the 1984 show jumping World Cup winner in Sweden. Denmark also has the Absatz son, Allegro (1972). He proved his worth as a sire over a number of years in Denmark, producing numer-

Argentan (1967), a prolific bay stallion owned by Celle and one of Absatz's last and best sons at stud, being the sire of Aramis, the World Cup show jumper.

ous mares graded into the top stud books as well as medal mares at the Danish Elite Show. He has Diamond (1982) and Picandt (1983) as fully graded stallions, both of whom show exceptional dressage talent, with Diamond working at Prix St Georges level as an eight-year-old. Allegro was also the sire of the 1990 Danish stallion grading champion Arizona Alfarvad, and his progeny are usually full of presence with a very good elastic action but often have a tendency to a rather long loin.

• **Watzmann** by Weingau. Chestnut Hannoverian (1968). This stallion has come to the fore as the sire of the top international show jumper Waltzerkönig, ridden by Franke Sloothaak, and a winner at Aachen, Berlin, Zurich, Stockholm, Bremen, Amsterdam and London. At the 1989 stallion licensing, Celle selected two sons of Watzmann to be bought in. One, the grey Foxhunter (1987) has already started his own successful jumping career. As yet there are not many of his graded sons available for export, but Denmark purchased Weinberg by Watzmann in the early 1980s and is one of the few countries to be ahead of Germany in this respect.

• **Wenzel I** (liver chestnut, 1976) and **World Cup I** (liver chestnut, 1977) both by Woermann. Both these sons of Woermann (1971) have the really outstanding action passed down from their grandsire Wöhler. They have excellent temperaments and are easy to ride. Wenzel I was Reserve National Champion at the DLG Show and World Cup I won the ridden performance test in 1980 at Adelheidsdorf. World Cup I's son, Weltmeyer (1984) out of an Absatz mare, was placed first at his licensing and awarded a gold medal from

PEDIGREE OF **WENZEL I** – LIVER CHESTNUT HANNOVERIAN, 1976			
Wenzel I 314510876 (Hann)	Woermann 310426571	Wöhler 3880	Flügeladjutant
			St Pr St Flozia
		Mandat H 59881 (Hann)	Marabou (XX)
			St Pr St Abendfriede
	Mon Cherie H 311802872	Matador 4149	Marconi 4020
			St Pr St Landtanne
		Diola H 70880	Don Carlos
			St Pr St Fanal

Wenzel I (1976) by Woermann. A leading sire in his own right, his outstanding action can be traced to his grandsire Wöhler, an 'action trotter' for the Celle Stud.

the FN. Weltmeyer was the German National Champion three-year-old riding horse in 1987, which – with his outstanding pedigree – pushed him in to being one of the most sought-after stallions at stud. Two of Weltmeyer first sons to complete grading, Wittinger (1989) and the privately owned Weltbürger (1989) won the Riding Horse Championships of their districts. Walt Disney I (1986), also by World Cup I but out of a StPrSt dam by Grenadier convincingly won the ridden performance test from a class of 38 stallions and was awarded the Buchard Müller Pries in 1990 for the best stallion of his year as well as a Gold Medal for his breeder Hans Joachim Krause. The Wöhler bloodline is also well represented in Australia, Belgium, Brazil, Canada, Denmark, Great Britain, New Zealand and the United States. Australia has Winterkönig (1979), World Cup IV (1984) stands in Ontario, Denmark has Woernitz (1977), the Wenzel I son Victory (1985) and Weltlöwe (1989) by Weltmeyer, whilst the United States has no fewer than four graded descendants at stud.

- **Wanderer** by Wagner. Hannoverian (1980). Coming from the Wendekreis line (which returned to the F initial again in 1990 to differentiate it from the Wöhler W-line), the colts from this stallion

Weltmeyer (1984) by World Cup I. A German National Riding Horse Champion and an extremely popular sire with high grading marks, he is an excellent example of the modern Hannoverian.

have been highly placed at the licensing and ridden performance testing. Notably, they have an exceptionally good jumping technique, and are medium-weight quality youngsters with harmonious, powerful top lines and outstanding action.

Thoroughbred blood has always been brought in to improve shoulders and withers and to give more elegance, but in 1990 Celle took the unusual step of licensing no fewer than seven Thoroughbred stallions at one time. Amerigo Vespucci XX (1982) by Akari XX was the champion stallion at the Thoroughbred Show in Köln in 1988. Foaled in West Germany, he ran forty-one times with a Timeform rating of 96.5. Another Thoroughbred of unusual interest is Prince Thatch XX (1982) by Thatch XX, who completed his ridden performance test alongside the Warmblood youngsters, ending up in a very respectable third place. Star Regent XX (1975) by Prince Regent sired the Best Mare at the Ihlienworth Show, and this three-year-old later sold (in foal to Walt Disney I) for a new record price at the Broodmare Auction 1994.

Lauries Crusador XX (1985) by Welsh Pageant is very popular having no fewer than thirteen sons selected for stallion grading in 1994,

Wagner (1975) by Gotthard. Leased from Spruce Meadows in Canada by the Celle Stud. His son Wanderer has founded a line of talented sons owned by Celle with great jumping ability and free movement.

and the champion foal at Freiburg in the same year.

Older Thoroughbred sires, notably Lemon XX (1971) and Augustinus XX (1976), have had a number of sons graded but only time will tell what influence their blood will have in the stud book; although during the 1970s and 1980s, two Thoroughbred sires unrelated but both beginning with the letter S – Sudan XX (1959) by Nizam XX and Shogun XX (1969) by Tamerlane XX – made a considerable impact.

Sudan XX was the sire of the Celle stallions Saluto (1969), Sansibar (1971), Smaragd (1971), Sudwind (1970) and Sultan (1973), as well as the international and Olympic event horse Sherry. Sudan XX has produced numerous competition horses, but as yet his sons have failed to make a mark in the Hannoverian breed.

Shogun XX was a very beautiful small stallion, who finished the 1980s as one of the best live sires in terms of the number of offspring selected for Verden Elite Auctions – only Der Löwe XX, Absatz and Cardinal XX can claim more. This popularity may in part be due to the fact that in 1982 one of his progeny won the three-year-old German Riding Horse Championship and that his daughter Shamrock (sold via the Verden auction) was in the gold-medal winning West German

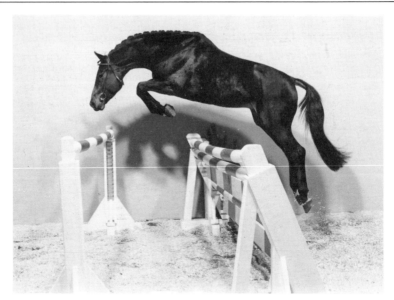

Wanderbursch I by Wanderer is out of a Shogun XX mare and shows excellent jumping talent.

three-day event team at the Seoul Olympics in 1988. At the time of Shogun XX's death in 1989, out of seven licensed sons none had been retained by Celle, although the graded Celle stallion Wanderbursch II (1986) by Wanderer, is out of a Shogun XX mare. There are, of course, other Thoroughbred and Trakehner lines that have produced well – for instance those of the Thoroughbreds Marcio XX (1947) and his full brother Maigraf XX (1948), Adlerschild XX, and of the Trakehner Lateran (1942) – but there are not many direct descendants currently founding stallion lines with those initials and it is difficult to see what effect they will have on future breeding generations.

In the 1990s the Hannoverian Verband have opened their stud books still wider and have bought in a number of outside bloodlines that have proved their worth in world competition and popularity. The Selle Français stallions Quasi Roi (1982) and Imperator (1980) and a number of Almé Z sons and grandsons are now recognised. (It is important to remember that Almé (1966) by Ibrahim and Almé Z are the same stallion. The Z was added when he stood at Leon Melchior's famous show jumping stud Zangersheide in Belgium.) More Trakehner sires are also being used and for the first time Holstein stallions have become popular, with the blood of Landgraf I (1966) and Lord (1967) by Ladykiller XX, Ramiro (1965) by Raimond, and the Holstein-

Walt Disney I (1986) by World Cup I. A convincing winner of the 100-day performance test with high dressage and jumping marks.

graded Selle Français stallion Cor de la Bryère (1965) by Rantzau XX now being integrated into the Hannoverian stud book on quite a large scale. Many of the highest priced foals at Verden's auction are by these sire lines.

PRIVATELY OWNED STALLIONS OF INTEREST

Private stallions have to be very competitive to warrant their stud fees. Excellence is a top priority, as the state-owned stallions are reasonably priced and of a very good quality, which makes for stiff competition. While state-owned stallions stand at stud for members of their own breed society, privately owned stallions are usually graded with more than one breed society in Germany. All the societies are looking for new sires, which will improve the standard of their breeding areas, and by so doing, the stallion owners have a wider choice of mares and also a higher number of visiting mares than if they restricted themselves to one breeding area. Usually the foal takes the brand and the pedigree papers of its dam. Privately owned sires are identified by PB after their names.

Some outstanding stallions have stood privately in the Hannoverian breeding district and the list below gives details of some of the most important ones:

•**Furioso II** (1965) by Furioso XX, a Selle Français imported from France and based at the privately owned stud of G. Vorwerk. He has produced over fifty graded sons and his progeny include the Junior European Dressage Champion Fiorio (ridden by E. Koller) and the International show jumper Furry, initially ridden by K. Reinacher before being sold to Britain. The same stud also became the base for the French Anglo-Arab stallion **Inschallah X** (1968) by Israel, a tall grey stallion with excellent movement. He has a good reputation for producing competition horses and has sired a number of graded stallions.

•**Zeus** (1972) by Arlequin X has also been imported from France. His progeny have won over 1,000,000DM, which in the Hannoverian listings makes him one of the top ten sires of the late 1980s.

•**Grannus** (1972) (previously Granit), by Graphit out of a mare by the Trakehner, Ozean, has produced a number of famous winners and is outstanding as a show jumping sire. His daughter Burschikase was Reserve Champion in Oldenburg and he himself was a Grade A show jumper. His show jumping son, Grand Slam (1979), was in the World Cup team in 1990 for Britain with Nick Skelton; with other internationally famous sons in Top Gun (Jan Tops) Almox Grand Plaisir (Ludger Beerbam) and Everest Grannusch (John Whitaker) in the top ranks.

•**Godehard** (1976) by Gotthard out of an Artur mare, was jumped by Franke Sloothaak and his progeny's winnings in show jumping have topped 1,000,000DM, which is perhaps not surprising as he is owned by Paul Schockemöhle and used on mares with a proven jumping pedigree.

•**Goldstern** (1972), by Gotthard out of a Waidmannsdank XX mare, is not only the sire of progeny with winnings of over 1,000,000DM but has also produced a good crop of graded sons including Goldfürst (1980), the reserve champion at licensing in 1983. His offspring also do well at auctions with a filly foal being the top priced lot at Vechta in 1982, and Gitano by Goldstern being sold to the United States through the PSI Sale.

•**Pik Bube I** (1973) by Pik König out of a Frustra II mare, is a full brother to the Celle-owned Pik Bube II (1975) and stood at the

Grönnwohldhof Stud. Pik Bube I and Pik Bube II are both sires of dressage as well as jumping progeny – and by 1990 the combined earnings of their stock was over 1,000,000DM. The foals offered at Verden auctions attract great attention and are always amongst the highest priced there. Pik Bube I's daughter Pikantje became the German National Riding Horse Champion in 1981, and her son Picasso (by Wandersmann XX) was exported and graded in Denmark where he stands at stud. Pik Bube I was a Prix St Georges horse with Herbert Rehbein. Also owned by Grönnwohldhof are **Donnerwetter** (1977) by Disput and his son **Donnerhall** (1981), who is branded as an Oldenburg (as his dam is Oldenburg graded) but is also graded into the Hannoverian and Westphalian stud books. Donnerhall was the champion at the DLG Show in 1986, and is competing at Grand Prix dressage. He has produced a number of sons to carry on his line in both the Hannoverian and the Oldenburg stud books, including Davignon (1988), Don Gregory (1988), Dream of Glory (1989) and Donnerschee (1988).

PEDIGREE OF **PIK BUBE** – BROWN HANNOVERIAN, 1973			
Pik Bube I 314600373 (Hann)	Pik König 4187 (Hann)	Pik As (XX) 3845	Abendfrienden
			Pechfackel
		St Pr St Anina H 68195 (Hann)	Abhang II 3992
			St Pr St Fahra H 64794
	Franka H 69382 (Hann)	Frustra II 3027	Futurist I 3063
			Talweise H 28128
		Dohlenfürstin H 64320	Domspatz 3910
			Löwenherz H 40042

- **Salut** (1966) by Sender out of a Gong mare was one of the last sons of Sender still alive by the early 1960s. His progeny have also topped the 1,000,000DM line in show-jumping competitions.

- **Cardinal XX** (1964) by Off Key XX is in the top listing of sires producing dressage horses. In 1988 Cortino (ridden by Petra Ebbing) headed the West German list of earnings for Hannoverian dressage horses. Another of Cardinal XX's progeny, Chagall, ridden by M. Winter, was fifth, and Charmeur – by Cardinal XX's son

Cavalier (1971) – was fourteenth in the same year. These are certainly impressive results, only beaten by Grande, who had three progeny listed.

THE HANNOVERIAN INFLUENCE

The influence of the Hannoverian on Warmblood breeding is a huge subject as the breed hails from one of the largest breeding districts and its popularity is worldwide. Most of the major Warmblood breeding societies have at least a certain percentage of Hannoverian mares and stallions in their stud books, the main exceptions being those of the Selle Français, the Holstein and the Trakehner. The chief Hannoverian bloodlines present in each of the breeds discussed in this book are therefore mentioned only in the briefest detail here, being dealt with more fully in the relevant chapter. This section will therefore deal mainly with exported competition horses and their impact.

Not only is the Hannoverian market popular with breeders but it also sells enormous numbers of competition horses both directly from home and through the Verden auctions, which are now publicised worldwide. Hannoverians are constantly in the limelight everywhere and regularly appear in national teams; examples in show jumping are Hugo Simon's E.T. FRH by Espri for Austria, Thomas Frühmann's Grandeur by Gralsritter for West Germany, Thomas Füchs's Diners Dollar Girl by Dynamo for Switzerland who is now ridden by Nick Skelton in Great Britain, and Jan Top's Dorreen La Silla by Diskus for the Netherlands (this horse was a Verden auction purchase in 1984), whilst in dressage E. Max Theurer's Acapulco by Absatz, C. Egerstrom's Metternich by Marmor, O. Nakamata's Medina by Matrose, and C. Boylen's Anklang by Adlerfarn II, represented Austria, Mexico, Japan and Canada respectively at the Los Angeles Olympics, and Cynthia Ishoy's late dressage horse, Dynasty by Darling, for Canada kept the Hannoverian flag flying in Seoul, as did the West German team horse Koran by Kadett in the European Championships. Five Hannoverians were in the medal-winning West German three-day event teams during the 1980s: namely Salem by Sudan XX, Mannix by Mongole and Doran by Diolen, and the previously mentioned Shamrock by Shogun XX and Sherry by Sudan XX.

As eventing is gaining continually in popularity, the rider wishing a Hannoverian can now choose from a number of Thoroughbred and Anglo-Arab first generation youngsters. For the 1996 Olympics in Atlanta a number of Hannoverians will be in the running for a place on the team including Granat FRH (Enno Reinstorf) by Gardeoffizier;

Magic Boy by Matcho AA (Tim Rethemeyer) as well as Active Explosion by Azur who is already in the States with his rider Peter Thomson.

As well as the breeding stock discussed more fully in the chapter on Warmbloods in North America, the United States has had some outstanding Hannoverian competition horses such as the world class show jumpers The Natural by Diskus (ridden by Katherine Burdsall) and Aramis by Argentan. Crown Royal Artos Z, a grey stallion by Almé but carrying a Hannoverian brand, is in the top listings with Mark Leone and the graded bay stallion, Rio Grande (1986) by Raphael ridden by Eric Lamze was shortlisted for the World Equestrian Games. George Lindemann and Genesis by Don Juan (1971) has made the WBCSH (World Breeding Championship for Sport Horses) soon to be shortened to FSSB (the Federation of Studbooks for Sportshorse Breeding). In dressage Gifted by Garibaldi II (a son of Grande out of a Lombard mare) has made a name for himself at Grand Prix level with Carol Lavell.

In Canada, in addition to Gail Greenough's 1986 World Championship winner Mr T by Wohlan, one of the first Canadian-bred Hannoverians, Concorde, by Wodka (1972) out of a Thoroughbred mare, was highly placed in the 1989 World Cup Final in Tampa, Florida. Wodka by Wolfsburg (1963) is from the same sire line as Wöhler and has competed in show jumping very successfully. Cindy Ishoy's gelding Dakar by Darling (1971) competes internationally at Grand Prix level.

Australia stands a number of Hannoverian sires, including a good Woermann son Winterkönig (1979), out of a Pik As XX mare. At the Seoul Olympics in 1988, Jeff McVean competed for Australia on Fürst Z from the Ferdinand line and Whisper Grey by Widerhall.

In New Zealand the stallions imported from West Germany are selected for their suitability to be crossed mainly with Thoroughbred mares. Olympic horseman Mark Todd competed in Seoul in the show jumping on a horse bred this way – Bago (NZ) by Winnebago (1970) by Winnetou – and won the Nescafé Derby in Auckland on this home-bred gelding.

Britain, the Netherlands and Denmark in particular have imported considerable numbers of competition horses and breeding stock, all discussed elsewhere, but in the context of the influence of the Hannoverian breed, the country of Belgium deserves a special mention. Belgium has based most of its breed on the top jumping lines available today. The stud book reads like a *Who's Who* of popular bloodlines and most of the best ones can be found there. Gardestern II (1975) (otherwise known as Goldspring de Lauzelle) by Gotthard is a leading show jumping sire. They also have stallions by Winnetou, Wendekreis, Bolero's sire Black Sky XX, a Der Löwe XX/Ramzes X grandson, a World Cup I son and a Matcho X son.

FUTURE DEVELOPMENTS

Since the advent of the single European market in 1992, horse breeding has become even more competitive and imports and exports are much easier. Despite some quarrantine restrictions for stallions, frozen semen has found an export market. The European Breed Shows have also become the showcase for horses, attracting buyers from both inside and outside the EU. Numerous stallions with impressive competition backgrounds from other countries are being recognised by the Hannoverian Verband and their foals from Hannoverian mares will be branded with the H and issued with pedigree papers. As a herald of this, in February 1990 Brussels held the first-ever championships of Europe's riding horse breeds. The Hannoverian Verband sent three mares – Ballerina by Bolero out of a Wendekreis mare, Baccarole by Bolero out of a Waldhorn mare, and Pirol by Pik Bube out of a Weltmeister mare. The international judging commission awarded Baccarole the championship, with the two other mares being placed second and third. Many more international competitions are being scheduled with the breed societies' support and backing in Belgium and Holland with special awards going to the country which has bred the winning animals.

These placing results confirmed the Hannoverian as one of the top breeds in Europe, and there is little doubt that it will continue to be extremely popular and that its reputation for excellence as both a stable foundation on which to improve other breeds and as a well marketed and talented competition horse will continue.

Chapter 3

The Holstein

by

DEBBIE WALLIN

IN THE NINETEENTH and early twentieth centuries Holstein breeding was not only the concern of the Landstall at Traventhal, which already existed by 1874 and is generally regarded as the birthplace of the breed, but also of a number of smaller organisations, such as the Verband der Pferdzüchtvereine in den Holsteinischen Marschen (1883 to 1935), and the Verband de Pferdeszüchtvereine in der Schleswig-Holsteinischen Gestlanden (from 1897 to 1922). These were superceded by the Verband der Züchterdes Holsteiner Pferdes (Holsteiner Verband), which still exists today, although sadly the Traventhal stud ceased to function as a breeding centre for Holstein horses in 1960.

The Verband der Pferdezüchter der Holstein Marschen, under the economic leadership of Georg Ahsbahs, founded the Reit-und Fahrschule Elmshorn eV in 1894. Jumping and driving were the main pursuits and under D. Hans Fellgiebel, the stud manager from 1926 to 1935, driving expanded and Holsteins competed with great success at the DLG shows in the 1930s. For driving, rather high, rounded knee action was sought, which might explain the tendency for the much rounder action found in the Holstein breed today when it is compared with the action of other modern Warmblood breeds. This action was also believed to be desirable in a jumper, and the next phase of popularity for the Holstein as a competition horse was just that.

In the years between 1949 and 1961 Fritz Thiedemann dominated the show jumping sport. He won no fewer than five Hamburg jumping Derbys, with Loretto (in 1950), Meteor (in 1951), Diamant (in 1954), Finale (in 1958) and Retina (in 1959).

Meteor was foaled in 1943 by the stallion Diskus, and had many of the foundation lines in his pedigree, notably that of Tobias, which

73

appears four times in the first five generations. Meteor was an exceptional performer by any standards, winning not only the above-mentioned jumping Derby, but also two gold medals at the Olympic Games in 1956 and 1960, a bronze at the 1952 Olympics, a gold at the European Championships in 1958 and the King George V Cup in London in 1953, to name but a few of his many successes. He also did invaluable publicity work for the rather small breeding area of Schleswig-Holstein.

Today the riding school at Elmshorn, which is now the home of the Holstein breeding stallions, is run by the Verband der Züchter des Holsteiner Pferdes, whose stud book offices are in Kiel.

BREEDING POLICY

Compared to the larger breeding areas that produce the Hannoverian, the Westphalian etc., the Holstein breed has a small nucleus of broodmares and has therefore managed to produce a quality stamp of horse unique to its area. Possibly due to the small numbers involved, and the importance of publicity to catch the eye of world markets, a prominent feature of the Holsteiner Verband is that it actively competes both its breeding stallions and other stock at international level. Today at Elmshorn there are three competition stables which always have a selection of talented youngsters for sale.

The trainers and riders are well known on the international circuit: Herbert Blocker is at the eventing yard, Dr Michael Rüping rides for the show jumping section and H.P. Mohr competes on the dressage horses.

Elmshorn is also the venue for the Elite Mare Show, where the best mares from each regional inspection (grading) show compete.

The Holstein stud book is divided into four sections and entry is gained by an inspection or grading done by a panel of judges. Points from 1 to 10 are awarded for type, topline, depth and breadth, forelegs, hind legs, and correctness, swing and impulsion of gaits. Eligibility for the four stud books is as follows:

• *State Premium (HSP Symbol)* These are awarded at three years. Mares must have a minimum height of 16hh/162cm (or 16.1/164cm if older when presented) and must gain a minimum of 45 points. Owners of premium-winning mares receive a money prize and agree to keep their mares in breeding for at least two years. Mares gaining a state premium are branded on the left side of the neck with a flattened triangle.

• *Main Stud Book (Hauptstutbuch) (H Symbol)* Mares in this book must be 15.3hh (160cm) high at three years old (or 16hh (162cm) if older when presented) and must gain a minimum of 40 points.

• *Stud Book (Stutbuch) (S Symbol)* Mares in this book must be 15.2hh (158cm) at three years old (or 15.3hh (160cm) if older when presented) and must gain a minimum of 40 points.

• *Register (Vorbuchstuten) (V Symbol)* Mares entered in this section fall into one of the following categories:

(a) no pedigree, but a height of at least 16hh (162cm) at three years and 45 points or above at grading;
(b) 50% known pedigree, a height of at least 15.3hh (160cm) at three years and 40 points or above at grading;
(c) a height of less than 15.2hh (158cm).

Foals sired by graded sires out of graded mares by recognised graded sires receive the Holstein brand on their left thigh, and since 1970 a number has been added underneath the original brand for more positive identification.

At one time stallion licensing/grading was held at Elmshorn, but now it takes place in a large indoor hall, called Holstenhalle, in Neumünster during the winter before the colts reach the age of three. Elmshorn usually buys in three to five colt foals as potential sires and they too attend the licensing at Neumünster along with the privately owned colts. In conjunction with the licensing there is a spectacular evening gala show and the following day an auction of young Holstein competition horses is held. Colts that do not receive their licence will also be offered for sale at this time. Successful youngsters must receive a minimum of 45 points in their conformation, correctness and action. No score in any category must be lower than 7. Soundness and a full vetting go hand in hand with a run up on hard ground, which starts early on the first morning. Every colt must be measured for height, girth and bone. In the 1980s the height of the colts was found to be over-tall, but now (due to careful selection), a more medium-sized animal with a modern action for dressage has found favour. The stallions are judged for type, exterior, limbs, bone and action, and the impression and harmony of the horse as a whole are important factors in the final decision.

Once through the initial licensing, the stallions have to complete successfully the 100-day ridden testing. This starts on 1 August of the stallion's third year and the Holsteiner Verband recognises only two testing stations, that of Adelheidsdorf (near Celle) and Mendigen (near Lüneberg). Since 1977, stallions who are going to focus on a career in the competition ring have been allowed to show their ridden talent by their winnings in various classes at M and S level, instead of competing in the 100-day ridden testing.

The Holsteiner Verband firmly believes that mare testing is also of importance when trying to evaluate the potential of the distaff side of pedigrees for producing potential competition horses. It believes that as colts are already very carefully monitored so as to continue the improvement of the breed, mares should also be scrutinised in the same way. Once again, possibly due to the relative smallness of Holstein numbers compared to other larger breeding districts, the Holstein Verband has quickly adapted the FN's format to one suitable for the ridden testing of young mares. The established mare families in Holstein are now also given a number. The lower the number, the better the line – 18b is particularly favoured as a good mare line. After a young stallion has stood one year at stud, at least ten per cent of his foals are inspected at the side of their dams, to be awarded premiums. This gives a clear and easy guideline as to the improving potential of the sire and the type and bloodlines of the mares he suits best. A decision as to his breeding future (if any) is then made by the breed organisation.

Still seeking to improve their breed and its reputation, an auction for outstanding four-year-olds was initiated at Elmshorn in 1987. This is now held annually in mid-April and has become an extremely successful international event. By 1990 just under fifty per cent of the horses sold were already being exported to other lands.

GENERAL DESCRIPTION OF THE HOLSTEIN

The Holstein is a well-built, often blood-type of horse with an elegant neck and quality head. The breed has big lines and good withers, but can sometimes be a little long in the loin, although this is compensated for by an excellent, long, muscular croup. Clean, hard limbs and hard hooves are also a feature. Holsteins are almost always bay or grey without many markings, but the occasional chestnut is to be found, although this is not a popular colour. The average height is from 16-16.3hh (162-170cm). The action is powerful with plenty of impulsion from behind, with rather a high knee action in front, but when combined with elasticity has outstanding extension as well.

The Holstein today is a modern horse with excellent riding points.

There is not nearly the same disparity of type within this breed as can be found in the numerically and geographically larger breeding areas, such as the Hannoverian for instance. (Interestingly, Holsteins often have inbreeding in one or more generations, which may also enhance the consistency of type.) The breed also has a very willing and active temperament, but due to the large amount of Thoroughbred blood now present, it can sometimes be rather hot.

IMPORTANT BLOODLINES

The Holstein breed was founded on three imported stallions – Brillant, Burlington Turk and Owstwick – in the mid-nineteenth century. All three stallions were bay, which is still the preferred classical colour of the Holstein today, too many white markings being discouraged.

- **Brillant** was the founder of the Achill line and was foaled in 1842. He stood at stud from 1847 to 1867, was of Yorkshire Coach Horse origin and was said to have won a first prize at the Yorkshire Show at Beverly. He was entered into the Yorkshire Coach Horse stud book as number 5381, being by a stallion called Baylock out of an Arram Trajan dam.

- **Burlington Turk** by the Thoroughbred Harpham Turk out of a Newton dam, was born in 1825. He was also imported from England and stood at stud in Germany between 1832 and 1845.

- **Owstwick** by Dreadnought was born in 1834 in England and was also entered into the Yorkshire Coach Horse stud book. He worked in Germany from 1846 to 1859.

The foundation sires foaled in Holstein are as follows:

- **Achill 1265** by Herkules (1877) was an inbred descendant of Brillant, his sire being a grandson of Brillant and his dam being a daughter of Achill 582 by Brillant. This particular inbreeding caused Achill 1265 to breed an extremely consolidated type of horse, and his best son Tobias and other descendants Favorit, Fanal, First and Fanatiker (known as the F-line) can be found in the pedigrees of most modern Holsteins today. Inbreeding is not recommended, however, because of the risks involved. The case of Achill 1265 may have proved to be a success but whilst one can double up the good points of an animal by inbreeding, one can all too easily double up the poor points as well.

•**Ethelbert** by St Fagans XX(1874-1898) was by an imported English Thoroughbred.

•**Adjutant** by Midas (1886-1913) was out of a dam by Brilliant.

•**Cicero** by Julius (1889-1916) was out of an Ethelbert mare.

•**Fusilier** by Nordlicht (1892) was by a Hannoverian sire out of a Brillant mare; he was removed from stud in 1907 after being found to be a roarer.

•**Amurath** by Amurath OX (1896) was foaled in Hungary and stood for many years in the Holstein breeding district before taking up a stud career in Celle in 1917. This line introduced the first greys.

EARLY BLOODLINES

As has been mentioned previously, members of the F-line are given a name beginning with F (similar to the Hannoverian practice). However, although some of the old sire lines listed above can be found in pedigrees today, letter changes have sometimes occurred as a new line has developed or an original letter became overloaded. This enabled some stallions to start their own lines should they prove exceptional, rather than keeping to their particular sires' first initial. However, references to the foundation lines are often so far back as to be of little relevance to the initials being used now.

The Ethelbert line's most famous grandson is Elegant (1913), who was the sire of Lorbeer (1919), Mackensen (1920) and Nordhauser (1921). The Lorbeer line is today the Holstein G-line (nothing to do with the Hannoverian G-line) and Mackensen, whose grey colour came from his dam whose blood traced back to Amurath's Arab influence, remains a founder of one of the M-lines. Today many Holsteins with M-line in their pedigrees still inherit the grey colour. Confusingly, another M-line of more recent origin, which traces from the Thoroughbred, Manometer XX is also grey. Finally, Nordhauser founded the N-line and produced twenty-seven graded stallion sons, the best known being Nordmark and Nordlicht, whilst Heintze (1925), a grandson of Ethelbert, founded his own H-line, which exists today. It is not possible to go into great detail with these old bloodlines as there are numerous branches and offshoots, and the breeding policy that developed the modern Holstein as we know it today was really based mainly upon using Thoroughbred stallions with the original mares from the 1950s onwards.

MODERN BLOODLINES

Until the 1960s the Holstein was – like most other Warmblood breeds of that time – a rather heavy, strong animal suited to farm work, cavalry service and driving. However, once the market changed, with machines taking over from the horse in most areas, Holstein breeders had to cope with the new idea of producing an animal mainly for sport and competition, suitable to be ridden by amateur and professional alike. This new breeding policy had to be consolidated, as many countries without a Warmblood breeding tradition looked to West Germany both for their foundation breeding stock and competition stock, and some breeding areas were modernising the look and performance criteria of their horses already. Without a doubt, the reason Germany is now in the enviable position of having so many good horses to choose from is due to the tough competition between its own breeding areas to capture the sales market. To cope with this changing market, Holstein breeders adopted the policy of using Thoroughbred stallions almost exclusively to establish their riding and sports horse model. The stallions used included:

• **Anblick XX** by Fero XX. Thoroughbred (1938). At stud from 1954 to 1965 he sired fourteen graded sons and founded the Holstein A-line of today. He was renowned for having an exceptionally good wither and shoulder, features which the old type of foundation mares needed to improve in their foals. Not a very big horse (15.3hh/161cm), his best-known son, Aldato (1958), produced numerous graded sons, and such competition horses as Venetia, the 1972 Munich Olympics bronze medal winner in the dressage, ridden by Josef Neckermann; and Albrant, Herbert Blocker's team silver medal winner in the three-day event at the Montreal Olympics. Alibi (1962), an Anblick XX grandson, was exported to Denmark where he has produced a number of Grade A show jumpers, and two graded sons in Alladin and Astaire.

• **Cottage Son XX** by Young Lover XX. Thoroughbred (1944). Cottage Son XX was imported from England and sired fourteen graded sons. He is the founder of one of the C-lines in the Holstein breed today. His most famous grandson, without a doubt, is Ramiro (1965), whose dam Valine was by Cottage Son XX. Ramiro (also known as Ramiro Z) was an international show jumping stallion when ridden by Fritz

Ligges and took the R initial from his sire Raimond (1960) by
Ramzes. Ramiro blood is found in almost every country in the world
involved in Warmblood breeding and competition riding. Most of the
Cottage Son XX line's outstanding talent seems to come through the
dam's line – the international show jumper and graded stallion Rocca
(out of Uganda by Cottage Son XX) and the outstanding sire of com-
petition-winning stock Lord (1967), who is out of Viola by Cottage
Son XX, are but two examples of this. The most famous dressage
horse of the early 1980s, Christine Stückelberger's Granat, is also
from this line, sired by Consul by Cottage Son XX.

- **Frivol XX** by Patrizier XX. Thoroughbred (1946). Whilst not so pre-
  dominant a sire as either Anblick XX or Cottage Son XX, being the
  sire of only three graded sons, the fame of Frivol XX was earned by
  the outstanding record of his progeny under competition riders. He
  produced hardy stock with good nerves, the best known being Fidux
  (who was ridden first by Manfred Kotter and then by both Piero
  d'Inzeo and Mancinelli for Italy), Fortun (who won the King George
  V Cup for Hans G. Winkler) and Format (the high-jump record holder of South Africa) ridden by Peter Levor.

- **Manometer XX** by Abendfrieden XX. Thoroughbred (1953). This
  line is quite closely related to that of Anblick XX, as Abendfrienden
  XX was his full brother. Manometer XX himself was a prominent sire
  of show jumpers, Marengo and Maximus probably being the best
  known on the international circuit. He also founded a sire line (again
  bringing in the grey colour) and his grandsons, mainly through
  Maximus (1963) and Moltke I (1967) continue the M-line today.
  Manometer XX was sold to Denmark in 1968 and produced some
  good show jumpers but nothing of exceptional talent. In 1973 he was
  sold back to West Germany.

- **Marlon XX** by Tamerlane XX. Thoroughbred (1958). Imported from
  Ireland in 1965, he is one of the 'big names' in Holstein breeding. He
  sired twenty-one graded stallions and numerous daughters who were
  awarded a state premium. Marlon XX stood at stud between 1965 and
  1981, and produced such outstanding competition horses as Karl
  Schultz's Montreal Olympics three-day event bronze medal winner
  Madrigal (1968) and Uwe Sauer's Grand Prix dressage horse
  Montevideo (1971) (who combined a successful stud career with
  achieving an individual gold medal in the 1983 European
  Championship at Aachen). Marlon XX's grandson Marmor (1972) by
  Marengo (1966), also a graded stallion, won twenty-three champi-

Montevideo (1971) by Marlon XX, a very talented bay stallion who combined a successful Grand Prix dressage career with his stud work, and seen here ridden by Uwe Sauer.

onships in Grand Prix and Grand Prix Specials. One of the most beautiful sons of Marlon XX, Martell I (1966) (who had three full brothers – Martell II, Martell III and Martell IV who were all graded as stallions), was exported to Denmark where, although he did not produce any graded sons, he did earn a reputation for talented competition progeny, and found mainly in the dam's line today.

• **Ladykiller XX** by Sailing Light XX. Thoroughbred (1961). Imported from England, Ladykiller XX stood at stud from 1965 to 1979, and is still one of the most sought-after names in pedigrees of both breeding and competition stock. His blood is found in every country interested in breeding show jumpers. There are only a handful of world-famous sire lines and Ladykiller XX's is one of them, which puts him in the same elite group as Gotthard for the Hannoverians, Almé and Furioso XX for the Selle Français, and Ramzes X for the Holsteins and Westphalians; the Selle Français Cor de la Bryère is also arguably a candidate because of his influence on the Holstein breed. Ladykiller XX sired twenty-three graded sons and one of them, Landgraf I (1966) (out of an Aldato dam), was the leading West German sire of 1989 with the highest progeny earnings in competition. Lord (1967) by Ladykiller XX out of a Cottage Son XX dam was ranked ninth in

Ladykiller XX (1961) by Sailing Light XX, founder of one of the most talented and famous bloodlines within the Holstein breed. His sons Landgraf I and Lord are world-famous sires.

the same list. Competition horses sired by Ladykiller XX are exceptional, including Ladalco (1969), who won a bronze medal in the three-day event world championships at Lexington; Landgräfin, the international show jumper who holds the Austrian high-jump record with Hugo Simon; and Eddie Macken's Boy, who was second in the Hamburg Jumping Derby in 1976 amongst other successes.

Two other sires must be mentioned here, as their influence in modern Holstein breeding is almost as important as that of Ladykiller XX, although neither is Thoroughbred and both were imported. The two stallions are:

- **Ramzes X** by Rittersporn XX. Anglo-Arab (1937). A grey stallion imported from Poland, he founded the R bloodline in both the Holstein and Westphalian breeds as well as being a sire of show-jumping horses. Ramona by Ramzes was jumped by Alwin Schockemöhle before his retirement, and Robin (1964) was in the gold medal show-jumping team when ridden by Fritz Ligges, who also jumped the Ramzes grandson Ramiro (1965). Ramiro has stood at stud for a number of years, and is also known as Ramiro Z when used at Leon Melchior's stud at Zangersheide, and sometimes as G Ramiro Z in

The Netherlands.

•**Cor de la Bryère** by Rantzau XX. Anglo-Norman (1968). This stallion has Furioso XX in his dam's pedigree and was imported from France. Within just a few years of starting to stand at stud he became one of the most popular sires of his age group. He produced award-winning stallions and mares at the grading shows and he also produced top-level competition horses. These include Contrast ridden by Herbert Blöcker in the three-day event world championships in 1982, the international show jumper Costa (ridden by Michael Rüping), and the leading Grand Prix dressage horse Corlandus (ridden by Margit Otto-Crépin for France) to name just three. His record for producing stud book animals for breeding is impressive, as is his record for siring competition horses. In 1980 he sired the champion stallion at Neumünster's licensing with Caletto II, as well as the champion two-year-old filly, at Elmshorn. In 1981 he again sired the champion stallion with Cordino, plus the highest-priced auction horse, Catania, and the supreme champion mare at the Elite Mare Show. In 1989 Cor de la Bryère is found as the dam's sire of the

Cor de la Bryère (1968) by Rantzau XX, imported from France. His progeny have an exceptional jumping technique and his bloodlines are well-established and sought throughout the world.

PEDIGREE OF **COR DE LA BRYÈRE** – DARK BROWN ANGLO NORMAN, 1968			
Cor de la Bryère 210398168 (SF)	Rantzau (XX)	Foxlight	Foxhunter
			Chouia
		Rancune	Cavaliere d'Arpino
			Rockella
	Quennotte (SF)	Lurioso (SF)	Furioso (XX)
			Riquette (SF)
		Vestale du Bois Margot	Landau
			Kristine du Bois Margot

reserve champion stallion at licensing with Locato (1987) and the same for the reserve champion two-year-old filly at the Elite Show at Elmshorn during the same year. Cor de la Bryère can give rather more knee action than most, but as this is combined with a good shoulder freedom his progeny can 'snap up' their forelegs for jumping and extend them for dressage.

Other modern stallions of note include:

• **Silbersee** by Silver Matal XX. Selle Français (1973). Another Anglo-Norman import from France, he competed in international show jumping in the 1980s at the World Championship in Aachen, and was twice winner of the Grand Prix at Neumünster under Dr Michael Rüping. Because of his travels, Silbersee was available by artificial insemination, and by the beginning of the 1990s his graded son Silvester (1978) had already entered the list of Holstein sires whose progeny are competition winners of some note.

• **Landgraf I** by Ladykiller XX. Holstein (1966) out of an Aldato mare. By the end of the 1980s, Landgraf I was first in the list of all sires that have stood at stud in West Germany in terms of money earnings of progeny. He rates as a world-class sire, and his sons can be found at stud or in competition in most countries. Libero H (1981) won all three of the World Cup qualifiers in 1994 ridden by Jos Lansink for Holland. Other well known superstar show jumpers by Landgraf I are Lucky Luke ridden by Otto Becker, Lacros (1978) with Dirk Shroder, Landlord (1977) with Willi Melliger, and Taggi (1981) who was on the German Olympic Team in Barcelona ridden by Soren von Ronne.

Landgraf I (1966) by Ladykiller XX, one of the most famous names in show jumping. He tops the German FN list for his progeny's high winnings in competitions.

PEDIGREE OF **LANDGRAF I** – BAY HOLSTEIN, 1966			
Landgraf I 310391966 (Holst)	Ladykiller (XX) 210384761	Sailing Light	Blue Peter
			Solar Cygnet
		Lone Beech	Loaningdale
			Fartuch
	Warthburg 210320903 (Holst)	Aldato 210377658 (Holst)	Anblick XX
			Kreta H 1608
		Schneenelke 210284503	Fangball
			Blümchen

•**Lord** by Ladykiller XX. Holstein (1967) out of a Cottage Son XX mare. Lord was ninth in the rankings of West German sires in 1989, just behind Cor de la Bryère.

•**Ramiro** by Raimond. Holstein (1965) out of a Cottage Son XX mare. This stallion became one of the most successful jumping horses on the

PEDIGREE OF **RAMIRO** – DARK BROWN HOLSTEIN, 1965			
Ramiro 210389565 (Holst)	Raimond 210380760 (Holst)	Ramzes 210365437 (X)	Rittersporn (XX)
			Jordi (X)
		Infra H 210145903 (Holst)	Fanatiker
			Lining
	Valine H 210313603 (Holst)	Cottage Son (XX)	Young Lover (TB)
			Wait Not (TB)
		Holle H 210129103 (Holst)	Logenschliesser
			Ilona

international scene, when ridden by Fritz Ligges. His progeny include Donau (ridden by Thomas Frühmann), and Ramiro's Girl and Rodney (ridden by Fritz Ligges). Two of the horses topping the lists for The World Breeding Championship for the Horse (WBCSH) are Ratina Z (1982) ridden by L. Beerbaum and Visa Rinnetou Z (1982) ridden by Piet Raymakers for Holland. Ramiro stood in Belgium for a time and also has progeny registered in The Netherlands, where he is also known as Ramiro Z or G Ramiro

• **Tin Rocco** by Tin Rod XX. Holstein (1970) out of a Roman mare. Tin Rocco is also graded into the Oldenburg stud book and has a graded Oldenburg son, Traumtanzer, in the United States. He has sired over twenty auction horses for Vechta, but his talent as a dressage sire has produced no fewer than seven youngsters selected for the PSI auctions by Ulrich Kasselmann and Paul Schockemöhle. In 1989 the German National dressage champion was Traic by Tin Rocco.

It is really quite exceptional that so many of the best show jumping sires in the world come from one of the smallest breed societies. The Holstein has a remarkable success rate. There are not many bloodlines and those that do exist have to prove their worth or they are phased out by the Verband. Today the Holstein has also taken in a few stallions with Almé blood from France, including Ahorn (1979), Aloubé Z (1979) and Athlet (1979). Gotthard blood from the Hannoverian Verband's top show-jumping line is also found on the dam's side of the pedigrees of both Aloubé Z and Athlet. If one excludes the most recent Thoroughbred sires to have entered the Holstein stud book, and a limited number of representatives of the old F foundation line, one can

Ramiro (1965, also known as Ramiro Z) by Raimond. An international show jumper and outstanding sire, he has stood in numerous countries and his progeny are to be found in the stud books of almost all the major Warmblood breed societies.

safely say that three quarters of the best Holstein bloodlines can be found within the Ladykiller XX (L), Ramzes (R) or Cor de la Bryère (C) lines, both at stud and in the competition world.

THE INFLUENCE OF THE HOLSTEIN

Holsteins can be found in most lands.

Hungary imported Toborzo (1975), a chestnut from a very good old foundation mare line (18b). (The established female lines in Holstein breeding are given a family number, the lower being considered the better.) Torborzo was originally called Tarento, and as such he was reserve champion of his grading year. His dam has produced the graded sire Constant (1972). Ramzes Junior by Ramzes stood twelve years at the stud in Mezöhegyes. His son Ramzes III (1969) followed his sire to the stud. Aldato (1958), the sire of Albrant, also stood there between 1971 and 1977 and sired a son, Aldato II, out of a Furioso/ North Star mare who did well in competition before retiring to stud in Enying. Fokus (1966) (formerly Freeman) by Frivol XX was imported in 1976, and in 1979 seventeen Holstein in-foal mares were imported to the Mezöhegyes Enying Stud.

The Netherlands has been importing Holsteins for a number of years. Some of the most prominent are listed below:

•**Normann** by Heidelberg. Holstein (1949) out of a Loretto mare. Normann had established the Ethelbert line with seven graded sons and some good jumping horses by as early as the 1950s.

•**Amor** by Herrscher (Trak). Holstein (1959) out of a Loretto mare. This stallion produced sixteen graded sons and became a well-known bloodline in international sport as well as a sire noted for broodmares.

•**Rigoletto** by Ramzes. Holstein (1960) out of a Logarithmus mare. He produced graded sons in both the Netherlands and West Germany. He was extremely popular as a sire, covering on average 200 to 300 mares per year in 1976 and 1977. He is the sire of the international show jumper Santa Monica for H. Quellen. A Rigoletto daughter called Queen of Diamonds also won the Rome Grand Prix for Jan Clood Vanenburghe in 1989, despite being only 15.3 hh (160cm).

•**Farn** by Fax I. Holstein (1959) out of a Monarch mare. A rather old-fashioned type, he earned a reputation for producing show jumpers. His son Nimmerdor is probably the most famous of his progeny. Interestingly, in 1987 one of his Dutch-owned Holstein sons, also called Farn (1984), returned to West Germany to complete the 100-day ridden test, as did another Dutch-owned Holstein, Cor d'Amour (1984) by Cor de la Bryère.

As the original mares in the Netherlands were rather heavy in type, the next stallions to be imported all carried Thoroughbred blood, and these included four sons of Sable Skinflint XX as well as young sires by Ladykiller XX, Manometer XX, Anblick XX, Marlon XX and Tumbled XX. However, three other more recently imported stallions should also be noted in conclusion as well:

•**Libero** (1981) by Landgraf I. Holstein out of a Ronald mare. A fully graded stallion, he won the Rotterdam Grand Prix in 1989 with Jos Lansink. Now called Libero H he is one of Holland's top money earners and exceptionally sought after by the show-jumping studs.

•**Calando III** by Cor de la Bryère. Holstein (1976) out of a Colombo mare. A full brother to Calando I (1975) (ridden by the Belgian international show-jumping rider H. Cuepper), this graded stallion also stands in The Netherlands.

• **Ladalco** by Ladykiller XX. Holstein (1977) out of an Aldato mare. This successful sire of competition horses, whose son Lenard (1982) now stands in Britain, was exported to The Netherlands in the late 1980s.

Joost (1971) by Consul, and Kommandeur (1969, known as Manchester in the Holstein stud book and in the United States where he was imported towards the end of his career) by Marlon XX also founded important breeding and competition bloodlines in the Netherlands.

The United States has gone into Holstein breeding in a fairly big way. Some good stallions have been imported, and with the top-quality Thoroughbred mares of substance available there, it will be interesting to see the progress of the breed. Fasolt (1969) by Farnese, Laredo (1974) by Ladykiller XX and the 1981 licensing champion at Neumünster, Cordino (1979) by Cor de la Bryère – whose dam is by Rigoletto – were among the first imports. Recently, in 1989, two more stallions entered an already growing list: they were Saceur by Silvester with the mother line being closely related to Michael Rüping's show jumper Costa, and Landslide by Landgraf I. Mares by Caletto I, Cor de la Bryère, Ahorn and Lacapo were graded into the stud book.

In the competition field, Lendon Gray rode the Holstein Later On by Lester for the United States in the dressage at the Seoul Olympics, and in 1987 Dianna Rankin on New Ladykiller was the national dressage champion and also qualified for the Seoul Olympics.

Sweden has only shown mild interest in the past for Holstein horses, but in the late 1980s – because of a new management decision to change the image of the Swedish horse from that of a mainly dressage animal to a dual-purpose Warmblood – some good Holstein blood has been imported. The stallions used so far have included Romantiker (1971) by Ramiro, who stood in Sweden from 1985 to 1989; Robin Z (1983) by Ramiro, out of an Almé dam, standing at the Flyinge State Stud; and Limelight (1974) by Landsturm who was leased from Denmark in the 1980s. The Swedish stud book therefore now has a pool of some of the best jumping blood in the world on which to draw.

Denmark has always been keen on Holstein blood. Danish breeders imported such stallions as Alibi (1962) by Aldato, Raimondo (1970) by Ramiro and Martell (1966) by Marlon XX to name but three. Later on they were followed by Romano (1975) by Roman, Flamingo (1975) by the now American-based Fasolt, and Lagano (1978) by Leander – who stood at stud only for a short time due to his early death, but even so managed to produce the winner of the National Riding Horse Championships and a graded son to carry on his line. Sandro (1974) by Sacramento Song XX out of a Wahnfried dam did not pass the Danish Warmblood grading but earned his place in the stud book by becoming an international show jumper. He was sold back to Paul Schockemöhle in West Germany in 1985, and soon won over 50,000DM when ridden by Franke Sloothaak. He became a popular sire and was used extensively in the Hannoverian, Oldenburg breed societies as well as the Holstein. His foals and youngsters were exceptional, bringing very good prices when sold at auction. In 1992, no fewer than eight of his progeny qualified for the Federal Championships in Verden, and he has produced sixteen graded sons since returning to Germany. Sandro did not produce anything of note in Denmark, maybe as the mare material is so variable, but he was listed in 1994 as being owned by the Zangerheide Stud in Belgium so his progeny will have a spreading influence on the continent.

Sao Paulo (1987), a bay stallion by Sandro (Holst) out of a Hannoverian dam by Gepard. Just one example of Sandro's excellent pedigree being integrated into the breeding programmes throughout the German societies.

The stallions Leonardo II (1981), Latino (1976), Lavallo (1979), Lincoln (1979), Lancier (1971), Leandro (1985) and Leuthen (1983) – all from the Ladykiller XX line – have stood at stud in Denmark at some time, with Lavallo returning to West Germany after coming out in the progeny winnings' list as a young sire of show jumpers of note in 1989. Another Ladykiller XX son, Locarno (1972), did not make much of an impression at first in Denmark, but by 1990 he had produced numerous highly graded mares and started his own L-line in stallions. Next came the sons and grandsons of Cor de la Bryère, Chamisso (1981), Calimero (1980), Corlando (1989), Castro (1981), and Churchill (1989). By the late 1990s we should be able to see whether these lines will be as successful in producing show jumpers outside of Germany as the Ladykiller line has been.

In Switzerland, the show-jumping Horse of the Year in 1988 was the nine-year-old grey gelding Corso by Capitol (1975), ridden by Willi Mellinger. The Landgraf I son, Lanciano (1976), competed at the Seoul Olympics with Philippe Guerdat for the Swiss team, and a representative of one of the best show-jumping families, Calando II by Cor de la Bryère, has been purchased by the Avenches Stud under the director Dr Poncet.

Yugoslavia imported a number of Holstein mares in 1980 with pedigrees mainly of the R-line, to be used with the stallion Fridericus (1974) by Farnese out of a Ladykiller XX mare. Fridericus was imported from Holstein after building up a good progeny record there. When put to the imported mare Maya by Roman he produced Faust I, a very large stallion of 17.1½ hh (177cm) in height but with great elasticity. Faust I won the title of Champion of Yugoslavia in 1988 for his jumping successes, whilst a second son Famos I was exported to Hungary, and the new lines of Ahorn/Capitano, Calypso I/Tin Rod XX and Silbersee/Romantiker were imported in 1987.

Britain has unfortunately had the bad luck to lose two very well-bred Holstein stallions before their potential was realised. In the 1980s Rinaldo (1970) by Ramiro was imported. He was exhibited during the Royal Show on the West German stand, but after only one year at stud he died of a twisted colon. Lawdon by Landgraf I was originally imported as a show jumper, and he was not licensed in Holstein for breeding. At some time in his career he suffered a back injury and was sold on to various owners until he was finally put to stud after being graded with the British Warm-Blood Society, but he died the same year. However, in 1990, the young stallion Lenard (1982), by Ladalco out of a Moltke I mare, was imported and graded with the British Warm-Blood Society. He had previously been owned by the Holsteiner Verband, licensed in Neumünster, and graded and performance-tested in Denmark before coming to Britain. He was subsequently joined by the Ronald son Saluut (1976), known as Rebell in the Holstein stud book, who had already proved himself in The Netherlands as a competition horse in Grand Prix show jumping. Saluut's competition record abroad in show jumping has given him a good following of British breeders, but his input on the future show jumpers of England can't be judged as yet as his first season at stud was in 1990.

British and Irish show-jumping riders have also had a succession of top-quality Holstein show jumpers including Boy by Ladykiller XX for Eddie Macken, Amigo by Farnese for Ted Edgar, and Sanyo Technology by Fasolt for Harvey Smith.

FUTURE DEVELOPMENTS

There is little doubt that the Holstein bloodlines are in demand for breeding as well as competition horses. With the introduction of the riding horse auctions in April and the winter auction combined with the licensing at Neumünster, all factors point to an expanding market. The breed is consolidated and the strict breeding policy with some clever inbreeding and line breeding has paid off. Holsteins are found wherever breeders are trying to expand their pool of jumping pedigrees.

Chapter 4

Other Major German Breeding Districts

by

CELIA CLARKE

with a section on the stud books of the New Germany

by Jane Kidd

THERE IS NO QUESTION that the principal foundation breeds in Germany are the Hannoverian, the Holstein and the Trakehner. Between them, they are the source of most of the Warmblood bloodlines found in other parts of Europe and the wider world, either through horses bred in those breeding districts or imported into them for breeding purposes. The expertise of breeders and judges in these areas is outstanding and their practices and selection procedures are emulated throughout Europe and beyond.

However, nowhere are the breeding systems that produced the Hannoverian, Holstein and Trakehner more closely followed than in the other breeding districts of Germany. Many of the stallions approved by one or more of the chief societies are also graded into one or more of the stud books of the other breeding areas. The use of the common state-controlled performance-testing areas of Adelheidsdorf, Mendigen and Marbach, prior to licensing or grading, encourages multiple registration of many of the privately owned stallions which – although it may seem strange to non-Germans – is merely a reflection of the federal nature of Germany in which each state is a separate entity for local government purposes but agricultural affairs are controlled by the federal government, with the Deutsche Reiterliche Vereinigung eV (or German FN) being the body responsible for horse breeding through its breeding committee. The legal terms of the Animal Breeding Law therefore stipulate that each state has its own selection commission (to grade stallions and mares), which must include a representative of the Federal government, usually the appropriate

Lanstallmeister, as director of a state-owned stud farm.

Because of the similarity of their histories, their closely related bloodlines and their near uniformity of structure in breeding industries and selection procedures (including the holding of gradings and auctions), it is probably best to deal with horses bred in Baden-Württemburg, Bavaria, Hesse, Oldenburg, Rheinland-Pfalz-Saar (also known as the Zweibrucken stud book), the Rheinland, and Westphalia as one group, identifying the common features amongst them but also stressing the differences when they occur. This is therefore the approach of this chapter, in which each of the breeding districts listed above will be covered in alphabetical order.

The newly incorporated stud books of what was formerly known as East Germany are discussed at the end of this chapter.

BADEN-WÜRTTEMBURG

This breed was developed in its original form at the Marbach Stud following German unification in 1871, although there had been a stud based on Spanish, Hungarian and Turkish lines in existence during the sixteenth century, and the eighteenth and early nineteenth centuries saw an approach based on Spanish and East Friesian imports.

For the last one hundred years the breeding area has been enthusiastic in its support of the East Prussian and then Trakehner bloodlines, and most of the important stallions of the present day reflect this taste.

BREED DESCRIPTION

Though not particularly tall in Warmblood terms, the Württemburg (as the horse bred in this district is known) is nonetheless often quite deep, with good limbs and a reputation for soundness, hardiness, a quiet temperament and thriftiness. The most usual colours are brown, black or chestnut.

IMPORTANT BLOODLINES

The blood of the Trakehner **Julmond** (1938) by Julianus has been the most powerful influence on the development of the Württemburg since the Second World War, and is regarded as its foundation sire. Although brought to the state stud at Marbach at the late age of twenty-two and dying there three years later, he sired many riding horses and founded a highly thought-of sire line. The other Trakehners to

The Pregel (Trak) son Prünk (1976) out of a Julmond mare. A typical representative of the modern bloodlines being used in the Baden-Württemburg breeding district.

stand in the district include Pregel (1958) by Tropenwald, Kornett II (1964) and Amor (1970) by Maharadascha, and Tassilio (1958) by Lateran. A little Holstein blood has also been introduced through Labrador (1972) and Laertes (1966), both by Ladykiller XX, and Montanus (1972) by Moltke I, but apart from the Pik Bube I son Pikfein (1978) and the Sesam son Seladon (1975), Hannoverian sires do not appear to be particularly popular. Because of the relatively recent development of the Warmblood horse in Baden-Württemburg, few native-born stallions have yet made a mark at stud. Those that have are usually from mainly Trakehner bloodlines – Indigo (1977) by Ingo, Pikeur (1978) and Prünk (1976) by Pregel being typical examples but the Don Carlos son don Rico (1984) and the Ramin son Radius (1983) do seem to be making their mark as sires as well.

BAVARIA

Another state-based breed developed relatively recently, the Bavarian Warmblood relies very heavily on traditional and modern Hannoverian bloodlines, particularly those of the D-, F/W- and G-lines, plus occasional influxes of Trakehner and R-line Holstein blood. Interestingly, although a number of highly graded pure-bred Trakehners such as Istanbul (1972) by Flaneur – who was exported to Britain at the end of his stud career – have stood in Bavaria in recent years, they seem to have been patronised mainly by Trakehner breeders rather than by local mare owners, whose long tradition of cold-blood breeding right up to the early 1960s perhaps makes them a little resistant to such a light type of horse. However, Komet (1952) by Goldregen and Kassio (1963) by Abglanz did have more widespread appeal.

BREED DESCRIPTION

As a newly developing breed based on the Hannoverian in all its diverse types, and as one with a percentage of Holstein and Trakehner blood, it is difficult to generalise on what a Bavarian Warmblood looks like, except to say that it is usually a middle-sized, middleweight horse of a solid colour.

IMPORTANT BLOODLINES

The most popular sires of competition horses in Bavaria in recent years include the two Hannoverians Donar (1968) by Don Carlos, and Duell (1964) by Duellant; the Trakehners Kassio (1963) by Abglanz, Latent (1963) by Lateran and Prince Condé (1967) by Prince Rouge XX; but the most popular by far have been the Selle Français Jalisco Jun (1981) by Jalisco B and 'new style' Oldenburg Fugato (1969), one of the many sons of the Selle Français Furioso II at stud throughout Germany. The R-line Holstein Rasputin (1961) by Ramzes X made an impact in the late 1960s and early 1970s, and his near relative the Westphalian Rasso (1971) by Ramiro has proved popular in more recent years. Bavaria has also contributed to the 'Bolero boom' by purchasing Bolschoi (1984) and Bordeaux (1987) by Bolero to stand at stud.

As yet, successful Bavarian sire lines are a little hard to detect, although Nordus XX (1951) produced both competition horses and stallions, such as Nordfalk (1971), who have been moderately successful, and Wolfhard (1970), the Bavarian-born son of Wodka (1966) by Wohlan, has sired some good competition horses. More recently, Acord's Son R (1981) by the international show jumper Acord B, the grading champion Coriograph B (1988) by Coriolan, the two Lord Incipit sons Lord Bavaria (1987) and Lord Charles (1988) – not forgetting Lord Extra W (1987) by Lord have all been proving to have potential as sires of show jumpers.

HESSE

This German Warmblood breed has only come to the fore since the early 1960s, due to a change of policy from breeding Oldenburg-based coach horses to competition horses. Most of the successful bloodlines used in the Hessen in recent years have relied at least to some extent on a percentage of Trakehner or Thoroughbred blood. This may come in directly, as was the case with Adonis XX (1952) or more usually through Hannoverian stallions with Trakehner, Thoroughbred or Anglo-Arab sires, with breeding activities being centred around the state stud at Dillenburg.

BREED DESCRIPTION

It is difficult to describe a typical Hessen horse for the same reason that it is difficult to describe a typical Bavarian Warmblood. As a rule, though, the Hessen is usually slightly lighter than the 'average' Warmblood horse because of the amount of 'refining' blood close up in the pedigree. However, the bloodlines are not yet consolidated enough to establish whether this will continue to such a marked degree in future generations.

IMPORTANT BLOODLINES

Like most of the recently improved breeds, the usual A-, D-, F/W- and G-line Hannoverian blood is present and the blood of the Selle Français Furioso II is evident through the Oldenburg Furioso's Sohn (1970), and the breeders of Hesse have also used Trakehner blood in the form of Imperial (1967) by Impuls and the two Thor sons Mandant (1964) and the home-bred Tango (1978). Der Löwe XX blood from Hannover is also very popular, through the Lugano I son Lotse (1960), whose reputation as a sire was established by his competition horses and by the progeny sired by his two Hessen sons Lord (1965) and Logos (1968). The Lugano I son Luetzon (1961) also produced good competition horses in Hesse but failed to make his mark as a sire of stallions, whereas Matrox (1975) by Matrose has already produced a successful graded son for Hesse in Matreat (1979). The popular Westphalian line to Ramzes via Romadour I is present through Raphael (1965) by Radetsky, and Le Charmeur E (1989) by Lordon, Reflektor (1986) by Rescator and Ams (1988) by Augustinus XX and doing much to enhance the Holstein and Thouroughbred lines available. Finally, the spectacularly coloured show-jumping stallion Ico (by Marco Polo) was bred and graded in Hessen, and his son Illasso (1988) made history

The European dressage team gold medallist, Floriano (1976) by Fiothor (Trak), was competed internationally for both Germany and Britain, and was one of the best Hessen competition horses so far.

when he became the first coloured Warmblood to win the performance test at Mendigen in 1992.

OLDENBURG

The Oldenburg used to be the main coach horse of Germany. With the collapse in the market for coaching horses in the early twentieth century, the old type developed from crossings between Friesians, Hannoverians, Normans, Cleveland Bays and Thoroughbreds was updated to an all-round agricultural horse, and remained so during the inter-war years. After the Second World War concentrated efforts were made to lighten the breed still further, which accelerated even faster from the early 1970s onwards when the outstanding merits of such new

The Selle Français stallion Furioso II (1965) by Furioso XX, one of the most important stallions in the Oldenburg breed and the sire of over 50 graded stallions and 150 broodmares worldwide.

stallions as Furioso II (1965) by Furioso XX, Kronprinz XX (1960) by Nizam, Inschallah X (1968) by Israel, Ultraschall (1978) by Ultra Son and Tiro (1972) by Tremolo began to be appreciated. With such a thorough overhaul of type and quality, the Oldenburg breed has now become one of the most successful for its numerical size in Germany. Its youngstock are widely in demand both as competition horses and breeding stock, and its graded stallions are being exported throughout the world – particularly the United States where the blood of Furioso II is very highly regarded. The future looks very bright for the Oldenburg.

BREED DESCRIPTION

Oldenburg horses are generally between 16hh (162cm) and 16.3hh (170cm) high and are generally dark coloured. Their heads can be a little plain, because of their coaching ancestry, but their conformation is generally good, with a long, sloping shoulder, powerful deep body and strong quarters. The limbs, which used to be fairly short and heavy jointed, are now lighter and longer. Some members of the breed tend

PEDIGREE OF **FURIOSO II** – CHESTNUT SELLE FRANÇAIS, 1965			
Furioso II (SF)	Furioso (XX)	Precipitation	Hurry On
			Double Life
		Maureen	Son-in-Law
			St Prisca
	Dame de Ranville (SF)	Talisman	Le Royal
			Créole
		Que je suis Belle	Lord Orange
			Comédie

to have a little too much knee action for some riding purposes, but careful use of good-moving, lighter stallions is eradicating this.

IMPORTANT BLOODLINES

By far the most important stallion to stand in the Oldenburg breeding district in recent years was the Selle Français **Furioso II** (1965) by Furioso XX. In fact, not only was he the most important Oldenburg stallion, he is arguably one of the more important Warmblood stallions of all time, siring over fifty graded stallions spread throughout practically all the Warmblood breeds in the world, and being the top money earner through his progeny for all stallions at stud in West Germany born before 1969. The majority of his competition stock are Oldenburgs, although substantial numbers also come from the Hannoverian and Westphalian breeding districts, as is also the case with his graded stallion sons.

Even with such an impressive stallion available to mare owners, it says something for the breadth of the breeding operation in the Oldenburg district that some very high-quality stallions have been able to stand to lucrative books of mares despite the opposition. Notable stallions such as **Inschallah X** (1968) by Israel, **Kronprinz XX** (1960) by Nizam, the three Gotthard sons Gepard (1974), Goldpitz (1972) and Goldstein (1972), and the two Der Löwe XX line Hannoverians Löwen As (1966) by Lugano and Luciano (1971) by Lukas, were all well patronised. Equally popular have been the Trakehners Herbsturm (1962) by Komet and Magister (1964) by Major, the Westphalian Prinz Gaylord (1974) by Perlkönig (exported to the United States in the mid-1980s), Tiro (1972) by Tremolo, Ultraschall (1978) by Ultra

Son, the two Neckar XX sons Vierzehnender XX (1965) and Vollkorn XX (1961) and Vollkorn's famous eventing son **Volturno** (1968) – arguably the best stallion so far bred in Oldenburg and destined to die tragically soon after his arrival in the United States. The Volturno son Voltur (1981) also looks like following in the illustrious footsteps of his sire and grandsire as he is already getting competition horses. Finally, the show-jumping talent that derives so often from Selle Français blood has been enhanced by the addition of Zeus (1972) by Arlequin and his KWPN-registered son Beach Boy (1988) to this list of Oldenburg-graded sires.

With the quality of stallions born outside the breeding district that are made available to mare owners there, it is perhaps not surprising that specifically Oldenburg sire lines have been a little slow to develop. However, a number of home-bred stallions as Volturno, Figaro (1972) by Futuro and the Weltmeister sons Welt As (1977) and Wanderfalk (1980) are now making names for themselves and sire lines are beginning to be more consistent.

Finally, the outstanding World Cup dressage stallion and DLG show champion of 1986, **Donnerhall** (1981) by the Hannoverian

Donnerhall (1981) by Donnerwetter, a DLG prizewinner, Grand Prix dressage horse and sire of graded stallions from his first crop of foals.

Donnerwetter, is an Oldenburg through the Oldenburg origin of his dam, and he is graded not only with the Oldenburg Verband but also with the Hannoverian and Westphalian societies. A beautiful, good-moving stallion, he is already proving extremely popular.

In the competition field, Oldenburgs have been making a name for themselves at top level being consistently listed in the top four or five stud books for dressage horses in the World Breeding Championships through the successes of such horses as Donnerhall, Cameleon Bonfire (by Welt As), Dondolo by Don Carlos and Fun by Furioso II. In show jumping the West German horses Otto (1975) by Kronprinz XX, Liberal (1976) by Luxus and the American-based Fridolin (by Freiherr (1976)) have all done much to promote the breed.

THE RHEINLAND

The modern Rheinland horse is probably the district Warmblood breed in Germany that is most heavily influenced by Trakehner blood. This preference for animals with an ancestry tracing to East Prussia has roots going back to the early nineteenth century when Prussia absorbed the former episcopal electorates of Mainz, Trier and Köln, all of which are to be found in the modern Rheinland. With this tradition and background, it has therefore been relatively easy for Rheinland breeders to develop and consolidate a definite breed type during the period since the 1960s and to establish consistent sire lines fairly swift-ly. Judicious use of the Westphalian branch of the R-line has also helped in this process.

BREED DESCRIPTION

In many respects the Rheinland is a variant of the Trakehner. It is sometimes a little larger than the present-day Trakehner and occasion-ally proportionally longer in the leg and lighter of bone, but its overall conformation, temperament and movement are very similar to its close relative.

IMPORTANT BLOODLINES

Trakehner blood, such as that of Garamond (1964) by Gabriel, Bernstein (1964) by Gunnar, Achat (1968) by Malachit, Patron (1967) by Tranzyt and Rubin (1969) by Flaneur – the sire of the 1979 Adelheidsdorf 100-day performance testing champion Rembrandt (1976) – has been vital to the development and upgrading of the

Grand Gilbert by Glückslee, one of the top dressage horses produced in the Rheinland and ridden by Nicole Uphoff-Becker.

PEDIGREE OF **RHEINGOLD** – BAY RHEINLAND, 1974			
Rheingold 430053774 (Rhld)	Romadour II 1848 (Westf)	Romulus 1618	Remus I
			St Pr St Fabriana
		St Pr St Gunda H 15075	Grünfink
			St Pr St Dorette
	Piroschka H 935 (Rhld)	Abendregen 1590 (Trak)	Altan
			Abenglocke
		Donna H 607 (Rhld)	Fabriano
			Almfee

Rheinlander and a number of the home-bred Rheinland stallions such as Faehnrich (1976) by Faharadscha and Pasternak (1971) by Patron carry at least fifty per cent of Trakehner blood. However, the bulk of the successful competition horses bred in the Rheinland are by Westphalian sires, as these lines have been used enthusiastically in recent years. In fact, a number of top Westphalian stallions are graded into the Rheinland stud book as well as with their own breed society, chief amongst them being Aarstein (1960) by Aar (who enhances the Trakehner bloodlines being by the Trakehner stallion Abschaum), the top show-jumping sire Bariton (1967) by Blairspecht XX, Perlkönig (1975) and Polydor (1972) both by Pilatus, and Romadour II (1969) by Romulus (1978) whose grand-sons Rythmus (1978) and Rassul, both by Rheingold, are also well patronised by Rheinland mare owners. Romadour II's full brother Romadour I is represented chiefly by Rhodos (1974) by Remus I, and another specifically Westphalian bloodline – that of Fruehling – 15 present through his son Foxtrott (1974) and grandson Fittipaldi (1981). From the Hannoverian breed, the qualities of Gotthard progeny are much desired – as they are through most of Germany – and his son Goldcup (1975) and Rheinland grandson Golan (1975) by Gottschalk have proved very popular in recent years. Two other young Rheinland stallions, Mephistopheles (1980) by the Trakehner Mackensen and Frediecke (1981) by Furioso II, are also making their mark, as is Amant (1981) by the Hannoverian Amazinos.

In the competition field, the Rheinland is well established enough, and well bred enough, to have been able to compete at the highest level in recent years. The top Rheinland competition horses so far have mostly been by Hannoverian and Westphalian sires with Romantico (1974) by Romadour II and Grand Gilbert (1982) by Gluckslee representing Germany and the United States repectively in dressage, Pirat (1979) and Pirol, both by Polydor (1972) being successful in top level national show jumping, and Flagrantus (1974) by Aarstein representing West Germany in Nations' Cups.

RHEINLAND-PFALZ-SAAR (ZWEIBRUCKEN)

Probably the smallest breeding district in West Germany in terms of both numbers of horses and choice of bloodlines, and itself the result of combining two even smaller districts, Rheinland-Pfalz-Saar (also known as Zweibrucken after the state stud) has not yet really made a mark in Warmblood breeding. There are also few home-bred stallions at stud that have yet proved themselves either as sires or stallions, or as sires of competition horses, although the district is making great efforts to establish its horse-breeding credentials more firmly.

BREED DESCRIPTION

Slightly heavier than some animals produced in other districts, the

Warmblood bred in Rheinland-Pfalz-Saar tends to be the product of cross-breeding between D- and F/W-line Hannoverians and Holsteins, with some Trakehner blood used for lightening purposes. It is therefore generally a powerful, good-moving horse, but sometimes a little old-fashioned in type with a tendency to a straight shoulder and a flat croup.

IMPORTANT BLOODLINES

The two most popular sires of competition horses in recent years in the district have been the Grande-line Hannoverian Grandus (1973) by Graphit and the 'modern type' Oldenburg Intervall (1973) by Inschallah X. Two Woermann sons also stood with some success: Woernitz (1977), who was afterwards exported to Denmark, and Woerth (1976); as did the Wendekreis son Weltmann, whose graded son Welspiegel (1979) is already siring competition horses. Holstein blood is represented at its best by the Landgraf I son Labrador (1976) and Marlo (1971) by Marlon XX, and Trakehner influence has come through Schöne Abend (1958) by Abendstein and Isenstein (1964) by Hessenstein. Alpha D (1983) by the Almé son Alexis has also made a considerable impact recently, and it was Alexis who also produced the most successful Zweibrucken-bred competition horse to date – the phenomenally successful show jumper Apricot.

WESTPHALIA

In terms of competition results, the Westphalian is definitely in the 'big league' of West German breeding districts. This is perhaps not surprising as the area around Warendorf, the central stud farm for the breed, has a long tradition of Warmblood breeding, going back to 1826 when thirteen East Prussian stallions were made available to mare owners, with the number increasing to fifty by 1830. The development of the breed suffered the usual problems caused by diminishing military demand in the mid-nineteenth century, increasing agricultural use in the late nineteenth century (including a decree that bloodstock breeding be conducted in the 'Oldenburg manner'), and an influx of an ill-assorted mix of Oldenburg, East Friesian, Hannoverian, Anglo-Norman and Trotter blood. However, in 1920 it was decided to concentrate chiefly on Hannoverian bloodlines and the foundations of the modern Westphalian were laid.

The breed is now very closely related to the Hannoverian, with all the modern Hannoverian bloodlines being present, but it also has three particularly strong lines that have been developed purely in Westphalia, that of Fruehling (1960) who comes from the Hannoverian F-line through his sire Fruehschein I, that of the R-line (best known through Romadour I and Romadour II) which traces back to Ramzes X, who was also the founder of the R-line in Holstein, and the P-line of the Thoroughbred Papayer XX (1954) by Persian Gulf XX through Paradox I and Paradox II and their descendants. Confusingly, there is another popular Westphalian P-line in existence, that founded on Perseus (1959) by Pluchino XX. It is such prepotent sire lines as these, which have all had outstanding success as producers of both graded stallions and competition horses, that have made the Westphalian breed the popular breed it is today.

BREED DESCRIPTION

The Westphalian is a high-performance multi-purpose horse, with a good character and temperament and a proven ability in dressage and jumping. It is perhaps slightly longer in the leg than the more old-fashioned type of Hannoverian, but it still retains its powerful, correct movement and outstanding athletic ability. As with most other Warmblood breeds, it can be of any solid colour and chiefly ranges between 15.3hh (160cm) and 16.3hh (170cm).

IMPORTANT BLOODLINES

As might be expected of such a successful breed, all the usual Hannoverian bloodlines – the A-, F/W-, D- and G-lines – can be found somewhere amongst the breeding and competition stock being produced in Westphalia, and we will concentrate on these in due course. However, what makes the Westphalian special is the importance that the blood of four stallions not generally found elsewhere has played in the development of the breed, and its outstanding record as a source of competition horses.

Alphabetically, the first of these original lines is that coming from the home-bred **Fruehling** (1960) by the Hannoverian Fruehschein I. Strictly speaking this is therefore a development of the Hannoverian F-line, but judicious crossing with Westphalian mares has meant that Fruehling and his many graded sons, such as Fruehlingsrau (1971), Foxtrott (1977) and Fruehlingsball (1970), and grandsons such as Fruehlingstraum I (1964), Fruehlingstraum II (1973) and Fortissimo (1978), have proved outstanding producers of both international competition horses and breeding stock.

The second original line is the line founded by **Papayer XX** – which

The outstanding Westphalian dressage horse, Rembrandt (by Romadour I), winner of gold medals in the 1988 Olympics and 1989 European Championships, ridden by Germany's Nicole Uphoff-Becker.

is sometimes known as the Paradox line, because of the two full brothers Paradox I (1964) and Paradox II (1970) who played such an important part in the promotion of this line of top competition and breeding horses. The other P-line appearing in Westphalia, that of **Pluchino XX**, chiefly through his son Perseus (1959), and the Perseus son Pilatus (1965), is almost as important as that of Papayer XX and its most successful two stallions to date are Pilot (1974) and Polydor (1972), both by Pilatus, and outstanding sires of competition horses.

The fourth, but arguably most important line, is that founded on the Anglo-Arab **Ramzes X** (1938) by Rittersporn XX, who also founded a related line in the Holstein breed. The Ramzes X son Radetsky (1951) is the senior Westphalian-born representative of this line, which through his sons Remus I (1958) and Remus II (1963) and their descendants Romadour I (1967), Romadour II (1969), Romulus I (1961), Romulus II (1962) and the Dutch-graded American-based Roemer (1969) amongst others, has spread the reputation of the Westphalian far and wide. Indeed, by 1990 the Romadour II son Renoir I (1981) was already the most successful sire of competition horses of his year, based on the first year of competition of his progeny, so the merits of this line are obviously still as powerful through each ensuing generation as has been proven by the outstanding success of

PEDIGREE OF **PARADOX I** – CHESTNUT WESTPHALIAN, 1964			
Paradox I 1697 (Westf)	Papayer (XX) 1565	Persian Gulf	Bahram
			Double Life
		Seaway	Fairway
			Chachlot
	St Pr St Arnika H 13596 (Westf)	Almfreund 1439	Almschütze
			Diktatin
		Schwälbin H 11129	Schwips
			St Pr St Fanny

the stallion Rubinstein (1986) whose sire Rosenkavalier is also by Romadour II.

The bloodlines derived from the more conventional Hannoverian lines favour, in particular, Aktuell (1973) by Absatz, who sired many progeny in Westphalia (as well as in the Hannoverian and Oldenburg breeds) and whose son Affekt (1977) is particularly favoured; another Absatz son, Amor (1973), has also found popularity with mare owners, as has the Absatz grandson Artwig (1974) by Argentan.

In the D-line, Damokles (1971) by Davos has proved himself an outstanding sire of competition horses and his son Debutant (1976) looks to be following in his footsteps. Two sons of Ehrenschild (1956) by Eindruck II, namely Ehrensfried (1966) and Ehrensold (1969), also found support amongst mare owners.

Apart from the Fruehling branch discussed earlier, the F/W-line is most strongly represented by Wohlklang (1962) by Wöhler and Wunderlich (1974) by Wedekind. The Thoroughbred W-line of Waidmannsdank XX is also strongly present through his two sons Waidmann (1969) and Waidmannsheil (1967).

In the G-line, the family developed in Westphalia through Gruenspecht is particularly strong through the three full brothers Gruenhorn I, Gruenhorn II and Gruenhorn III by Gruenschnabel. Equally popular are several Gotthard sons, with Gottschalk (1969) consistently producing top competition stock. Goldlack (1968) by Goldfalk also left some outstanding progeny in Westphalia.

The Der Löwe XX line's main representative is the outstanding stock-getter Löwenstein (1973); and Milan (1966) has also proved a superb ambassador for his own sire Marconi (1957) by Marcio XX.

In addition to the R-line developed in Westphalia, the other

Holstein branch of the R-line can be found in Westphalia through the descendants of Ramiro (1965) by Raimond, a stallion whose stud career not only made a great impact on Holstein and Westphalia, but also on Belgium, the Netherlands and (through his graded sons) Denmark and Sweden. Confusingly, this stallion is sometimes known as Ramiro Z, or even G Ramiro Z in some stud books, but in the Westphalian breeding district he is referred to by his original straightforward name of Ramiro.

Thoroughbred blood has also played an important role in the development of the Westphalian, not only through the previously mentioned Papayer XX and Pluchino XX, but also through Angelo XX (1962) by Oliveri XX, Octavo XX (1966) by Miralgo XX, and the noted competition-horse sires Sinus XX (1949) by Ticino XX – who has founded a consistent sire line through his sons Sinatra (1971) and Sioux (1959) – and Taipan XX (1968) by Darling Boy XX.

Finally some Trakehner blood from Bernstein (1964) by Gunnar and Garamond (1964) by Gabriel has been introduced to supplement the influence of Semper Idem, Lateran and Abglanz found in many Hannoverian pedigrees.

The bloodlines listed in the Westphalian district therefore provide the classic modern blend of the Trakehner-derived A-line Hannoverian, with D-, F/W- and G-lines plus top quality Thoroughbred and a dose of proven quality Holstein blood. This carefully planned mixture has produced an admirable Warmblood competition horse, successful and in demand throughout the world.

The international competition record of the Westphalian since the mid-1970s has been superb. To name just a few in show jumping: Romadour I sired Gerd Wiltfang's world champion show jumper Roman; and Fruehlingstraum II was responsible for Norbert Koof's world champion Fire, while Everest Two-Step (1983) by Polydor, Lamborghini (1983) by Lowenstein, Piamos (1982), Almox Rush On (1982) and many more have ensured a consistently high placing for the Westphalian breed in the jumping section of the World Breeding Championship for Sport Horses. In dressage Ahlerich by Angelo XX won the Los Angeles gold medal, where three other Westphalians also competed – Amon by Angelo XX for the Netherlands, Satchmo by Sinus XX for Canada, and Civian by Cyrian for Mexico. More recently Rembrandt (1977) by Romadour II has been Olympic and European champion and has returned to top-class international competition after an horific hock injury. Such well-known dressage horses as Goldstern (1981) by Weinburg, Bollvorm's Wempe Jewel (1985) by Weinburg and Adrett (1978) by Adlerfels are all Westphalians, which is an indication of the sheer strength and depth of talent available

PEDIGREE OF **ROMADOUR II** – DARK BAY WESTPHALIAN, 1969			
Romadour II 1848 (Westf)	Romulus I 1618	Remus I 1547	Radetsky
			St Pr St Fidelia
		St Pr St Fabriana H 11799 (Westf)	Fabriano (Hann)
			St Pr St Maritta (Westf)
	St Pr St Gunda H 15075	Grünfink 1518	Grünspecht
			St Pr St Almuth
		St Pr St Dorette H 13066 (Westf)	Dorn (Hann)
			St Pr St Abendfee (Westf)

within the breed. Finally, Westphalian eventers have also scored well with the outstanding stallion Volturno competing at the highest level, and Angelus by Angelo XX being a member of the West German European gold medal team.

With successes such as these it is perhaps not surprising that Westphalians have become popular as imported sires in the newer Warmblood breeding districts. Of particular note are Roemer I (1969) by Romulus I, who was exported first to The Netherlands – where he became the top dressage sire of all time – and then on to the United States where he has proved extremely popular, and Fruehling (1982) by Fruehlingstraum II who was exported to Denmark and founded a popular line which eventually found its way to Britain by the Danish Warmblood Fulton (1987) to give just two examples.

The reputation of the Westphalian is assured. It was the only West German breed, apart from the Hannoverian and the Holstein, to be invited to Brussels to compete in the first European Breeding Championships in 1990, and its foals now fetch record prices both in Germany and abroad. In competition with other breeds in performance tests it often comes out top, and its competition record is extremely impressive. Its long-term development has been a credit to all concerned and will surely continue, given the firm basis on which it is built.

THE STUD BOOKS OF THE NEW GERMANY

Breeders in what was the German Democratic Republic have not enjoyed the stimulus of producing for a thriving equestrian sports market. Surprisingly, in a country in which there was such a great emphasis on sport, riding was neglected. Riders were given little encouragement and few became good enough to represent their country internationally. This meant there was relatively little demand for high-class Warmbloods, and compared to the other districts of Germany, few were produced. In 1989 there were about 99,500 horses and ponies and this included Thoroughbreds, coldbloods and Trotters.

The country was divided into three, with the administrative centres and stallion depots being at Redfin in the north, Neustadt/Dosse in the middle and Moritzburg in the South. State-owned stallions were based at the three stallion depots, and only the ponies stood privately. Most of the mares were also owned by the state and were kept either at the state studs or on the agricultural communes. Since 1988 these mares have had to pass tests before being graded for breeding.

The national Warmblood was known as the Edlen Warmblood, and was based on the Hannoverian/Mecklenburg and the Trakehner, but there was also a heavier type known as the *Schweres Warmblut* which was a close relation to the Oldenburg. The Trakehner was maintained in its own right and used to improve the Edlen Warmblood, and at the Neustadt stud the most influential sires were **Tertzky** by Hyperion, **Insgeheim** by Pythagoras and **Sturmwind** by Sturmer. Thoroughbreds and occasional Anglo-Arabs and pure-bred Arabs were also used.

Since unification of Germany in 1990 five new breeding associations have been founded in the new Federal states of Mecklenburg, Brandenburg, Sachsen-Anhalt, Sachsen and Thuringen. They have been made members of the breeding department of Germany's National Federation with the same rights as the breeding associations in what was West Germany.

At present about 180 of the best of the 1500 colts born each year are selected as potential stallion material and brought up under supervised conditions. Further evaluations lead to 40 of this group going forward for eleven months of performance tests at the central station of Neustadt every year. Of these about fifty per cent finish the tests and are considered suitable to stand at one of the three stallion depots, and even then they are subjected to further examinations every two years to ensure they are fit to stay as licensed stallions. In the long term, after the disturbances caused by the unification of Germany settle down, the breeding in this eastern sector is likely to enjoy the stimulus of a much more bouyant demand and more international influences. In fact, the Sachsen-Anhalt-bred stallions Abendwind (1982) by Adept B, Akzento (1987), Goldschatz (1985) by Gotland and Kolibri (1979) by Kobold I are already becoming popular with more owners throughout the newly enlarged country.

Chapter 5

The Warmbloods of France

by

JANE KIDD

FRANCE IS A great horse-breeding nation with top breeds for all
branches of equestrianism, from racehorses to heavy horses. They
are all administered by the Service des Haras, founded in the seventeenth century, and this has helped to ensure that pedigrees, the
foundation of selective breeding, have been kept for generations. The
Service administers over six breeds of blood horses as well as nine cold
bloods and thirteen ponies, but it is the Selle Français, France's sport
horse, which is the major concern of this book. Mention should be
made too of the Anglo-Arab, which must be considered a Warmblood
under the broader definition, because in France indigenous mares were
used that were not pure Thoroughbred or Arab, and because many
Anglo-Arab breeders produce specifically for the sport-horse market.
Certainly there have been some great Anglo-Arab performers, like the
Olympic gold medallists, Ali Baba X (in show jumping) and Aiglonne
(in eventing), and with such great breeding stock as Inschallah X,
exported to be a major influence in Germany.

It is the Selle Français, however, that has dominated the sporting
honours. Created as recently as 1958 with the amalgamation of the
regional breeds under one title, it had the largest number of representatives of any breed in the show jumping at the Los Angeles Olympics,
including such great names as World Cup winners Galoubet and I Love
You, 1988 Olympic gold medallist Jappeloup, and 1990 World Cup
gold medallist Quito de Baussy. It has been an important influence on
other Warmbloods, particularly the Holstein with Cor de la Bryère (or
Cor de la Bruyère as his name is written in France), the Oldenburg
with Furioso II, the Dutch with Le Mexico, and the Belgian which
benefited from the great Almé standing there for some seasons.

The Selle Français excels as a show jumper, and its breeders have

112

concentrated on production for this market. An extensive range of young-horse jumping classes (for the three age groups, four to six years) with remunerative rewards (£75 for a clear round at the regional contests in 1991), has encouraged production specifically for this well-developed market and enabled breeders to show off their produce and prove their breeding stock at a very early stage. This, together with the collection of extensive data from the large number of shows and show jumpers competing in France, has facilitated the analysis of genetic jumping characteristics. This has further promoted the breeding of horses for show jumping, and with fewer competitions in dressage, eventing and driving, data about these activities is less valuable and selective breeding in these spheres therefore more difficult.

Success has bred more success as the excellent records of the French show jumpers have created a better market and encouraged producers to concentrate more and more on breeding them. The Selle Français has become the most specialised Warmblood in Europe.

There is yet another incentive to specialise in show jumpers, as the government gives the breeder a percentage of the prize money earned by produce even after they have been sold, and prize money in show jumping is higher than that in any other of the disciplines.

THE ANGLO-ARAB

The Anglo-Arab's development was based in the south and particularly around the national stud of Pompadour. Although foundations for the breed go back to the eighteenth century, the main spurt started in the mid-nineteenth century. The breed was defined in 1880 (a minimum of twenty-five per cent Arabian blood) and a special section of the French stud book was created for it a few years later. From then on, the percentage of stock produced from Anglo-Arab sires grew faster than from the foundation cross between Arab and Thoroughbred. This helped to establish it as a breed with a consistent type of produce.

In the nineteenth century too, much use was made of the halfbred mares in the Limousin and south who were dominantly Arabian. Their produce were popular first as cavalry horses and later in competitions. The stallion Kephir was a particularly successful producer of competition horses, and in 1942 it was decided to include these half-bred Anglo-Arabs in a section of the stud book.

Today about twelve per cent of French sports horses are Anglo-Arabs, including the Olympic show jumper Jiva, the Boekelo winner Djerk, and top dressage horse Hava. Selective breeding to increase their size and robustness has made them more popular as riding horses.

They have played an important part in the development of the Selle Français – up to twenty per cent of Selle Français horses being by Anglo-Arabs. Today Selle Français breeders with heavier mares often use Anglo-Arab stallions in preference to Thoroughbreds as the cross-breeding is then less extreme and less likely to lead to unexpected results. The Anglo-Arab features which are in demand are speedy reactions, an easy character, a big heart and fast recovery after stress, strong but fine bone, and small hooves.

THE SELLE FRANÇAIS

The Selle Français is a new breed named by decree in 1958; its stud book was first published in 1965 when it included offspring from 1950. The origins of this Warmblood, however, date back hundreds of years. Like Germany, France classified horse breeds originally produced for farm work and the cavalry but now refined into sports horses, according to the area in which they were born. Thus there was the Charolais, Corlay, Vendée, Anjou, Ain, Ardennais, as well as by far the best known and most influential, the Anglo-Norman. Nearly ninety per cent of today's Selle Français trace back to the Anglo-Norman rather than the other regional breeds.

There is one category within the Selle Français, but it is not a regional breed. The AQPS (Autre Que Pure-sang), which is very close to Thoroughbred is used for racing mainly over fences, often against the pure Thoroughbred. It has also proved to be a very good eventer.

Originally the regional types varied considerably with the closest to Thoroughbred being the Charolais, which was used in races for the AQPS. The success of the Anglo-Norman, however, led to most regions introducing plenty of this blood, which resulted in the breeds becoming less distinguishable and making the establishment of the Selle Français a logical step.

The soil and climate of Normandy is particularly conducive to the production of horses with good bone and muscles. It has always been a well-known breeding area and the Anglo-Norman traces back to the medieval Norman war-horse. Its horses have been refined to suit the demands of the time. In the eighteenth and nineteenth centuries, Arab, Thoroughbred and Trotter blood were used, leading to two distinct divisions – the French Trotter and the Anglo-Norman cavalry horse, and it was the latter that became the foundation for the Selle Français, although Trotter blood, like the Anglo-Arab but to a lesser extent, has been used in the development of this Warmblood. The great jumpers Galoubet and Jappeloup both have Trotter blood.

Galoubet is an example of the most successful use of Trotter blood when it is on the dam's side and two generations back, but Jappeloup is by the Trotter Tyrol II. Today a little over one thousand Trotter mares are covered each year by Selle Français stallions.

As the Selle Français establishes itself as a distinguishable type of Warmblood, more and more of the breeding is from Selle Français dams and sires. At present about half the matings are like to like, with the cross-breeding with Thoroughbreds, Anglo-Arabs and Trotters, so important in the early years, declining. Today there are fewer of the big heavy mares that made such a good cross with the Thoroughbred and enabled those great Thoroughbred sires of the 1950s and 1960s, Furioso XX by Precipitation, Fra Diavolo XX by Black Devil, and Rantzau XX by Foxlight, to lay the foundations of the Selle Français. A little earlier, in the inter-war years, it was another Thoroughbred, Orange Peel XX by Jus d'Orange, who became so important for the Anglo-Norman and, subsequently, the Selle Français. His greatest son, in terms of the Selle Français, is Last Orange who was responsible for Ibrahim, sire of both Quastor (and in his turn the likes of Fair Play III) and Almé who, with produce like Galoubet, Herban, I Love You, Joyau d'Or and so on, would be considered by many the most famous Warmblood sire of the 1980s.

GENERAL DESCRIPTION OF THE SELLE FRANÇAIS

The aim is to produce a horse with substance and strength which has the 'class' of the Thoroughbred. Most have a strong, broad body with good limbs and particularly powerful hindquarters. The feet tend to be larger than those of other Warmbloods. The movement is loose and elastic, but may not be so rounded as that of other Warmbloods; and with the emphasis on show jumping there has not been the drive for the high-set neck and upward build, which are so popular for dressage horses. The 1990s, however, marked the initiation of a scheme – *Plus de Dressage* – to breed better dressage horses. A panel of experts that includes Wolfgang Niggli, Margit Otto-Crépin and Dominique d'Esmé select stallions worthy of the label 'Plus de Dressage'. These include some foreigners who are used through AI like Donnerhall and Gaugin de Lully but there are French sires like Hopal Fleury.

BREEDING POLICY

France's breeding policy for Warmbloods is much closer to that used for racehorses than that practised by any other European Warmblood breeding country. The breeder has great freedom to use his own initiative as there is nothing comparable to the pass-or fail grading system for stallions and mares used in the rest of Europe. Instead breeding stock are given plenty of opportunities to prove themselves in competitions, and the performance of their progeny and relatives is also taken into account. The emphasis is on competitive selection, with an extensive production of data derived from young-horse classes, show jumping, dressage and eventing, and its thorough analysis.

Stallions do still require licences if their stock is to be registered, and these are given annually for horses four years old and above. Shows for young stallions are held at the national studs of Saint Lô and Tarbes, where they are marked under saddle, in-hand and, when free, over fences. The top three-year-olds at these shows, usually about twenty-five a year, are bought by the national studs. There are also tests for both sexes of three-year-olds, when marks are given for conformation and paces. The best horses at local levels go through to the regional shows and the very best to the finals at Fontainebleau. Stallions accumulate marks in these conformation and gait classes as well as in further ones for four-year-olds. They also collect points if they are successful in show-jumping classes, or if their relations, and later their progeny, win money. The number of points earned determine whether an annual licence should be awarded to a privately owned stallion. The most important factor is, again, performance.

Mares have an automatic right to be entered in the stud book as long as their pedigree qualifies them, and they are given points to indicate their breeding value. These are acquired first in the conformation and gait classes for young horses, and secondly through the successes of their family (brothers, sisters, parents and eventually produce) and their own performances.

The Société Hippique Français runs a host of classes for four- to six-year-olds, and the results in these are an important basis of selection. There are classes in a wide range of activities so that particular talents can be exposed. There are conformation and gait classes, style (similar to American hunter classes), free jumping, cross-country events and dressage classes. But with France being so show-jumping orientated the most valued and valuable tests are the 'cycles classiques' for young show jumpers.

Finance for these classes, which are central to France's breeding programme, comes from the profits of the Pari Mutuel (racehorse tote). In France, profits from racing are ploughed back into the equestrian world and they help to give breeders the reasonable returns which are needed to encourage them to breed more and better horses. The administrators of the breeding policy are the Service des Haras, who are in charge of technical, economic and scientific aspects of equestrian matters, as well as the production, marketing and use of horses. By law they are responsible for 'the identification, registration and control of their ancestry, their progeny and their performances; the assessment of the genetic value of the stallions and the publication of any information that may concern them.'

The Service runs twenty-three stallion depots throughout France where all types of stallions stand, from racehorses to draught, but some are better known than others for a particular breed. Pompadour, for example, is most famous for its Anglo-Arabs, while Haras le Pin and Saint Lô are renowned for their Selle Français.

Over five hundred Selle Français and Anglo-Arab stallions stand at these depots, in addition to the Thoroughbreds and Trotters which are sometimes used for sport-horse breeding. The majority of the Thoroughbreds stand privately, but only about three hundred and fifty Selle Français and Anglo-Arabs do so. Many of these privately owned stallions stand at pretty substantial fees, having proved themselves as top competitors. Galoubet's service fee was over £2000 in 1990, but Warmbloods at the national studs are available at extremely reasonable fees, below £100.

A central part of the breeding policy is SIRE (Système d'Identification Repertoriant les Equidés), whose headquarters is at Pompadour. This organisation manages computer data concerning identification (documents and stud books) and selection (breeding competitions and index ratings). It also analyses that data and distributes findings to the breeders. The basis of its policy is a booklet known as a *Cartes d'accompagniment*, for which about 10,500 sports horse foals apply each year. This document contains important information about an individual – authenticating the pedigree; providing an identification certificate and a registration certificate to the relevant stud book (unless of unknown origin or of known origin but not eligible, when it is a Cheval de Selle); a health certificate and record of vaccinations. All data on the horse's performance is also kept by SIRE but is not included in this booklet.

SIRE keeps records of the breeding classes run by the national studs for broodmares, and gait and conformation tests for two- to five-year-olds. The results of show-jumping, dressage and eventing competitions are recorded on another computer in Paris at the Société de Steeplechases, and it is these that form the basis of a simplified rating system for stallions and their progeny. On another computer at the National Institute of Research (INRA) winnings are used to compile indexes for the purpose of proving genetic value. There is an individual index for the horse's own performance in each discipline – show jumping (ISO), eventing (ICC), and dressage (IDR). An average horse is rated 100, and a very good horse above 140.

In 1988 a 'BLUP' index was started to assess the genetic potential of breeding stock. Calculated from the ISOs of relatives, the mare/stallion (if and when they compete), and of the progeny, there are plenty of allowances even for the standard of mare covered. A horse may have this genetic index when he is born, based on assessing his/her genetic potential through the ancestors', brothers' and sisters' performance ability. At present this is done only for show jumping as there is not yet sufficient data attached to each sire in dressage and eventing to make it valid. Show jumping's index is known as the BSO and has become an important aid to selective breeding in France.

SIRE also produces many publications including genealogical books, statistics on coverings and births, lists of selected sires, etc. Data from their central computer is available to the general public through a Minitel/Teletel system so it is very easy for French breeders to collect and study the data necessary to breed selectively.

One of the great features of the French system is that the classes for three- to six-year-olds provide extensive data about the young horses. This makes it easier to prove the genetic value of mares and stallions at the earliest possible stage.

The pivot for this system is the *grand semaine de l'élévage* – a week for breeding in September at Fontainebleau. More than one thousand three- to six-year-olds, most of whom have gone through prior qualifying events, compete in a wide variety of championships for each age group. There are jumping classes, gait and conformation classes, cross-country and dressage tests. The results are used to help show which mares and stallions are producing the best stock, with much analysis of the pedigrees of winning stock.

The trend is towards more and more of the successful stock being the result of a Selle Français mating to another Selle Français, and about threequarters of the top young horses at Fontainebleau finals are the result of this approach. There were, however, some high-class representatives of Thoroughbreds with Selle Français mares, Trotters with Selle Français mares, Anglo-Arabs, and Anglo-Arabs with Selle Français mares.

The wide variety of type in the stallions available is one of the features of French Warmblood breeding. The other is that apart from the English Thoroughbred they are all French. It is only the occasional mare that is 'foreign', but this trend is on the increase with Hannoverian blood in particular being used to help the Selle Français meet the demand for dressage horses.

IMPORTANT BLOODLINES

The strongest influence on the Selle Français has been the Thoroughbred and its crossing with the heavier native mare, but after thirty years
of Selle Français breeding most of the breeding is Selle Français to
Selle Français, with cross-breeding, which was the basis of this
Warmblood, becoming rarer. There are now top stallions like Narcos II
(1979) who go back through three generations of Selle Français. His
sire was Fair Play III, who was by Quastor who was by Ibrahim.

The most famous Thoroughbred foundation sires Orange Peel XX,
Furioso XX, Fra Diavolo XX, Rantzau XX and Ultimate XX are found
again and again in the pedigrees of leading French horses:

- **Orange Peel XX** who stood at Saint Lô from 1925-1940, was by Jus
  d'Orange out of Rirette by Ajax. He produced nineteen sons who
  stood at stud, but particularly influential were Jus de Pomme, a producer of top broodmares, Plein d'Espoirs and, best of all, **The Last
  Orange** (1941), who sired the great **Ibrahim** (1952). Out of a Porte
  Bonheur mare, Ibrahim is considered the patriarch of the Selle

*Orange Peel XX (1922) by Jus d'Orange XX, whose blood appears
in many Selle Français pedigrees through his nineteen graded sons,
including Jus de Pomme XX, Plein d'Espoirs XX and The
Last Orange.*

Ibrahim (1952) by The Last Orange XX, often thought of as the founding sire of the Selle Français, being the sire of many important stallions, including the great Almé.

Français. He produced almost fifty stallions, including top sires **Quastor, Elf III** (1970), who produced Olympic show jumper Kaoua, Dynamique, **Double Espoir**, whose dam's grandsire was also Orange Peel XX, and, greatest of all, **Almé** who, like Elf, was out of an Ultimate XX mare. Quastor produced **Fair Play III**, who was a successful competitor but sadly died at the age of nine, although fortunately he left some good sons, including Narcos II, a regular member of the French team in the late 1980s who has Ibrahim twice in his pedigree and Furioso XX once.

• **Almé** (1966) was the greatest of Ibrahim's progeny. He, like Elf, has Ultimate XX on his dam's side. He stood in France from 1971-1974, in Holland from 1978-1983, and in Belgium from 1984-1985 before returning to France. He was an international show jumper, representing Holland in the 1977 European Championships. Many of his sons followed in his footsteps, three of them competing in the Olympics. His great show-jumping sons, who are all stallions, include **Galoubet** (1972), the World Cup winner whose granddam, Ida de Bourgouin, produced winning Trotters. Galoubet, like Elf, has Orange Peel XX on both sides of his family. Then there was **I Love You** (1974), the

Almé (1966, also known as Almé Z) by Ibrahim out of an Ultimate XX mare, not only an international show jumper himself, but also the sire of such top show jumping stallions as I Love You (1974) and Galoubet (1972).

		PEDIGREE OF **ALMÉ** – BAY SELLE FRANÇAIS, 1966	
Almé (SF)	Ibrahim (SF)	The Last Orange (SF)	Orange Peel (XX)
			Velleda (SF)
		Vaillante	Porte Bonheur
			Querqueville
	Girondine (SF)	Ultimate (XX)	Umidwar
			No Go
		J'Vins Mars (SF)	Cyrus
			Mazette

1983 World Cup winner for America, who returned to stand in France in 1987, and **Jalisco B** (1975), out of a Furioso XX mare, who represented Portugal in the 1988 Olympics and has produced such good jumping stallions as **Onyx IV** (1980), **Papillon Rouge** (1981) and **Quito de Baussy**, the 1990 world champion. There is also **Quidame de Revel**, who is proving to be one of the best jumpers in France of his generation. This is not all. Almé was also responsible for Jolly Good, full brother to I Love You and Puissance world-record holder, **Joyau d'Or A** (1975), who represented Italy at the Olympics, and he is grand dam sire of the great mare Ratina Z.

Almé is one of the great Warmblood sires of the world, having had a major influence directly in France, Belgium and Holland, and via his sons in practically every major Warmblood breeding nation. His

PEDIGREE OF **QUITO DE BAUSSY** – BAY SELLE FRANÇAIS, 1982			
Quito de Baussy (SF)	Jalisco B	Almé	Ibrahim
			Girondine
		Tanagara (SF)	Furioso (XX)
			Delicieuse (SF)
	Urgande	Prince du Cy (SF)	Ultimate (XX)
			Vaudoise (SF)
		Jolietta	Brûle Tout
			Quiryda

success marks the turning point in the history of Warmblood breeding in France, as he, together with others from his generation, have made it into the equal of any country in the world for the production of show jumpers.

His history does, however, show the vagaries of breeding, as he was allowed to go out of the country because he was not rated as a potential top sire. It seems that the only reliable guide to a top sire is the success of his progeny, which shows the need for countries to develop systems to expose these as soon as possible.

Almé's great son Galoubet did not have a good start to his future as a stallion as he was not successful in the Saint Lô stallion selection as a three-year-old, and his illustrious career began when he won the five-year-old show jumping championship. His stud career had been notable for pioneering the use of AI (artificial insemination) first used with him in 1981 when he was still competing. He now belongs to a French-American syndicate, and his frozen semen is flown across the Atlantic. Amongst his first crop of foals he had seven finalists at Fontainebleau.

Rantzau XX (1948) by Foxlight, best known as the sire of Cor de la Bryère, a Selle Français stallion who has founded a line in the modern Holstein breed.

- **Rantzau XX**, by Foxlight and out of Rancune by Cavaliere d'Arpino, stood at Saint Lô from 1951-1971. He sired many successful show jumpers and stallions, the best in France being **Kalmiste**, **Phoenix** (1959), **Quelqu'un** (1960), **Starter** (1962) and **Erioso** (1970). His most famous son, **Cor de la Bryère** (1968), was exported to Germany to become one of the Holstein's most important sires of modern times.

- **Furioso XX**, born in 1939 by Precipitation and out of Maureen by Son in Law, stood at Le Pin from 1946-1967. Probably the greatest Thoroughbred sire of show jumpers in the world, in his own performance tests on the racetrack he never won a race. He sired top competitors, which included more than thirty international winners and ten Olympic show jumpers, as well as leading broodmares and stallions. He was the father of the 1964 Olympic champion Lutteur B and the 1966 World Champion Pomone B. His most famous sons are **Mexico** (1956), who stood at Le Pin, sire of the great Dutch stallion **Le Mexico**, as well as top show jumping stallions **Texico du Parc**, who jumped for Spain at the 1984 Olympics, and **Laeken** (1977), out

Furioso XX (1939) by Precipitation, photographed at twenty-nine years old. A poor performer on the racetrack but an outstanding sire of show jumpers, he has influenced many pedigrees throughout the world, principally through his Oldenburg-graded son Furioso II (1965).

of the Dutch mare Herta, and who has been a member of a number of winning French Nations Cup teams. Mexico was a full brother to **Furioso II** (1965), who was exported to Germany and helped Oldenburg in particular to produce top competition horses with winnings well over one million Deutschmarks. In the long term he will, however, have an even greater influence through his sons, more than fifty-five of whom have been made graded stallions. **Futuro** was another of Furioso's great sons who also joined the Oldenburgs, and he was responsible for one of Britain's top international show jumpers, Everest Forever.

The Dutch and Germans were major benefactors of Furioso's blood and, apart from Mexico, his best sons who did stay in France were **Brilloso** (1967), who stood privately and sired the Olympic show jumping stallion **Je t'Adore** (1975), who had one of the highest ever ISO indexes of 173, and like so many other good horses has Ultimate XX on the dam side, and **Surioso** (1962) who produced another Olympic jumper in Belle de Mars.

•**Fra Diavolo XX** by Black Devil and out of Frayeur by Blandford was

Laeken (1977) by Mexico. A half-brother to Le Mexico, he has combined a successful stud career with international show jumping at the highest level.

another Thoroughbred who stood at Saint Lô (from 1945-1969) and sired such good stallions as **Nykio** (1957), a multiproducer of top stock including Elyria, the dam of I Love You, and **Nankin** (1957) who produced such top show-jumping stallions as **Uriel** (1964).

• **Ultimate XX** (1941), by Umidwar, stood at Sartilly and was a big influence on the Anglo-Norman, being found in the pedigree of such top Selle Français stallions as Almé, whose dam was by Ultimate XX; I Love You, whose grandsire was Ultimate XX; and many of the top new stallions like the international show-jumping stallions **Prince d'Incoville** (1981), **Quidame de Revel** (1982) and **Lama des Landes** (1977). The latter is a son of one of the best sires of recent years, **Grand Veneur**, who died in 1988. He was by Amour du Bois and

Inschallah X (1968) by Israel X, a Hannoverian- and Oldenburg-graded sire of top dressage horses and broodmares.

traced back to Orange Peel XX via Jus de Pomme. He had one of the highest ever 'BLUPS' of +30 and was one of the most popular stallions to stand at Saint Lô. He left many high-class sons, including the international show jumper **Le Tot de Semilly** (1977), who was the only other stallion in 1989 to earn a +30 'BLUP', Love Love who jumped for Portugal, and Montblanc for Belgium. Not one of the most handsome stallions, it took some years before his potential was realised and good mares were sent to him. His progeny tend to be good, courageous horses that are easy to ride. In recent years he has often headed the stallion ratings for successful horses in the Classique jumping series for young horses.

- **Night and Day XX** (1957), by Soleil Levant, was another influential Thoroughbred. He was a very good racehorse coming second in the Prix du Jockey Club. He stood at Haras du Pin from 1962-1984. His best stallion son is **Ithuriel** (1974), who was out of the Kesbeth mare Keslante X. He jumped internationally for Portugal, before returning to France. Other successful Night and Day XX produce include Tokyo

(ISO 141) and Ascot (ISO 156).

The Thoroughbred influence continues, but is less important. One of the best recent Thoroughbreds is **Laudanum XX**, born in 1967 by Boran. He raced before becoming the only Thoroughbred stallion to win the show-jumping Grand Prix. He has gone on to produce many successful show jumpers, including the successful stallion **Oberon du Moulin** (1980), who has a 'BLUP' of +22.

Of the Anglo-Arab sires, **Denouste X**, whose produce won so much just before World War II, has been very influential and is found in the pedigree of such top stallions as **Lotus VIII**, **Royal Nostra**, **Kesbeth**, **Nithard** and **Thouland**. Also there was **Velox X**, who produced such stallions as **Farceur**, who is in the pedigree of World Cup runner-up Jiva, who was by **Amiral** (1969), and **Israel X**, the sire of **Inschallah X**, whose grandsire was the Thoroughbred Persimmon.

INFLUENCE OF THE SELLE FRANÇAIS

The influence of the Selle Français is concentrated on show jumping. Some exported stallions like Cor de la Bryère and Inschallah X have produced top dressage horses, but homebreds have not as yet shone in this sphere. Ironically Cor de la Bryère's most famous dressage horse, the 1988 Olympic silver medallist Corlandus, competed for France although he is a German Holstein. The successes of the event horses are a little better than for dressage but are still totally eclipsed by those of the French show jumpers. No other Warmblood that is produced in such large numbers (about 10,000 per year) has become so specialised – they dominated the 1990 World Show-Jumping Championships, taking both the individual and team gold medals, and Quito de Baussy made it a double by taking the 1991 European title. The mare Quinta C by Cyrus (Ibrahim grandsire) held the title for France in 1993. Then in 1994 the French star was another mare – Miss San Patrignano by Histrion who was a duel silver medallist (individual and team) at the World Equestrian Games with Michel Robert.

The other feature of the Selle Français' influence is the high number of stallions that have become top-class performers in the show-jumping arena before reverting to stud duties. This idea is becoming increasingly pronounced, with most privately owned stallions, not those of the Service de Haras, having to prove their worth as show jumpers before being accepted as good sires.

France exports more than one thousand sports horses a year for use as breeding and competition stock. Italy and Spain are particularly dependent for their show jumpers and eventers on French horses, and these include the Italian champion Gitan P by Bill de Vargenil, Joyau d'Or A by Almé, Impedoumi by Dynamique, and Jexico de Parc by Almé.

In Belgium the French horses have been used for sport, but even more importantly as the foundations for the increasingly successful Belgian Warmblood. There is Fantastique, a Selle Français by Ibrahim, who produced the Canadian show jumper Ian Millar's great World Cup winner Big Ben by Etretat. Most influential of all was Almé who stood there as Almé Z before his greatness was fully recognised and he was taken back to France.

In Switzerland Selle Français stallions are used at the national stud and Swiss show jumpers have such successful French partners as Jeton du Charme by Eden.

In The Netherlands Le Mexico, the son of Mexico, has been very influential with such good produce as Sievano. Almé was also there for three seasons, and Millerole XX, a French Thoroughbred, produced international winners Jumbo Design, Larramy and Dutch Courage.

Germany has imported some great French stallions, notably Furioso II and Futuro, who became mainstays of the Oldenburg, but Bonjour by Bibelot and Alméo by Almé have also been an influence on this breed. Cor de la Bryère, by Rantzau XX and tracing back to Furioso XX on his dam's side, has been a major influence on the Holsteins. So too has Silbersee, by the Thoroughbred Silver Matal XX and out of a Quastor mare, and he is a top performer as well as a stallion graded successfully in the Holstein stud book.

French Anglo-Arabs have been used with great success in Germany, the best known being Inschallah X, born as Josselin by Israel X and out of another Anglo-Arab Resena. He produced some Olympic medal-winning dressage horses. Zeus by Arlequin has been popular and has much Anglo-Arab blood, and Matcho X by Pancho II X is being used to produce Hannoverians with increasing success.

The USA has bought many top French horses, which include stallions like Galoubet; the World Cup champion I Love You, who is also by Almé, and Noren, who was the 1982 Horse of the Year with Kathy Monahan and who won Grand Prix classes all over the USA. They have also had many top show jumpers, like Valde Loire by Ibrahim, Janus de Ver by Uriel and Krischna III by Night and Day XX.

England has imported some Selle Français stallions, which include the Grade A jumper Dallas by Brilloso, who is yet another good stallion with Ultimate XX on the dam's side.

French horses go to other less expected places like South America, Japan, and the Middle East, and the total numbers exported are so large that about thirteen per cent of the foals born go abroad. It is an impressive success story and one brought about in an individualistic manner and not by conforming to normal European approaches to Warmblood breeding. The French have avoided importing other breeds and have developed methods of selective breeding more associated with the Thoroughbred than Warmbloods.

Chapter 6

The Swedish Warmblood
by
CELIA CLARKE

E VER SINCE THE twelfth century when Bishop Absalon of Den-mark chose to raise his cavalry remounts in the Skåne area of what is now southern Sweden, the country thereabouts has been noted for its horse-breeding skills. In fact, when Charles X acquired it from Den-mark in 1658, one of his first acts barely three years later was to found a Royal Stud at Flyinge – an establishment which still exists well over 300 years later, and which is still devoted to breeding riding horses.

Those 300 years have seen the development of one of the top Warmblood competition horses in the world, the Swedish Warm blood. This breed, which is noted for its lively but tractable tempera-ment, extravagant athletic paces and correct conformation, has not only enjoyed considerable favour in its own domestic market but has also been sought by top dressage riders elsewhere and has played a key part in the upgrading of some of the newer Warmblood breeds. However, as with all successful Warmblood breeding, these achieve-ments have not been accidental and are the result of many years of careful planning.

Probably the first significant step towards the development of the modern Swedish Warmblood was the appointment of Crown Prince Adolf Frederik as director of Flyinge in 1747. This resulted in many of his own Holstein stallions being used at the stud, and an increasing percentage of Hannoverian, East Prussian, Thoroughbred, Arab, Oldenburg and Frederiksborg blood also finding its way into the breed's genetic bank over the next 150 years. The organisation of the stud at Flyinge, of the other main Swedish state stud at Stromsholm, and of the breed in general, was strengthened by the Stallion Inspection Law passed in 1884 and the codification of the duties of the central stud farm laid down in 1923.

By the mid-1920s, the native Swedish Warmblood mares were being covered by a considerable number of high-class stallions, both home-bred and imported. The bloodlines of the best of these imported stallions can still be found in many Swedish pedigrees and include the Hannoverians Schwabliso, Tribun and Hamlet, the East Prussians Attino, Sonnesänger, Kyffhäuser and Humanist, and the Thoroughbred Hampelmann XX.

Probably as a result of the success of these importations, relatively few foreign stallions were introduced into Sweden between 1930 and 1945. However, shortly after the end of World War II a significant group of East Prussian (as distinct from Trakehner) stallions found their way to Sweden, and during the following twenty years a number of these stallions – including Hartung (Ilmengrund/Altan), Heinfreid (Paradox XX/Camoens), Heristal (Hyperion/Haselhorst), Humboldt (Hutten/Paradox XX), Polarstern (Portwein/Alibaba) and Unikum (Traumgeist XX/Aquavit) along with the home-bred Drabant (Kokard/Pergamon), Gaspari (Parad/Haffner), Jovial (Bohème XX/Trotz XX), Lansiär (Niger/Florett), and Varolio (Novarro/Florett) formed the basis of the increasingly popular breed, Stromsholm having ceased to function as a stud.

These imports blended well with the existing broodmare band, which had had significant inputs of East Prussian blood during the

Drabant (1946) by Kokard, founder of a famous line of dressage horses and sire of many top graded stallions.

previous eighty years, so much so that Dr Aaby Ericsson, who was responsible for the import of many of the modern East Prussian stallions commented that no other blood had been found to be as dependable genetically as the East Prussian, and that all stallions born in Sweden have some East Prussian blood in their veins. Dr Aaby Ericsson was also responsible for the introduction of top-class Arab blood into the Swedish breeding programme. This venture was so successful that Nerox (Nigro/Mersuch I) was sold to the Hannoverian state stud at Celle, and Son au Sverge (Onkel/Nigro) was sold to the Polish state stud. The grey Flyinge stallion Urbino by Drabant is probably the most famous descendant of this bloodline, being out of Nella by Nerox.

Originally, the riding model of the Swedish Warmblood was developed as a cavalry horse, both at home and latterly for sale to the Swiss market. However, when the purchasers from the army declined in numbers, private buyers replaced them and Swedish breeders changed their breeding policies to fulfil this need.

Although Swedish horses were notably successful in competitions in all equestrian disciplines and at the highest level during the inter-war and immediate post-war period, in the 1960s and 1970s the Swedish Warmblood was thought of chiefly as a dressage horse.

However, breeders in Sweden then discovered that show jumping could also provide a lucrative outlet for their horses, and they went to considerable lengths to introduce some top jumping blood through subsequent imports. These included the Holsteins Conte (Cottage Son XX/Marder), the much-travelled Limelight (Liguster/Narciss) and Modesto (Marlon XX/Cromwell), the F-line Hannoverian Windwurf (Wendekreis/Wohlklang), the G-lines Goldgraf (Goya/Bounteous XX) and Grandsudan (Grande/Sudan XX), as well as Fasching, Fremoor, Furidant II, and the Dutch Warmblood Voltaire (all by the Selle Français Furioso II), and the Bolero son Bold Grande. In addition, the closely related Dutch Warmbloods Robin Z (Ramiro Z/Almé Z), Ralmé Z (Ramiro Z/Almé Z) and Aladin Z (Almé Z/Good Bye XX), who all trace to the top French show jumping sire Almé (sire of I Love You and Galoubet) were acquired, as were Marcoville's sire Irco Marco (Irco Polo/Sportsman) and his show-jumping son Irco Mena. Several Danish-bred horses from proven dual-purpose lines, namely Racot (Raimondo (Holst)/Pik As XX), Galanthus (Gunnar (Trak)/Wöhler (Hann)), Rastell (Raimondo (Holst)/ Gotyk (Wlpk)) and Midt West Ibi Light (Ibikus/Limelight) have been leased to Sweden in recent years, and Swift (Zeus/Weltmeister) has been imported from West Germany.

The long-term success of this venture is a matter of debate, but

The Dutch warmblood stallion Irco Mena (1982) by Irco Marco (KWPN) out of a Menelek XX mare, imported into Sweden to improve show-jumping bloodlines.

Swedish breeders are optimistic about this change of emphasis, which took place shortly after control of the breed was transferred to the partly privately funded Swedish Equestrian Breeding and Sports Foundation at Flyinge in 1985.

These Warmblood imports are additional to the regular numbers of new Thoroughbred stallions (about half a dozen per year) that are brought to Sweden for use on both Thoroughbred and Warmblood broodmares. These Thoroughbred stallions have an impact on the Warmblood breeding process as well, with such sires as Cosmos XX (sire of the stallions Karakoll, Indus and Jasper), Hurricane XX (sire of Gaston and Orkan) and Bohème XX (sire of Jovial) being particularly notable.

In the near future, however, Sweden will probably still be seen mainly as a source of dressage bloodlines and with the constantly increasing interest in the sport at all levels, the future popularity of the Swedish Warmblood looks assured, even if the venture into show-jumping does not prove to be as universally successful as their record in producing dressage horses has been.

BREEDING POLICY

Graded stallions in Sweden must have four proven generations in their pedigrees and broodmares must have three. In addition, both sexes must pass a performance test, a rigorous veterinary examination and an exacting assessment of type, conformation and action. About thirty foals are selected every year for probationer stallions at Flyinge, the majority of which are purchased from private owners, who are also given generous additional payments as the youngsters develop successfully. Re-inspections take place at eighteen months old and then again twelve months later, when a number of privately owned and raised stallions are also looked at. Those still remaining are then broken to saddle and are performance tested in the autumn of their fourth year. Culls are gelded and sold as quality riding horses, and now that increasing importance is being laid on jumping, an occasional older stallion may also be rejected if he is not showing sufficient ability in that sphere. Information on the plusses and minuses in quality of a stallion's progeny are freely discussed and available to mare owners seeking breeding advice. Finally, when the full results of progeny testing and assessment of four-year-olds are available, any stallion whose progeny show a continuing, recurrent fault in temperament, vice or conformation is liable to be removed from breeding and either be gelded or put down, however correct or successful he appears to be himself. Further information on the competition potential of the progeny of the younger stallions is also gleaned every year from the results of the nationwide Swede Horse Breeders Cup young horse championships.

Nearly 200 five- and six-year-olds qualify for the dressage and show-jumping finals every year and the prestige of any stallion with a proven record of successful progeny in this competition is very high. It is by these clear and open testing procedures that the quality of the Swedish Warmblood is upgraded and help is given to breeders in steering clear of problem areas.

The foundation maternal bloodlines in Sweden are numbered, and of nearly fifty so honoured. The majority are old Swedish Warmblood, with the remainder being divided almost equally between bloodlines of East Prussian and Hannoverian origin. About 6000 Warmblood mares are covered annually by just under 200 stallions, about 45 of whom are based at Flyinge, the rest being privately owned.

The aim of these matings is to produce an easy-to-manage, multipurpose riding horse with a pleasant temperament and easy, generous paces. In addition, Flyinge sees its primary goal as providing Sweden's horse breeders with superior stallions, and to this end each year covers some highly qualified mares free of charge under the Free Access scheme, on condition that it has first refusal on the resultant foals. The increasing use of frozen semen, which is exported throughout Europe and America, is also making Swedish bloodlines more accessible to the outside world.

Both the graded stallions and the graded mares who are entered into the breeding stud book are classified upon grading as either Premium AB or Premium B, and this information is duly recorded in the stud books. Once the results of progeny testing are known, those stallions and mares with outstanding offspring are elevated to Premium A or Elite status.

GENERAL DESCRIPTION OF THE SWEDISH WARMBLOOD

Because of the changing demands of the market over the years, and the mixed origins and types that have been used to develop the breed (which was originally designed to be a cavalry remount), it shows a considerable variation in height, bone and temperament across the different bloodlines, from the high-spirited Drabants, through the compact but slightly calmer Gasparis, to the taller eventing Jovials and on to the powerful show jumping Lansiärs. However, despite these variations, nearly all members of the breed have a kind eye and a wide generous forehead, a generally harmonious conformation and athletic paces. The most common colours are bay, chestnut, black and grey, and some bloodlines have a tendency to throw a lot of white on face and legs (as is often the case in animals with Gaspari blood). There is also a tendency for some of the older bloodlines to produce somewhat straighter shoulders and flatter croups than is currently desirable, and although in most cases these do not inhibit the paces of the horses concerned, efforts are being made to eradicate these characteristics as much as possible to suit the modern buyer. The temperament of the breed can range from willing and unflappable to brilliant but highly strung, the former being popular with the less serious competitor and the latter being thought to provide that flash of presence and ability so essential to top-class work.

IMPORTANT BLOODLINES

The bloodlines found in most successful modern Swedish Warmbloods, be they competition horses, broodmares or stallions, tend to trace to one or more of the following stallions:

•**Drabant** (Kokard/Pergamon). Bay (1946). Drabant, whose progeny were known as being difficult to ride, but were often brilliant performers, was the sire of 9 graded stallions and 96 broodmares. His progeny includes Urbino (sire of four graded stallions, including the successful international dressage horses Flyinge Tolstoy and Flyinge Flamingo, and 150 broodmares), Vagabond (sire of 9 graded stallions and 113 broodmares) and Brisad (who competed in Grand Prix dressage in West Germany before returning to stud in Sweden). Drabant was also responsible for William Chammartin's Wald, the Swiss Olympic dressage silver medallist in Rome, Linda Zang's American dressage horse Fellow Traveller, and Harry Klugmann's international eventer for West Germany, Verberot.

PEDIGREE OF **URBINO** – GREY SWEDISH WARMBLOOD, 1962			
Urbino 430 (SV)	Drabant 315	Kokard 135 (SV)	Humanist (Trak)
			Miss G 2117 (SV)
		Tomona 4268	Pergamon 197
			Torna 1891
	Nella 4763	Nerox 207	Nigro 138
			Judit 2925
		Irsa 2049	Brûleur
			Irma 1407

•**Gaspari** (Parad/Haffner). Chestnut (1949). The sire of 11 graded stallions and 96 broodmares. Probably one of the world's greatest producers of dressage horses, and a competitor himself in the Rome Olympics, he was the sire of Piaff (World, European and Munich Olympic champion), the dressage stallions Elektron, Gassendi and Flyinge Herkules (sire of five stallions and 70 broodmares as well as being a regular competitor in international and World Cup competitions), and the Los Angeles Olympic show jumper Flyinge Imperator. Gaspari was also a noted sire of broodmares, one of his daughters being the dam of Christine Stückelberger's Gauguin de Lully (World Cup final winner, silver medallist in the 1986 World Championships and bronze medallist in the Seoul Olympics). Since retiring to stud in Switzerland, Gauguin de Lully has been used as an AI sire in Sweden on a limited number of high-class mares.

PEDIGREE OF **IMPERATOR** – BAY SWEDISH WARMBLOOD, 1972			
Imperator 529 (SV)	Gaspari 340	Parad 194 (SV)	Humanist (Trak)
			Musette (Ostpr)
		Russi 3359	Haffner
			Rusette 2773
	Donetta 6885	Biarritz 294 (SV)	Hamlet (Hann)
			Maritza 3338 (SV)
		Dongola 6088	Tokajer 240
			Dorothea 5408

Gaspari (1949) by Parad, an Olympic dressage horse himself and the sire of the World, European and Olympic dressage champion Piaff, as well as eleven graded stallions.

•**Jovial** (Bohème XX/Trotz XX). Brown (1952). The sire of several graded stallions, including Flyinge Stud's Olympic bronze medallist Nebraska (international eventer), Labrador (international show jumper and sire of two Flyinge stallions himself), and the all-round producer Ceylon. He was also the sire of Ajax, who was a team dressage Olympic bronze medallist in Munich in 1972 and was also the champion Scandinavian show jumper at one time. Because of the high percentage of Thoroughbred in his pedigree, he was primarily used to produce eventers (one of his progeny competed in the Olympics in this sphere) and was noted for his ability to add elegance and endurance to the heavier bloodlines. His graded sons standing at stud privately include the dressage sire Caracas as well as Jocer, Carat, Mix and Neva.

•**Lansiär** (Niger/Florett). Chestnut (1954). Lansiär has a noted reputation as a producer of high-quality broodmares and show jumpers, and was also the sire of the stallions Langos, Caviar and Ambassadeur, who competed successfully in international three day events such as Chatsworth and Boekelo as well as being short listed for the Montreal Olympics.

Lansiär (1954) by Niger, an all-round sire of graded stallions, good broodmares, show jumpers, dressage horses and eveenters.

•**Utrillo** (Ernö/Anilin). Dark bay Hannoverian (1962). Utrillo was the sire of a number of graded stallions, including Chagall (father of over 130 broodmares and competition horses in all disciplines,

The international dressage stallion Amiral (1985) by Napolean, who is one of the current top representatives of the Utrillo line which also produced the World Cup winner Gauguin de Lully.

PEDIGREE OF **CHAGALL** – BROWN SWEDISH WARMBLOOD, 1966			
Chagall 455 (SV)	Utrillo 432 (Hann)	Ernö 3959	Astflug 3564
			Fugosa H 54287
		Anisett H 60267	Anilin 3371
			Havanna 49951
	Efrodite 6211 (SV)	Frondeur 333	Salvator 226
			Kickan 4196
		Edelweiss 5530 (SV)	Heinfried 206 (Trak)
			Erica 5008

including the competing stallions Gauguin de Lully and Chirac), Kaliber and Maraton.

• **Varolio** (Novarro/Florett). Brown (1942). The sire of four graded stallions and sire of the dams of the graded stallions Brisad (by Drabant) and Gassendi (by Gaspari).

THE SWEDISH INFLUENCE

Despite the growing interest in show-jumping bloodlines, Swedish Warmblood breeding is still chiefly concerned with meeting the requirements of the dressage arena, as befits a country where riders seem to have only an incidental interest in any sport other than dressage. This has proved both a benefit and a limitation – a benefit in that the horses have been allowed to compete in a field where many of them excel, and a limitation in that only now are the show jumping abilities of the breed beginning to be appreciated. Of necessity, therefore, the prime influence of the Swedish Warmblood so far has been in those countries, such as Switzerland, who have historically purchased the bulk of their cavalry horses from Sweden and used the best of their imports as dressage and riding horses, or in countries like Britain, where the growing interest in dressage has generated a demand for proven competition horses and breeding stock. Swedish influence is therefore most strongly felt in the following countries:

Switzerland. Between 1948 and 1960 the Swiss army bought over 1400 young Swedish horses, all of whom were renamed with a name beginning with the letter W. Swedish horses who have competed in or for Switzerland include the 1960 Rome Olympics dressage gold medallist Wald (by Drabant), Henri Chammartin's three horses Wöhler, Woermann and Wolfdietrich (all of whom have Attino in their pedigree, and who are nothing to do with the Hannoverian stallions of the same names) and the 1988 Olympic bronze medallist Gauguin de Lully (Chagall/Gaspari). In addition, a number of Swedish stallions have stood recently at the Swiss Federal Stud in Avenches, most notably the Vagabond son Vagant, and a considerable number of broodmares have also been imported into the country for breeding purposes.

Germany. Considering the numbers and ability of the home-grown product available to German riders, it is perhaps significant to note that when the Olympics were held in Munich the gold medallist in dressage was a German rider, Liselott Linsenhoff, riding a Swedish horse, Piaff (Gaspari/Ruthven). Other eminent German riders have also shown a marked preference for Swedish horses, including Frau Becher with Silver Dream (repurchased by Sweden as a present for the king) and Elektron, Herbert Rehbein with Mars, Magnus II and Gassendi (subsequently exported to the USA) and Harry Klugmann with his international eventer Verberot. Sales of horses to Germany still continue at a notable level and this is particularly true of entires who tend to compete at the highest levels and then often return to Sweden to be used at stud afterwards. However, because of their heavy competition commitments, few of these horses are used at stud whilst in Germany, and the Swedish influence on German breeding is minimal.

Denmark. In past years, both Danish riders and Danish breeders drew upon the resources of their near neighbour to a considerable extent. The Danish national Warmblood breeding policy is closely modelled on the Swedish approach, and during the early years of the development of the Danish Warmblood both Swedish horses (such as Donau by Onkel) and Swedish judges played a vital part. Indeed, the Danish authorities used the facilities of Flyinge for the first few years of stallion performance tests and twenty-six graded Swedish Warmblood stallions have stood at stud in Denmark in the last twenty-five years, many of them being of considerable influence in the outstanding progress the breed has made. Probably most notable are Mozart (sire of the graded stallion Titian), Herzog (the sire of the World Champion dressage horse Marzog) and Pilar (all Heristal/Samos), Gladiator (Heristal/Onkel) and the noted broodmare sire Epok (Tintoretto/Salvator) but even so few Swedish sires have founded their own stallion lines in Denmark to date. A number of outstanding mares were also exported to Denmark, including Eliza (Dragos/Frondeur and a half sister to Gauguin de Lully's sire Chagall), whose son Elizar by Unikum (Trak) produced the outstanding graded stallions May Sherif (who himself was represented by four progeny at the Seoul Olympics) and May Black (Elizar/Securius). A second son of Eliza, Tasano by Rousseau, also stood as a graded stallion in Denmark. Drabant blood is also evident in Danish breeding through the Brabant son Ibsen (Brabant/Frondeur), who is a half brother to Eliza, and a number of other horses also carry significant amounts of Lansiär and Unikum blood.

Britain. Until about 1978 no organised Warmblood breeding took place in Britain, and dressage riders tended to use Thoroughbreds, Anglo-Arabs or the occasional foreign import. Even so, at least three of the top British dressage horses of the late 1970s (Sarah Whitmore's Junker, Domini Lawrence's San Fernando and Tanya Larrigan's Salute) were Swedish, and this helped highlight the importance of the breed to the small but growing numbers of Warmblood breeders in Britain at that time. Since then, several Swedish stallions have found their way to the UK, chief amongst them being the well-known international Grand Prix dressage horse Apell (Cordon Bleu/Abhang II) and the talented Maximilian (Martini/Utrillo) but so far they have tended to cover only a limited number of mares due to competitive and training commitments. However several other British-based stallions, such as Rabinowitz (Go On Then XX/Gladiator), Durfee Augite (Atlantus (DV)/Drabant), Tallents Wellesley (Weibfang (Hann)/Gaspari) and Alizar (Atlantus (DV)/ Elizar) also represent Swedish bloodlines, but in this case through their dams. Eliza also found her way to Britain at the end of her illustrious stud career, but unfortunately she died before she was able to make an impact on the British scene. However, her grand-daughter Ostrea (Elizar/Securius, and a full sister to May Sherif and May Black), who was imported a few years later, is in fact the dam of the BWBS-graded stallion Alizar and has therefore helped Eliza's line to become well-established here.

United States and Canada. The lack of overall control by a national Warmblood breeding organisation in the USA makes it difficult to assess the total influence of the Swedish Warmblood there. However, the Swedish authorities are now examining American-born stock which are eligible for entry into the Swedish stud books and issuing pure or part-bred papers to them according to their bloodlines. Several fully graded Swedish stallions were exported to the USA during the 1980s, such as Elektron and Gassendi by Gaspari and Concarneau by Caracas and over 30 stallions are now graded with the Swedish Warmblood Association in North America. The Dressage at the Devon Show, which is the premier national showcase for dressage and Warmblood youngstock, now regularly features horses of Swedish bloodlines amongst its top champions, and plans to produce a home-grown dressage horse based on Swedish stock appear to be bearing fruit. In addition, American riders have also regularly drawn on Sweden for riding horses for the last few years, the most notable being the 1974 American Dressage Horse of the Year, the Drabant son Fellow Traveller who also represented the USA at the Dressage World Championships in Goodwood in 1982. A number of North American-based stallions such as Juvel (Flamingo/Utrillo) and Oskar II (Urbino/O'den) have also successfully combined stud careers with competition work on a regular basis.

Chapter 7

The Danish Warmblood
by
DEBBIE WALLIN

THE DANISH WARMBLOOD horse has been part of an organised breeding programme since 1962, known in Denmark as Dansk
Varmblod Avlsforbund (DVA).

Originally, Denmark had no real riding-horse breeding. Its main
native breeds, the Knappstrupper (a spotted breed) and the
Fredriksborg (a chestnut breed) were both more suited to driving, and
competition horses were imported from Sweden, West Germany,
Poland and sometimes to a lesser extent, The Netherlands and Great
Britain. There was therefore no uniform type of animal bred in
Denmark specifically for Danish riders, so Danish breeders formed a
new society, the Dansk Sportheste, which began to hold annual stallion and mare gradings in the early 1960s.

As it was a new venture, expert help was sought and willingly given
from experienced Swedish and German judges, who joined the Danish
grading panels as 'advice givers'. The new stud book was divided into
three sections: DH for the Head Stud Book for the best animals (for
graded stallions and the top 10-15 per cent of graded mares); DS for
the Main Stud Book (into which the vast majority of graded mares
were entered); and a register (Forr) for mares possibly lacking movement, pedigree details or a minimum height requirement. The stud
books were open to all mares, and a small percentage failed and were
not entered. There is also a small, relatively new Elite Stud Book
(EDH) into which previously graded mares can be entered if their
progeny record outstanding success either at gradings or under saddle.

Due to the wide variety of mare material in Denmark, a much
stricter, more concentrated, effort was made to ensure that high quality stallions were available to breeders, and from the beginning only the
best were approved for breeding. In the formative years mainly

Swedish, Trakehner, Hannoverian, Holstein and a few Polish stallions formed the basis of the stud book and ridden performance testing was done either in the stallion's country of origin or at the Flyinge State Stud in Sweden. However, in due course, the increasing numbers of stallions requiring testing and the growing financial strength enabled the testing to be done in Denmark controlled by the Danish breed society. The Danish breed society is not government-funded, so in its early years its progress was often restricted for financial reasons.

The Dansk Lette Heste (DLH) was another breed organisation in Denmark running in competition with the DSA (Dansk Sport Heste Avlsforbund) during the 1970s. Many stallions taken into the DLH association had already failed the grading process for the DSA, which complicated matters for both organisations. Later, in 1978, an agreement was reached between them and some previously failed stallions were then recognised by the newly formed and newly named Dansk Varmblod (DV), which took over control of the major portion of the riding-horse breeding in Denmark. Stallions which entered the DV from the DLH have an S in front of their stud book number.

Two further societies had a small influence on Warmblood breeding in Denmark. The Fredriksborg was the main native breed in Denmark. A dual-purpose animal, always chestnut, with a nice quality head and amenable temperament, it was used for pleasure riding and light draught work. It is a pure-bred breed with an active breed organisation in Denmark today. In modern Warmblood pedigrees, Fredriksborg blood appears only rarely, and then usually only on the female line.

There is also an Oldenburg Society in Denmark, as well as small Holstein society (Graeseegnens Holsteiner Hestealvsforening) which has broken away from the Danish Warmblood Society, both hold their own shows and gradings. Horses registered into the Oldenburg stud book carry the letters OL in front of their numbers.

Danish stallion owners have always been willing to pay large prices for top quality bloodlines and as a result many of the best, most highly proven Warmblood bloodlines from most Warmblood breeding nations can now be found in Denmark. Ibikus (1967) by Hertilas, Donauwind (1965) by Pregel, Herbsturm (1962) by Komet, Gunnar (1966) by Komet, and Schwarm (1966) by Traumgeist XX, who are all famous in Trakehner breeding, have stood at stud in Denmark, as have the East Prussian stallions Gabriel (1950) by Gygant, and Ackjonariusz (1953) by Sandor. Top Holstein lines are fully represented with Alibi (1962) by Aldato, and the Lord sons Lavallo (1979), now in Germany, and Leonardo II (1981) (exported to the United States), the Cor de la Bryère son Calimero (1980), the Ramiro sons Raimondo (1970), Royal Z I (1984) and Royal Z II (1985) and the Landgraf I son Lancier

(1984). Lagano (1978) by Leander out of a Roman damline, only stood a few years at stud in Denmark, but managed to produce a long list of top quality, and champion riding horses. His graded son Lucky Light (1985) is an enormously talented show jumper and reached Grade A at early age.

Lucky Light (1985) bay stallion foaled in Denmark by Lagaro (Holst) out of Majbritt, a gold medal winner. Lucky Light is a Grade A show jumper of pure Holstein pedigree.

The Selle Français stallion Almé (also known as Almé Z), probably the most famous of all show-jumping sires in the world, was represented by his short-lived son Zalméco (who died in 1990) and by his grandson Dwight (1985-91), as well as being the maternal grandsire of the previously mentioned Royal Z I and Royal Z II.

In recent years, new Hannoverian imports have carried the blood of Bolero (1975) by Black Sky XX, Wenzel I (1976) by Woermann, and the Hannoverian-graded French Anglo-Arab Matcho X by Pancho II X, whilst the earlier Hannoverian blood of Grande (1958) by Graf, Wedekind (1966) by Ferdinand, Absatz (1960) by Abglanz, and Argentan (1967) by Absatz, are well represented amongst the imports of past years. The Westphalian Dressage star, Rubinstein (1986) by Rosenkavalier is in the limelight the world over and sought by breeders of dressage horses, having reached Grand Prix at such an early age.

In 1994 two of his sons were imported and are now going through their ridden performance testing.

BREEDING POLICY

The Danish society has a reputation for excellence. Its grading process is very stringent, usually allowing only between three and fifteen young stallions per year to go forward to the ridden performance test, from the annual stallion grading show which is held every year in late February at Herning. In addition, older stallions imported into Denmark as mature animals are eligible to come forward for grading if they have already completed their ridden tests elsewhere and have been placed in the top third of animals doing that particular performance test that year.

Stallion grading in Denmark is strictly regulated and takes several years. In the first instance, young stallions (rising three-years-old) must pass a severe veterinary inspection (including X-rays), plus an assessment of conformation, loose jumping and action. Next, they must pass their ridden performance test with *very good* results, as average passes

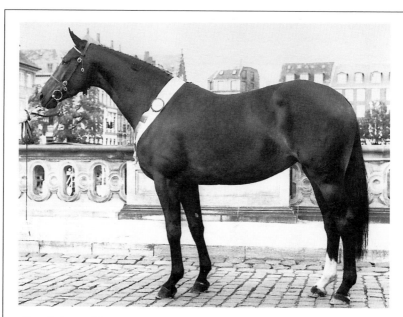

Øxenholm Gilda (1986), by Waldstern out of the silver medal mare Glabella Lundgård, who is a half-sister to Vola Lundgård. Gilda was awarded a gold medal at the 1989 Elite Mare Show.

will not suffice. In later years, points scored at foal and progeny inspections, as well as fertility results, must reach a certain standard, and finally the progeny must compete with success. In 1994, it was decided that any stallion which had not shown either outstanding talent himself, or managed to produce a goodly number of talented progeny or shown success through his breeding stock, would have his breeding licence within Danish Warmblood revoked and no longer used at stud. Surprisingly, May Sherif's full brother, May Black (1973) Weinberg (1979) the only Watzman son in Denmark, as well as a number of other imported sires of mainly show jumping pedigrees, Valentino (1977) by Winnaton, Weibfang (1972) by Waidmannsheil, Furore (1976) by Furioso II all failed to produce.

The Danish society holds a number of shows every year. The country is divided into seven regions, each with a district leader. In these districts, various activities are arranged from feeding and production lectures, stallion parades, to stud visits to Sweden, Germany, Great Britain and so on. Most importantly, every year each region holds large regional mare-grading shows (usually in July) as well as a foal show slightly later in the year. In the mare grading, mares are given points for type, conformation, limbs, correctness of gaits, elasticity and extension, plus a final general all round mark out of 10. A written critique is also given. Both the marks and the critique appear on the mare's combined pedigree and grading papers. Mares with high points (not less than 8 out of 10) enter the Head Stud Book (indicated by the prefix DH on the mare's stud book number). Mares with lower marks enter the Main Stud Book (DS) and others with missing pedigree information or insufficient marks go into a breeding register (Forr). Only about ten to twenty per cent of mares enter the DH book, and only these are branded on the neck. After the Danish grading shows, mares with the best results gain entry to the prestigious Elite Show, usually held at the end of July. Here gold, silver and bronze medals are awarded to the very top mares. Ridden performance testing for mares started in the early 1990s. Before Medal mares can claim their title, they are required to pass a ridden test. All mares going forward to Grading are eligible for this testing, and once successful will have the letter R added to their graded stud book numbers.

Foals out of two Danish Warmblood graded parents are branded with the Danish crown on the left thigh; for further identification purposes since the mid-1980s three digits reflecting the last three figures of the foal's registration number have also been included in the brand directly underneath the crown. Foals/horses with a Danish heritage which are unable to qualify on their pedigree/breeding for the DV brand are sometimes branded with the DK brand.

The foal shows are also run by each region, and the highest placed youngsters from each show go on to compete for the 'Foal of the Year' title. At these foal shows, the first progeny of stallions graded the previous year are also inspected and points are given to the sires for each improvement in the foal that the stallion has made in comparison to the mare (e.g. better limbs than the dam, better topline, better action) and a recommendation is made by the judges as to which type of mare (light, heavy, big, small etc.) would seem to be the best possible choice to send to the new stallion in future years.

In the mid-1980s the DV introduced regional qualifiers for a National Young Riding Horse Championship for four-year-olds rising five, with the Final Championship being held in conjunction with the Stallion Grading Show. At the same time, auctions were started at the Herning Show for horses entered at the show (stallions and riding horses). The auctions got off to a slow start but in 1990 the Riding Horse Champion, a DS graded five-year-old chestnut mare by Lavallo, out of a May Sherif dam, sold for £38,000 and a new precedent was set for future sales. The Danes continue to explore the use of auctions as a sales process, but as yet have met with little success when compared to the German, Dutch and French.

GENERAL DESCRIPTION OF THE DANISH WARMBLOOD

The aim of the Danish breeders is to produce a very harmonious animal with well-proportioned modern lines. Great attention has been taken to improve the wither and shoulder and thereby the walk and canter by the use of Thoroughbred blood. Swing and elasticity, with shoulder freedom and suppleness through the loin, rated very highly in the Danish grading process, but with the influx of Thoroughbred blood, (the model as a riding horse improves) elasticity and power is often lost unless the dam is extremely strong in both points. The Danish Warmblood ranges from 15.3-16.3hh (160-170cm) and is generally of medium weight with good, flat bone and a good frame. It should also have a quality head, a well-set-on long neck, a good shoulder with a well-pronounced wither, a muscular back and loin, a long croup and excellent free movement.

IMPORTANT BLOODLINES

Although Dansk Varmblod has only been established for just over a quarter of a century, a number of stallions have already made a considerable impact on Warmblood breeding in Denmark and through their exported progeny – to those countries such as Great Britain and the USA who are new to Warmblood breeding but wish to use the best modern types for their foundation stock.

Stallions who have had particular influence in Denmark and abroad include:

• **Securius** (Sender/Abendgold II). Chestnut Hannoverian, born 1960. He covered over 700 mares and was responsible for one of the best foundation mares in Denmark today – May Kignaes, a winner of both bronze and silver medals for progeny.

• **Alibi** (Aldato/Heidekrug). Brown Holstein born 1962, imported by Anders Andersen. He was the sire of another famous female line, founded on the broodmare Pari, as well as being responsible for both numerous Grade A show jumpers and a number of graded sons, including Alladin (1981) and Astaire (1982).

• **Solist** (Seelöwe/Domspatz). Black Hannoverian, born 1966. Also a

Alibi (1962) by Aldato. A pre-potent Holstein foundation sire in Denmark, he is the sire of the international show jumping stallion Alladin.

The gold medal mare Vola Lundgård (1973) by Weinbrand (Hann).
She was Mare of the Year in 1976 for her owner/breeder
Herr Ingemann Jensen.

founder of a line of exceptional broodmares, he is still prominent in today's Danish pedigrees. He was the dam's sire of both Kawango (by Ibikus) born 1978 and Gefion (by Go On Then XX) born 1978, who was short-listed in dressage for the 1988 Olympics, as well as a number of good international dressage horses, notably the Grand Prix dressage horse Stradivarius. Gefion is now competing in Great Britain.

•**Pilar, Mozart and Herzog** (all Heristal/Samos). These Swedish Warmblood full brothers, born 1958, 1955 and 1950 respectively, did a great deal to consolidate Denmark's female breeding stock in the early years, as did Gladiator (1949) also by Heristal. They also sired numerous competition horses, mainly in dressage, of which Anne-Grethe Törnblad's Olympic Grand Prix horse Marzog (by Herzog) is probably the best known.

•**Weinbrand** (Waldspecht XX/Dominus). Brown Hannoverian, born 1967. He stood in Denmark between 1970 and 1978 before being sold back to West Germany as a Grand Prix dressage stallion. He produced a number of top-quality foundation lines for mares, notably through the silver medal mares Vola Lundgård, Wenche and Vita Lundgård, and the bronze medal mare Vena Lundgård. Vola Lundgård was also later awarded the coveted silver medal in 1976 and 1977 at the Elite Mare Show. In the competition field, Weinbrand produced both Prix St Georges and Grand Prix dressage horses, notably Why Not (ridden by Ernst Jessen), and is also the grandsire of the graded stallion Limebrand (1980) which stood at stud in the USA but is now back in Denmark.

•**Raimondo** (Ramiro/Frivol XX). Bay Holstein, born 1970. Imported into Denmark in 1973 by Anders Andersen, this stallion founded an outstanding male line, being responsible for the graded stallions Ragtime (1976), Racot (1975), Rastell (1984, exported to Sweden), Rinaldo (1983), Radamas (1974) and Ramir (1983), most of whom won their performance tests, as well as a silver medal mare and five bronze medal mares. His progeny have also been particularly successful in the show-jumping arena. Racot stood a number of years at stud in Sweden until his graded son Faighter had such enormous success with an outstanding number of DH and medal mares at the annual gradings that Racot was brought back to stand at stud in Denmark. Racot also has the honour of siring the first graded stallion in Denmark to receive 10 out of 10 in the final points at grading in 1990. This stallion, Rambo (1986), is out of a bronze medal mare by Ibikus and won the ridden performance test by such a large margin that the grading awarded the maximum possible marks. His ridden career in Denmark is so successful that, young as he is, his semen is being exported to Britain and the USA.

•**May Sherif** (Elizar/Securius). Bay Danish Warmblood, born 1972. In

PEDIGREE OF **MAY SHERIF** – BAY DANISH WARMBLOOD, 1972			
May Sherif DH 250	Elizar DH 191 (DV)	Unikum 429 (Trak)	Traumgeist (XX)
			Amadea 1836 (Trak)
		Eliza DH 906 (SV)	Dragos (39) 316
			Efrodite (23) 6211
	May Kignaes DH 1046 (DV) Silver medal and Bronze medal mare	Securius DH 125 (Hann)	Sender 3983
			St Pr St Abendkätzchen H 56324
		Marinka DH 735 (Holst)	Nessus 3167
			Fatza 60303

May Sherif (1972) by Elizar. A leading sire of Grand Prix dressage horses throughout the world, including Matador (Finland) and Andiamo (Switzerland), both of whom competed in the Seoul Olympics.

1988 May Sherif was the only living sire represented by four progeny at the Seoul Olympics, and numbered amongst these were the dressage horses Matador, competing for Finland, and Andiamo, for Switzerland. May Sherif's sire Elizar (1967), by Unikum (Trak), was out of the mare Eliza, by Dragos, an imported Swedish Warmblood mare from one of the most influential and proven foundation lines in Sweden. Eliza was also the dam of another graded stallion in Denmark, Tasano (1970), by the Swedish stallion Rousseau. May Sherif's brother, May Black (1973), was also graded in Denmark and their full sister, the DH mare Ostrea, proved her worth when – following export to England and mating with Atlantus (1975), by Galanthus – she produced the graded British Warmblood stallion Alizar Kignaes in 1986. May Sherif is now exporting frozen semen to both Holland, Great Britain and the USA.

•**Go On Then XX** (Como XX/Navigate XX). Chestnut Irish Thoroughbred, born 1967. Ideal for those Warmblood breeders who by the mid-1970s were looking for good Thoroughbred blood to refine some of their heavier lines, Go On Then XX stood only five short years at stud but made a definite mark. His son Gefion topped the grading, and went on to win the ridden performance testing and become an international dressage horse. Go On Then XX is also the sire of Anne-Grethe Törnblad's Grand Prix dressage horse, Super max Ravel and the maternal grandsire of Silvester, who won the three-year-old grading in 1987.

• **Ibikus** (Hertilas/Impuls). Bay Trakehner, born 1967. Ibikus made an enormous impression both in West Germany, where he stood as a young horse, and in Denmark. He also has a number of graded sons in the USA, including the Danish Warmblood graded Trakehner Raubritter (1975), whilst his graded sons in Denmark include Kawango, Ibi-Bell, and Midt West Ibi-Light (1985), the winner of the 1988 ridden performance test, and now being ridden by Kyra Kyrklund in Sweden. Ibikus also sired numerous DH medal award mares and some outstanding young riding horses. He is without doubt the one of the most respected Trakehner stallions ever to stand in Denmark.

• **Donauwind** (Pregel/Boris). Bay Trakehner, born 1965. This much travelled stallion with an international reputation is probably best known for his World Cup and Olympic gold-medal-winning, grey show-Jumping son Abdullah (who was imported *in utero* into the USA). Whilst standing in Denmark, Donauwind sired Diana (EDH 1827), the first mare to be awarded a gold medal by the Danish breed society, and the graded stallion Dolomit (1979), as well as being the

PEDIGREE OF **DIAMOND** – BLACK DANISH WARMBLOOD, 1983			
Diamond DH 330 (DV)	Allegro DH 247 (Hann)	Absatz 4052 (Hann)	Abglanz 3534 (Trak)
			Landmoor H 53556 (Hann)
		Ottomane H 68980 (Hann)	Ozean 3923 (Ostpr)
			Miniature H 64692 (Hann)
	Dinah DH 1827 (DV) Gold medal mare	Donauwind (Trak)	Pregel
			Donaulied von Schimmelhof 2319
		Desiree DS 2067 (DV)	Atlantic DH 159 (Hann)
			Dinah DH 1153 (DV)

Diamond (1982), a champion stallion by Allegro (Hann) out of the gold medal mare Diana by Donauwind (Trak). Diamond sired the champion stallion at grading in 1991 and is a very talented dressage horse in his own right.

grandsire of three graded stallions in Donnovan (1984) (the 1987 grading champion) and Diana's two graded sons Diamond (1982), by Allegro (Hann) (performance test ridden champion in 1986) and Domino (1983), by Luxembourg (Hann).

• **Allegro** (Absatz/Ozean (Ostpr. Trak)). Bay Hannoverian, born 1972. Imported as a three-year-old by a dedicated Danish breeder, Johannes Nielsen, this stallion has been a producer of many highly graded progeny to whom he passed on his extremely good action, especially to his sons Diamond and Picandt (1983), plus innumerable DH and medal mares. Diamond and Picandt both won their performance tests and went on to compete successfully in dressage. Diamond was awarded a gold medal in 1988, after winning the Supreme Championship in

1987 at the Twenty-fifth Year Jubilee Show in Denmark, and Picandt was exported to Germany for a dressage career.

•**Elizar** (Unikum (Trak)/Dragos). Bay Danish Warmblood, born 1967. As well as being the sire of the graded full brothers May Sherif and May Black, who have been mentioned earlier, Elizar also sired a third graded son in Excellens (1974) and set a standard that was hard to beat by being responsible for siring the Supreme Champion mares at the Elite Show in 1976, 1977, 1979, 1980 and 1981 (all of whom were medal mares). Elizar was then sold to Sweden to stand at stud.

THE DANISH INFLUENCE

Worldwide, Danish horses are popular, but the marketing system and language in Denmark can make it rather more complicated to purchase a horse there than, for example, in Germany, which has developed an efficient organisation to meet the demands for export and has auctions throughout the year.

In the competition field, May Sherif's graded stallion son, Matador won the 1991 World Cup (dressage), a silver medal at the 1990 World Games and attended the 1988 Olympic Games for Finland, proving himself to be a world-class dressage horse in Seoul. Danish dressage horses have also scored well in the USA, where Danish Dancer, by Galanthus, was the top point earner in 1988, and Australia, where the two graded stallions Granada (by Goldfinger (Hann)) and Kilof McOhl (by Kilof) were successful in the Australian Dressage Championships in 1983.

In eventing Nils Haagensen won the gold at the Alternative Olympic Games in 1980 with Monaco by Forethought XX.

Although graded stallions were exported to both North America and Australia in the 1980s, the geographically wide-spread basis of Warmblood breeding in these areas has made it rather difficult for the stallions concerned to make the impact that they would normally make in a more concentrated breeding area.

In Britain on the other hand, Danish Warmbloods have been able to make a strong impression in a fairly short time. The Go On Then XX son Rabinowitz, imported from Denmark as a yearling and graded with the British Warmblood Society, became a successful dressage horse at Prix St Georges level (ridden by Richard Davison) and now stands at stud in Scotland. The BWBS-graded Atlantus (1975) by Galanthus, imported as a foal, has never competed himself but as a sire, his list of winning progeny is exceptional. His daughters have topped the mare gradings for many years and he has three BWBS-graded sons at stud, Wadacre Chicko (1980), Durfee Augite (1980) and Alizar Kignaes (1986) (who is out of May Sherif's full sister and was reserve champion at the BWBS Stallion Grading in 1989). His competition progeny include Byron, the show-jumping winner of the Donauschingen Grand Prix in West Germany for Jeffrey Welles of the USA, Everest Early Devil ridden by Michael Whitaker, and the eventer Avalanche ridden by Fiona Van Tuyll (Holland).

Diamond's half brother Diadem (1984) (graded with the BSHR) and his son Desmond (1986) (graded with the BWBS) began their stud careers in Britain in 1989 but have so far failed to make their mark as sires. Diadem had been highly placed in young-horse competitions in Denmark before being imported as a dressage horse.

Finally, a small number of Danish Warmblood stallions have reversed the original trend in the early years of the breed, by being exported to Sweden for use at stud. The most senior of these is Elizar (1967), by Unikum (Trak), whose dam Eliza was Swedish-bred herself. Another stallion of a slightly later vintage – Galanthus (1970), by Gunnar (Trak) – spent part of his stud career in that country, being brought back when his talent as a broodmare sire became obvious. In the late 1980s the highly graded Raimondo son Rastell (1984) was sold to Sweden, principally as a sire of jumping horses, a field in which he showed considerable talent under saddle himself. Most recently, Denmark is represented in Sweden by the Grand Prix dressage stallion Mid West Ibi Light, who also sired the Reserve Champion Mare and Gold Medal winner in 1994. By the mid 1990s, most of the original founders and well known judges of Dansk Varmblod have retired making way for a younger generation to steer the future of the Danish horse.

With the Common Market now firmly in place, a much greater importance has been placed on 'sales' by the Danish society. To this end, Danish Warmbloods are now being encouraged to be bred outside of Denmark. One has to ask how this new policy will benefit the breed in the long run. As the Danish Warmblood is not a 'purebred' race, but a mixture of many bloodlines, it will be very difficult to keep the standard and uniformity of type outside its country of origin.

Chapter 8

The Dutch Warmblood

by

JANE KIDD

THE WARMBLOED PAARDENSTAMBOEK Nederland (WPN) stud book was established in 1969 by combining a number of regional books. Since then the Dutch Warmblood has made a meteoric rise to fame to become one of the world's most popular Warmbloods. Riders from all over the world use Dutch Warmbloods at Olympic and international level for show jumping, dressage, eventing and driving. The foundations for this rapid success were laid over the previous century by Dutch farmers, who are the mainstay of the current breeding system, and who were then concentrating on producing an all-round light draught horse for use on their farms, and to carry their families on horseback or in carriages.

The important factor was that these farm horses were produced by selective methods. The first stud book was recognised by William III in 1887 and this stimulated the breeding of registered horses. At the same time a most effective method of selection was used: breeding stock had to stand up to the rigours of agricultural work. The result was a very sound horse with a tractable temperament.

Two distinctive types of these all-purpose horses emerged in Holland, the Groningen and the Gelderland. The Groningen, from the north of Holland, was a strongly built horse developed to cope with ploughing the heavy clay lands. As this area was close to Germany some of that country's breeds were used in the development of the Groningen, particularly the Oldenburg and East Friesian. The Gelderland was found in central Holland, where the soil was more sandy and a lighter horse could be used. French breeds, and English ones like the Yorkshire Coach Horse and its close relative the Cleveland Bay, together with the Hackney, were used in its development. Neither of these Dutch all-purpose breeds became a pure bred;

The foundation sire Domburg, typical of the more old-fashioned type of Dutch horse bred in the earlier years of this century.

outside stock was used to adapt or improve it according to the farmers' needs and each was used to improve the other as necessary. The Gelderland was used to lighten the Groningen when the latter became too coarse, and *vice versa* when the Gelderland became too light.

When mechanisation lessened the demand for these horses, there was some crossing with Thoroughbreds to produce a riding horse. In the main, though, the 1950s and early 1960s were an undistinguished period for horse breeding in the Netherlands, with the Dutch riders importing many horses to supply their own needs. The foundation to the current success of the Dutch Warmblood was laid in 1969 when various local stud books were merged to establish the WPN, and the results were so good that in 1988 'Royal' (K) was added to the title, to become KWPN.

The KWPN divides its stud book into three categories: the riding horse, which has become world famous in show jumping, dressage, eventing and FEI carriage driving; the basic horse, which is derived from the old breeds, predominantly Groningen and Gelderland, and is an all-purpose horse for riding and driving and useful foundation stock for breeding; and the carriage horse, known as the Tuigpaard. This latter is a high-stepping horse with tremendous presence, used by the

Dutch to pull carriages, originally on special family occasions, but after mechanisation for showing classes.

GENERAL DESCRIPTION OF THE DUTCH WARMBLOOD

The Dutch Warmblood is a well-built riding horse of 16-17hh (162 173cm) with clean sound legs and three good gaits. The conformation should meet with the demands made of a riding horse. His character and spirit makes him eager to work, co-operative, balanced, happy, friendly, intelligent and game. The emphasis is on performance, particularly dressage and jumping, but without forsaking the fundamental riding horse qualities of conformation, paces and character.

DEVELOPMENT OF THE DUTCH WARMBLOOD

The government has played little part in this development. Some laws have made a contribution, such as not allowing stallions to stand other than those that are recognised by a stud book (i.e., in the case of the Warmblood, those that have passed rigorous tests), but state finance has been minimal. For each foal produced in the 1980s the Dutch farmer receives only 165 Guilders, compared to 900 Guilders in Germany and 2000 Guilders in France. The administration is private and controlled by a council which is democratically elected by the breeders (there are about 27,000 members of the KWPN and about 40% of these are active breeders). The finance comes from membership fees and a percentage of the stud fee charged to each mare that is covered.

It was in the late 1960s that the first big wave of stallion importations started. Demand was growing quickly for a riding horse and it was realised that it would take too long to upgrade the existing national stock. The best way to produce the type required was to use Thoroughbred stallions on the Gelderland and Groningen mares. A smaller number of the most refined of the Warmbloods, the Trakehner, was also used for this purpose. The Thoroughbreds used in the development of the Dutch Warmblood came from all over the world. Ireland provided just one of the most influential sires, Uppercut XX (1960) by Fighting Don; but many more came from Britain, including Compromise XX (1954) by Nearco, El Guacho XX (1955) by Vilmorin, African Drum XX (1960) by Chanteur and out of a Fair Trial mare, Courville XX (1952) by Fair Trial, and Eratosthenos XX (1957)

Winner of a number of World Cup Qualifiers, Cameleon Cocktail (formerly Olympic Cocktail) by Purioso XX.

by Guersant out of a Fairway XX mare. America was responsible for Ishan XX (1958) by Nantallah. France provided Abgar XX (1964) by another sire of good jumpers, Abernant; Koridon XX (1950), a grandfather of Nimmerdor; Cartoonist XX (1968) by Gilles de Retz, a good sire to have in the mare line; and Millerole XX (1956) by Cobalt, sire of leading British dressage horses Dutch Courage and Dutchman. Sadly Millerole XX died after a very short time at stud. From Germany came Erdball XX (1956) by Abendfrieden, and he was the sire of Nick Skelton's Apollo. The best home-bred Thoroughbred was Lucky Boy XX by Compromise, although First Trial XX (1956) by Looc Mo produced many dressage horses. The best of the Trakehners were Marco Polo (1962) by Poet XX, and Intermezzo (1970) by Pelion. Doruto (1978) by Komet, who was a good mover himself, produced many dressage stars and at one European Championships there were six of Doruto's offspring.

During this period in the establishment of the Dutch Warmblood, the central policy was to cross local mares with the Thoroughbreds and Trakehners, but early on Holstein mares were imported and sold to farmer breeders. The most influential of these mares was Morgenster, by Gabriel, who founded a dynasty through her two sons by Groningen stallions. The eldest was Senator by Paladijn, who was the grandsire of the greatest WPN stallion, Nimmerdor. His younger half brother, Sinaeda, was born one year later in 1955 and was by Camillus, who was threequarter Groningen and a quarter Oldenburg. Many of Sinaeda's

Marius by Marco Polo (Trak), an international show jumper in his own right as well as being the sire of the world-famous show jumper Milton.

sons became approved stallions and his name is found in the pedigrees of a host of the top jumpers, including Britain's Marius and Apollo.

A study on the Thoroughbreds, completed by the Dutch, shows that the better the performance on the race track, the better the performance results of their Warmblood offspring.

This first stage of cross-breeding was followed by the second stage of consolidation, when horses of the type the Dutch wanted to produce, the Warmbloods, were used, but only those whose pedigrees were harmonious, i.e. made up of similar types for many generations. This helped to strengthen the type bred, increase the chance of the stock breeding true to type, and reduce the risk of throw-backs. The German and French breeds best fulfilled these conditions, and the breeds used with greatest success were the Holsteins, followed by the Selle Français. The Dutch, unlike most other societies producing Warmbloods, selected very few Hannoverians, and only the occasional Westphalian, although one of these, Roemer by Pilatus, was one of their best stallions, throwing some very good dressage horses before being exported to the USA.

In this second stage of consolidation of the Dutch Warmblood a top sire was the Holstein Farn (1963), who was by Fax who stood in England for one or two years in Sussex. He produced the first great, and probably even today the most famous, Dutch Warmblood sire, Nimmerdor (1972). Another great Holstein import was Amor (1959) by Herrscher (Trak).

From France famous imports included Le Mexico (1974) by Mexico, a Selle Français by the great Thoroughbred Furioso XX. Le Mexico was full brother to Furioso II. Then there were more Selle Français like Duc de Normandie, and Enfant de Normandie by the Thoroughbred Enfant Terrible XX, and his best produce were a high class of brood mares. A. Palatin (1959), by Fra Diavolo XX and out of a Selle Français mare, produced some all-round horses. Later, between 1978 and 1982, the great Selle Français Almé stood in Holland before moving on to Belgium.

Thoroughbreds were still used during this consolidation period with Hannassi XX (1971) by Nearulla coming from Britain, Ghyll Manor XX (1971) by Gilles de Retz (same sire as Cartoonist XX) from France, and, most important, from Holland, Lucky Boy XX (1972) by Compromise. The initial outcrossing led to considerable success in the

The coloured (tobiano/pinto) Grand Prix Warmblood stallion Samber by Pericles XX, who has several similarly marked graded sons at stud throughout Europe and North America.

competition arena, but in the consolidation period, when the aim was to establish a definite type and to breed true to it by putting like to like, there was a brief lull in the successes. The produce of a first cross is often a successful performance horse, but not the best breeding stock, as harmonious pedigrees lead to better results. The first of the successful stallions which were close to the type required included Notaris (1972) by Courville, Telstar (1977) by Nimmerdor, sold after two or three years to the USA, Formateur (1963) by Polaris, Garant (1964) by Farn, and Kristal (1969) by Wiesenklee.

Gelderland and Groningen blood was used less and less but there were successful KWPN stallions like Lector (1973), who was by the French Thoroughbred Cartoonist XX and out of Barola, a Gelderland mare. The striking coloured Grand Prix dressage stallion Samber, who has many coloured graded sons throughout the world is also half Thoroughbred being by Pericles XX.

For a decade relatively few foreign stallions were imported, but at the end of the 1980s demand grew for some outside stock, particularly from the more important bloodlines like Furioso II, Pilot, and Landgraf I. The feature of the selection policy for the Dutch Warmbloods, and Dutch breeds before it, was the willingness of the farmers to adapt to changes in demands and to use stock, if necessary foreign, which would help to breed out any weaknesses in their horses and consolidate strong points.

IMPORTANT BLOODLINES

The following stallions are the foundation sires of the Dutch Warmbloods being those most frequently found in the pedigrees of top Dutch Warmbloods.

• **Abgar XX** (1964-1986). A French Thoroughbred by Abernant and out of a Roc du Diable mare, he produced a large number of show jumpers. His best stallions sons are **Pele**, **Treffer** (KWPN stallion and Olympic show jumper) and **Pion**, who produced the dressage stallions **Aktion** and **Democraat** (stands in Westphalia).

• **Amor** (1962). An imported Holstein, he was by the Trakehner Herrsher (by Heristal) and out of the Holsteiner mare Barber Bij by Loretto. He is a legend in Holland and a statue has been built in his image. He was prepotent in the production of big movers and became very well known for his mares who produced show jumpers. His best sons were **Zandigo**, **Eros**, **Epigoon**, **Armand**, **Econoom**, **Ecrasiet** and

Akteur, an international jumping stallion, Gondelier and sire of the stallion **Creool**.

•**Courville XX** (1966). A British Thoroughbred by Fair Trial and out of Plouvien, he sired such great jumpers as Linky, who went to the USA, and Little One, who won the Hamburg Derby. His graded sons included **Notaris**, sire of **Bredero**, **Caruso**, **Jasper**, (who when show jumping was known as Little One), and **Renville**. He also sired many excellent broodmares.

•**Farn** (1963). A Holstein by Fax I out of Monarch mare, he produced excellent broodmares and show jumpers but not dressage horses. He was used with greatest success on the threequarter-bred mares who were by Thoroughbreds, and out of those foundation cross-breds between Thoroughbred and registered farm mares. His most famous son was **Nimmerdor**, who was out of a Koridon XX mare. Nimmerdor's produce includes **Bergerac**, **Consul**, **Wisconsin**, **Ahorn**, **Wellington**, **Amethist**, **Telstar** and **Aram**. Farn's other successful approved sons were **Safari**, **Amulet**, **Wolfgang** and **Garant**. With Groningen stock he produced some high-class foundation mares, particularly in his early years at stud, but his potential was not realised

Nimmerdor (1972) by Farn (Holst), one of the most famous sires of show jumpers in the Netherlands, seen here accompianied by the Dutch international riders Albert Voorn (left) and Henk Nooren.

PEDIGREE OF **NIMMERDOR** – BAY DUTCH WARMBLOOD, 1972			
Nimmerdor Pref Stb (WPN) 147	Farn 1467 keur NWP	Fax I 3720 (Holst)	Fanatiker 2319 (Holst)
			Margot H 14012 (Holst)
		Dorette H 2696 (Holst)	Monarch 3316 (Holst)
			Schelle H 2161 (Holst)
	Ramonaa 187 NWP	Koridon XX	Karamont XX
			Poutzi XX
		Friedhilde II NWP	Senator 1390 NWP
			Friedhilde 22202 NWP

until he was used on lighter mares with more Thoroughbred blood.

- **Joost** (1971-1988). A Holsteiner by Consul, sire of the great dressage horse Granat, Joost himself was by one of the best Thoroughbreds in Warmblood breeding, Cottage Son XX. Joost was an import who produced valuable licensed stallions like **Ultrazon** and **Palfrenier** and such good show jumpers as VIP, who is now an approved stallion in the USA.

- **Le Mexico** (1974-1988). By Mexico who was by the famous French Thoroughbred stallion Furioso XX. His offspring were mainly jumpers, many international, but there were plenty of good movers who were successful in dressage. His best graded sons were **Ulft** (sire of Conveyer and Boston), **Silvano** (champion jumper in Italy), **Zelhem** and **Expert**.

- **Marco Polo** (1965-1976). A Trakehner by the Thoroughbred Poet XX, he was small but produced excellent jumpers, particularly from Sinaeda mares, which have been successful all over the world and include Melanie Smith's top speed horse Vivaldi, and Marius, who won so much when ridden by the late Caroline Bradley and sired the world-famous Milton. His best sons to stand at stud are **Legaat**, sire of Adios and Cosmos, **Recruit**, and **Irco Polo**, sire of **Irco Marco**, a Swedish international jumper.

- **Lucky Boy XX** (1972). A Dutch Thoroughbred by Compromise, he is one of the best Thoroughbreds in Warmblood breeding. He produced a huge number of leading approved sires, which included

Naturel, **Candyboy**, **Derrick** (out of a Nimmerdor mare), **Nooitgedacht**, **Dutch Boy**, **Casanova**, **Obrecht**, **A Lucky One** (stands in Belgium), **Omega**, sire of **Belmondo**, **Octrooi** (known as Best of Luck when standing in the USA), **Beaujolais**, and **Columbus**. At the Los Angeles Olympics there were three sons of Lucky Boy, and his show jumpers include Calypso, Van Gogh and The Victor.

- **Sinaeda** (1958-1967). Of traditional origins with a threequarter Groningen sire, Camillus, and a Holstein dam, Morgenster, he founded a show-jumping dynasty. International British show jumpers Marius and Apollo trace back to him.

- **Uppercut XX** (1964-1983). An Irish Thoroughbred by Fighting Don, he had fifteen sons who became approved stallions, and many of his mares produced more approved stallions. His most famous sons are **Nabuur** and **Uniek** (Keur).

- **Doruto** (1965-1989). By the Trakehner Komet, he has been an outstanding producer of dressage horses like Banjo, Jungle Doruto, Ivar, Ideaal, Kitty, but of only a few stallions, the youngest of which is **El Corona**.

- **Ramiro Z** (1965). A son of Raimond, he was graded into the Holstein and Westphalian stud books and show jumped internationally before standing in the Netherlands and producing dressage horses and show jumpers the most famous of which must be the mare Ratina Z. Ramiro is also discussed in Chapters 3 and 4.

BREEDING POLICY

The Dutch have developed a highly efficient system which proves the breeding stock in terms of their own performance and that of their progeny, at the earliest possible stage. It is a performance orientated policy, with the stallions having to compete (some may be excepted) as well as having to go through the training reduced in 1994 from 100 to 70 days, and with the ability of their progeny being interpreted through a stallion index using the 'BLUP' method. There are two – sport indexes based on results in the performance test, competitions and of progeny; one being for dressage and another for show jumping. There is too a BLUP which assesses conformation as an inheritable factor. A linear scoring system has been developed to analyse the produce.

STALLION TESTING

In the region of 11,000 Warmblood foals are produced each year, and as in France their names must begin with the letter representing that year (i.e. alphabetically based year names). The best of these colts, between 600 and 800, are entered for local testing in January when they turn three years of age. Veterinary, conformation and action tests reduce this number to 200, which then go forward to the s'Hertogenbosch stallion show. Visitors from all over the world come to this event to watch these youngsters being examined on two separate occasions for their conformation and temperament, their paces and their free jumping. They show off their spectacular trots in demonstrations around the arena.

About 60 pass this test to go forward for blood tests, semen tests and x-rays, before undergoing the central training where their character, dressage and jumping talent and overall health are assessed. Marks are given for the walk, trot, canter, riding and jumping test, free jumping, cross-country, condition, character, behaviour in the stable, trainability, impression when being trained and in the stable, and general impression. These marks are published, helping breeders to assess in which spheres the stallions are weak and strong. The stallions that pass this test are admitted to the stud book and can stand at stud that summer. The foals they produce in their first year are subjected to random examinations. They must show that there are no consistent weaknesses and that the stallion is having a positive effect, i.e. raising the standard of the stock.

The stallion himself must (with few exceptions) then prove himself as a competitor. There are dressage and jumping competitions open to KWPN young stallions from four-year-olds upwards, through the winter (about seven are held), with finals at the s'Hertogenbosch stallion show in February.

Further progeny tests are made when a stallion's stock reach three years of age, and again when his stock are six or seven years. Still more assessments are made in terms of the progeny's results in competitions.

Even after passing all these tests a stallion may have his licence removed if at any time his results are disappointing. The KWPN examines its stallions annually to ensure that each fits in with their breeding policy.

Exceptions are made. Stallions which have not gone through all these tests but which prove to be outstanding performers, may be brought into the scheme. Thoroughbreds are assessed mainly on their track record, and foreign stallions imported into The Netherlands may be accepted if they have passed tests with societies recognised by the

Dutch. All these stallions are, however, expected to spend some time at the stallion centre to have that important aspect of the Dutch horse assessed, their character.

Those stallions which positively improve the Dutch Warmblood may be given the classification of '*keur*', and the very famous like Amor, Doruto, Joost, Lucky Boy and Nimmerdor, '*preferent*'.

MARE SELECTION

The selection system for mares operates through the summer, starting with the regional shows when the three-year-old mares are selected for the stud book and branded with the lion of the KWPN. The top mares at these shows go forward to twelve central shows, the best going to the national show at Utrecht in September.

At the central show the best mares are awarded the 'star' classification. To achieve a higher classification, '*keur*' status, the mare has to pass a performance test in dressage and jumping and produce a good foal. A mare who has produced three 'star' mares or three stallions who during the stallion show have proved their outstanding conformation and gaits can be given '*preferent*' status, and if she has three good performers then a '*prestatiemerrie*'.

There is no national stud, no rules or regulations governing the way breeders should select their stock. The KWPN simply does as much as it can to give data to the breeders so that they themselves can make informed selection. The KWPN publish the results of the grading, progeny tests and competitions to help the farmer make his decisions. A bi-weekly magazine distributed to 27,000 members provides as much information as possible, from critiques about the stallions after training and selection, to articles from the experts.

THE DUTCH INFLUENCE

As a young breed the Dutch horses' influence on other Warmbloods has been mainly in those countries starting to develop their own – New Zealand, Australia, USA and Britain.

In Britain, Dutch Courage (by Millerole XX) was first a top competitor in dressage, becoming the 1978 World individual bronze medallist, before establishing himself as a top sire and one of the main foundation stallions for the British Warmblood. Marius (by Marco Polo) was similarly a top competitor (show jumper) and leading sire with such great progeny as 1989 European Champion Milton.

Others who have stood at stud for a shorter time and could make their mark include Animo by Almé who jumped for Norway at the Barcelona Olympics; Renkum Arturo, a Grade B jumper, by Statuar; Vital, by Fresco, who was Joe Turi's international show jumper and a graded Anglo-Dutch stallion, and Jashin who came to Britain at the end of his career. The Holstein bred Dutch-graded stallion Saluut (1976) was also sold to Britain as a mature stallion and became immediately popular with owners of lighter mares. Two of Britain's best dressage horses are Dutch and both by the same sire, Kommandeur – they are Virtu who with Emile Faurie won a bronze and silver medal at the 1993 European championships and Cupido whom Jane Bredin rode for Britain at the 1994 WEG. In show jumping, Midnight Madness by Nurzeus has been ridden by Michael Whitaker to be the individual winner of the World Breeding Championship for Sport Horses in 1993 and the KWPN Horse of the Year.

By far the biggest influence has been in the USA where a new branch of the KWPN stud book was started in 1983, the North American Warmblood Stud Book of The Netherlands (NA/WPN). Horses registered in it receive European not North American registration papers and the brand is identical to that used in Holland, but can only be applied by an official of the KWPN.

The Holstein stallion Saluut (1976) by Ronald, who competed in Grand prix show jumping and produced graded stallions in the Netherlands before moving to Britain in 1990 to continue his stud career.

Dutch Warmbloods in America are eligible for the same grades as stallions, mares and geldings as horses in The Netherlands. There are, however, some additional foundation classifications, like for stallions, pre-evaluation, and for horses with Dutch blood but who are not eligible for KWPN papers, e.g. only one Dutch parent having a certificate of pedigree. There are three grades of stallions registered, licensed and approved – the latter are, or are corresponding to, stallions which have passed their 100 days' testing in The Netherlands.

There is close liaison between the KWPN and the NA/WPN, with one of the home country's most important services being provision of judges for the annual *keuring* tour when youngstock, mares and stallions are graded, offered premiums and even evaluated, in the case of two-year-olds, as to potential for being licensed as stallions.

Probably the best Dutch Warmblood stallion in the US earned all his credentials in Holland before being exported in 1986. He is Roemer, who was originally a Westphalian by Pilatus and was the leading producer of dressage horses in The Netherlands in the 1980s and early 1990s. In the US he has won Grand Prix dressage competitions and his son Winston, who also passed his tests in The Netherlands, has been successful up to Intermédiaire levels.

Another successful performer and stock producer is Argus by Pion who, like Roemer, passed all his tests in The Netherlands. He competes at FEI levels in dressage and show jumping and in 1988 had more 'First Premium' foals in the US than any other stallion.

Best of Luck, by Lucky Boy XX and out of a Koridon XX mare, became a champion green hunter when he came to the US after passing all his tests and producing six international show jumpers. Ommen, by Abgar XX and out of a Joost mare, has spent most of his time competing, earning amongst many awards a place in the 1986 World Cup finals. His foals are now winning premiums.

Rubinstein by Lorenz, who is by Ladykiller XX, is a Holstein but passed his stallion testing in The Netherlands and was a successful jumper there before coming to the US in 1982 when he turned to dressage, winning Grand Prix classes. He is producing some high class breeding stock, including approved and licensed stallions, in North America.

Several Dutch Warmbloods have been exported to the southern hemisphere. In Australia, Dutchman by Le Mexico, and full brother to the graded stallion Zelham, now stands at the Australian Equestrian Academy. In New Zealand, there are Ramzes by Rigoletto, Urban by Makelaar, Immigrant by Formateur and Polaris by Luclus.

With its short history, the main influence of the Dutch Warmblood horse has been at the competitive level: at the 1988 Olympics there were more Dutch horses competing in the jumping than from any other country, and in the dressage they had the second highest total. Probably the most astounding success was that three members of the German team competing at the 1986 World Championships rode Dutch horses: Ampere (by Amagun) with Gina Capellmann; Ideaal (by Doruto) with Johan Hinnemann; and Pascal (by Stranger) with Dr Reiner Klimke. At the 1988 Olympics, a German Olympic show jumping team medallist was mounted on The Freak (by Lucky Boy XX).

In Belgium, the show jumper Jean-Claude Vangeenberghe rides Queen of Diamonds by Rigoletto; in Switzerland another show jumper, Thomas Füchs, rides Jogger by Lektor, and even more successful for this country was Oran by Hanassi XX, who won the European Three-Day Event Championship for Hansueli Schmutz. In Columbia Mario Torres rides Zalmé by Almé, and they went to the 1988 Olympics; in Brazil André Johannpeter rides Heartbreaker by Liberto; and in Canada Mario Deslauriers has had great success with Box Car Willie by Le Val Blanc XX. In the US there have been great show jumping horses, like the World Cup winner Calypso by Lucky Boy XX, and in dressage the stallion Orpheus by Solaris XX went to the Seoul Olympics. The Approved stallion Libero H by Landgraf I has with Jos Lansink won numerous international show jumping classes and these include the 1994 World Cup. In dressage the Approved stallion who has excelled is Cameleon Cocktail by Purioso whom Anky van Grunsven has ridden to victory in Aachen, the Horse of the Year Show and s'Hertogenbosch.

In driving, too, the Dutch Warmblood has been exceptionally successful, particularly in the hands of their own country's whips. The World Champion at Appeldoorn in 1988 was Ijsbrand Chardon and he drove KWPN horses, as did Ad Arts who won the championship in 1990. For two years in succession, 1993 and 1994, they have been the winning stud book for dressage horses in the World Breeding Championship for Sport Horses.

Chapter 9

The Belgian Warmblood

by

DEBBIE WALLIN

A S WITH MOST OF the Warmblood breeding countries today, the roots of the present-day Warmblood bred in Belgium lie in the changing demands of the years since the mid 1930s.

The statistics for horse breeding in Belgium for 1935 show that more than 40,000 foals were produced, which were mostly destined to be working farm animals. Allied to the fact that a total of about 500,000 people were engaged in agriculture, and approximately 11,000 Belgian draught horses were sold abroad each year, it is obvious that the market for farm horses was immense.

The single most important factor in the development of the Belgian Warmblood was the forming of the volunteer Rural Cavalry at Boezinge (West Flanders) by Canon Andre de May in 1937. The men who became part of this Rural Cavalry were known as 'the Canon's horsemen'. The importance of the Cavalry to the history of Warmblood breeding in Belgium is that it did not supply the mounts, so each individual had to ride his own horse, and the wide variety of types and their lack of suitability for ridden work soon became obvious. This became particularly noticeable when, in 1938, the Cavalry held its first official riding tournament. Just 39 horses were entered and yet over 4000 people turned out to watch the new display, which included a dressage demonstration, various riding performances and jumping. Of the 39 horses entered, 25 were heavyweights and only 14 could be called lighter riding models. None of the horses represented any specific breed type and they were mainly the result of haphazard crossings of Thoroughbred stallions with heavy farm horses. Certainly, it was impossible with this material to produce an eye-catching, harmonious display of precision cavalry riding to compare with those already being held in the countries bordering Belgium, and two important decisions

172

were therefore taken immediately. The first was to promote equestrian education through riding associations and training programmes, principally aimed at the sons of farming families. Secondly, and most importantly for Warmblood breeding, a structured programme was drawn up, designed to produce the sort of riding horse required.

Unfortunately, it was impossible to make any substantial headway towards either of these goals before the outbreak of the Second World War, so they were sidelined for the duration. However, after the end of the war the breeding programme to create a Belgian Warmblood was finally launched and horses were imported from The Netherlands and the Hannoverian breeding area of West Germany. By 1953 this new breed was ready to hold its first stallion inspection, which took place at Waregam, and a month later the then Minister of Agriculture, Charles Heger, gave his approval for the continuing development of the breed, provided that all breeding results were documented and the first foals be entered into the stud book in 1954. (There were just 27!)

With the founding of an official stud book came the necessity of using the stallions on the original farm mares, and not just on the mares selected for the five-year breeding programme. Agriculture was mechanising quickly, and many people started to question the usefulness of a dual-purpose agricultural and riding horse at a time when farm use was fast declining. To try and promote interest and show its opponents the possible future market for these lighter riding types, four small demonstration shows were held in 1954 at Antwerp, Limburg, East Flanders and West Flanders, with a total entry of 82 horses. Whatever the reason, this new idea of horse breeding caught on and on 25 March 1955 the National Breeding Association of Agricultural Riding Horses (NFLR) was founded at Louvain. 1955 also saw five shows being held in the provinces, with entries jumping to a staggering 368 in one year. In 1958 the shows changed from displays and demonstrations to the riding competitions more usual today, and the Belgian Warmblood became firmly established.

Official recognition of the NFLR took place on 1 September 1960 and the new breed was added to the list of recognised stud books already in existence in Belgium, the others being for the Belgian Draught Horse, the Ardennais Draught Horse, the Thoroughbred Jockey Club and the Belgian Half-Bred (or Belgian Demi Sang). The Belgian Half-Bred is a riding horse whose bloodlines today are based almost exclusively on the Selle Français discussed more fully on the chapter on France. Because of their similar interests there were some problems and rivalry between Demi-Sang breeders and Warmblood breeders at the beginning, but by the late 1980s they were working together in a combined effort to present the best possible horses for their newly launched international riding horse and foal auctions.

Ten years later, with the collapse of the agricultural market and the greatly increased interest in riding, the new aim to produce a riding and competition horse *par excellence* resulted (in February 1970) in renaming the National Breeding Association of Agricultural Riding Horses, the National Breeding Association for Warmbloods (NFWP).

BREEDING POLICY

In 1959 the Landelijke Ruiterschool was founded in Oud Heverlee (Louvain) and the buildings and surrounding grounds became the venue for the main national Belgian Warmblood events, which include the National Mare Grading Inspection, the Stallion Licensing/Grading Show, the National Championships for Young Horses, the National Belgian Warmblood Presentation Show for Licensed Stallions and the National Foal Show (first held in 1988).

Mare gradings/inspections are run under the supervision of the Ministry of Agriculture on a regional, provincial and national basis. Mares can be presented every year and are therefore awarded a state premium annually rather than for life, as the title in West Germany denotes. For the newly registered mares, the National Riding Horse Championship plays an important part in establishing their value as a broodmare. Classes are held for four-, five- and six-year olds, which are based on strict selection throughout eleven provisional competitions. To qualify for the championship each horse must have been selected at least three times at different provincial rounds and the finals are held annually in July. Altogether the NFWP now has about 20,000 registered horses and 5,500 members. By the end of 1984 the first stallion stud book was ready to be published and it contained all the known details of the approximately 500 stallions to have been at public stud since the 1950s.

Stallion selection is very strict in the choice of bloodlines and performance ability, and the inspection/grading process is done in a number of phases. In March all new stallions appear for two days of inspection, which includes a visual veterinary examination and measurements for height, girth and bone. The young colts are judged by a panel for correctness of conformation and action, in hand at the walk and trot. Finally, during the last part of the first day, the stallions are observed free jumping down a lane, when the judges are looking for obedience, use of the back, leg technique, willingness to jump and calmness. Great care is also taken to study the natural carriage of the stallions in canter and gallop. Only the best colts are allowed to go on to the second day.

On the second day a more thorough examination of conformation and gaits on both hard and soft going is held. Interestingly, the colt can either be shod or unshod depending on the owner's preference. Again, in the afternoon, the jumping talent of each youngster is given a re-examination. Once more, the best are selected to go forward to the next phase to be held approximately two weeks later. This second inspection involves a detailed veterinary examination, with blood typing to control the pedigree details. The stallions who pass this inspection are then required to have their semen assessed by a recognised university laboratory. This fertility test must be completed by April, when the third inspection takes place at the Landelijke Ruiterschool at Oud Heverlee. The third phase involves ridden exercises at walk, trot and canter with attention being paid to the ease with which the horses work and carry the rider. Finally, they have to jump a small course of eight jumps including a double (no jump higher than 3ft 3ins/1m).

Those stallions which pass this inspection successfully go on to the final phase in May, which includes a dressage test to examine their balance and suppleness at the walk, trot and canter, and their calmness and willingness to relax and work. Finally, the young stallions have to do a cross-country test, comprising a course of 2760m with twelve natural jumps of 3ft 3ins (1m) in height. The minimum speed for this course is 450m per minute. Immediately after the cross-country phase comes an obligatory gallop at hunting speed over a distance of 920m. Whilst there are no jumps a speed requirement of not less than 500m per minute has to be met. During this phase very careful monitoring is in operation, the condition and fitness of the colts being the final part of the assessment as to whether or not they become breeding stallions.

There are a few cases in which exceptions have been made to the grading format. Thoroughbred stallions with a racing record can be excused from some of the phases but must complete phase one and two whatever their race record. Older stallions of nine years or more will have their previous records (or gradings in other countries if imported from abroad) examined by judges. A minimum standard of successful completion of phases one and two is required in all cases, but an exception to the loose jumping can be made in certain cases. On the other hand, any Anglo-Arab stallion wishing to gain entry to the stud book must complete all the phases successfully.

The main foundation stock in Belgium lies on the mares' side. Although a number of well-bred mares were imported in the 1970s – mainly from France and West Germany – by far the largest percentage of mares are traceable to the original stock or crossbreds bred from them. Bloodlines recognised by the NFWP are Dutch, French, Hannoverian, Westphalian, Holstein, Oldenburg and Trakehner, as well as occasional Thoroughbred and Anglo Arab mares. The main goal is definitely to produce a show jumper and all the very best show jumping pedigrees can be found in the imported stallions of the 1970s and 1980s.

GENERAL DESCRIPTION OF THE BELGIAN WARMBLOOD

The Belgian Warmblood stands between 16hh (162cm) and 17hh (173cm) on average. The old bloodlines were heavy-boned, plain of head, often rather thick-necked, with a roomy topline and a good strong croup. The old type was also rather short-legged and lacking in extension and elasticity of action. However, with the introduction of modern stallions, especially a number of good Thoroughbreds, a newer type is to be found, which is a more elegant, lighter-boned horse with freer movement and more calibre. The older model was very muscular and powerful – both assets in jumping – but now breeding in Belgium seems to be turning its attention to both the dressage and eventing markets in the development of the modern riding horse. It is interesting to note that the NFWP is one of the few newly emerging breed societies that have not used Trakehners with any regularity to refine the horse population.

IMPORTANT BLOODLINES

As the first stud book was a recent development, the Belgian Warmblood does not have the wealth of background bloodlines that can be found in many other breeds. Almost exclusively, the modern foundation sires to be found in the third and fourth generations of Belgian pedigrees are Hannoverian. Flügel van la Roche by the Hannoverian Firnis, Widikund de Lauzelle by Winnetou (1964) and Lugano de la Roche (1963) by Lugano I feature prominently in many pedigrees today, and the Lauzelle name in particular is regularly found in both international show jumping and breeding.

The most important stallions in modern Belgian Warmblood pedigrees include:

• **Drost** by Duft II. Hannoverian (1965). He was the first sire to bring Belgian breeding to the fore. His son Talky, winner of the Grand Prix at Peulis in 1980 with Christian Huysegens, was sold to show jumper Ian Millar of Canada, whilst Ferdi Tyteca's international horse Passe Partout is also a Drost descendant. Others that Drost produced, less well known except on the Belgian circuit, were Taxi (ridden by E. Blaton), Ulena (ridden by T. Molenaars) and Pallieter (ridden by P. Lienard).

• **Saygon** by Alcanar XX. Belgian Warmblood (1972). Out of a D-line Hannoverian mare, Saygon was a big, upstanding, good-looking and harmonious horse with an admirable shoulder and wither. When ridden by Paul Hermans he became National Champion in S class jumping. He won the bronze medal at the European Event Championships held at Ermelo. His progeny also show talent with Wiegand (ridden by M. Fuchs) competing in the puissance at Francanville in France in 1989.

• **Goldspring de Lauzelle** by Gotthard. Hannoverian (1975). He is out of an Amhugel III dam and a full brother to the Celle stallion Gardestern I. Goldspring is the sire of the gelding Cambronne de Lauzelle, which won the five-year-old National Riding Horse Championship and competed for Belgium at the European Championships in Fontainebleau and the Nations' Cup in Lisbon in 1987 with Eric Wauters. Once again, in 1989, the five-year-old National Championship was won by a Goldspring de Lauzelle son, Hermes. Goldspring de Lauzelle's progeny earnings between 1988 and 1989 made him second highest ranking sire of his year by progeny winnings. In 1990 Celle announced that they would be offering frozen sperm from this talented sire to mares in West Germany.

• **Wendekraus de Lauzelle** by Wendekreis. Belgian Warmblood (1976). The dam of this stallion is a Wolfsburg mare. He underlined the excellence of the Lauzelle breeding policy by winning the six year-old National Riding Horse Championship with his daughter Grace in 1989. Other impeccable show jumping bloodlines are represented in Belgium by stallions with the Lauzelle prefix, including the Hannoverians Goldfisch de Lauzelle (1976) by Gotthard out of a Winkel mare, and Picasso de Lauzelle (1976) by Pik König out of a Graphit mare, and the Belgian Warmblood Almhugel de Lauzelle (1977) by the international show jumper Widukind de Lauzelle out of a Flügel mother line. The newest imports of this successful stud farm are the Hannoverian Feo (1980), by Wendekreis with the Thoroughbred Jonkeer XX on the dam's side, and Skippy II (1984), a liver chestnut stallion of Selle Français bloodlines rather than

Hannoverian. Skippy's sire is the world famous Galoubet A by Almé – once again show jumping blood of enormous value.

•**Darco** by Lugano van la Roche. Belgian Warmblood (1980). Codex, the maternal grandsire of this stallion, was by Cottage Son XX. An international show jumper in his own right with L. Philippaerts, Darco is an excellent ambassador for the Belgian Warmblood having won a Grand Prix in London and already being a sire of promising young stallions in Kimball (1987), Klimex (1987) and Kafka (1987). He has been used on a wide base of mares with a jumping pedigree in mind, but certainly his best looking progeny come from the lighter and more elegant type of mare. Darco's talent and great muscle development seem clearly to be inherited by his progeny.

•**Oula Owl XX** by Tachypous XX. Thoroughbred (1980). This lovely stallion stood at stud in Britain but was unfortunately not used in Warmblood breeding there. Sold to Belgium in the late 1980s, his foals on the heavier mares are outstanding.

Not only are the best Hannoverian bloodlines present in Belgium, there is also Holstein, Dutch and Selle Français blood available. For instance, Ibrahim (1952), the Anglo-Norman stallion who is the sire of Almé (1966) and is one of the world's top show jumping sires, is represented in Belgium by four sons and a number of grandsons of the Almé line. The Netherlands have also provided good sires from the Lucky Boy XX line, which are not particularly big or heavy but are extremely elastic and elegant and ideally suited for the plainer mares – Brown Boy (1983), Bonheur (1983) and A Lucky One (1982) are examples. Finally, the Holstein blood is represented by the well known names of Landgraf I through Landadel (1986), Latano (1985) and Laredo (1987), Ramiro Z, through Raphaelo (1980), Redford (1985) and Romeo (1979) and of course Cor de la Bryère through the mother line of Jadalco (1986) and as the sire of the Westphalian Concorde (1987).

Finally, mention must also be made of the famous Zangersheide Stud owned by Leon Melchior. All stallions that stand at this stud (including both Almé and Ramiro at various stages of their stud careers) and the animals bred there or bought in, carry the suffix Z after their names. Confusingly, until recently, the progeny have been mainly graded and registered in Germany and carry Hannoverian pedigree papers. Stallions bred at the stud and carrying the Z suffix can be found in Germany, Sweden, Denmark, Britain and Hungary which has recently purchased Feo (1980) and Kafka (1987) by Darco.

This has all changed with the forming of Zangerheide's own stud book which is recognised as a section of the FSL (Federation des Studbooks Luxembourgeois). With the new 'Z' Studbook firmly in place, their pool of show jumping sires has expanded rapidly. The pedigrees used to concentrate almost exclusively on Ramiro Z, Almé Z, and Gotthard, with many being quite closely inbred to one or another of these stallions. Holstein and French bred stallions now predominate, with both Landgraf I and Cor de la Bryère much in evidence. Double Espoir (1969) by Ibraham presented a number of sons for entry into the new studbook and the foals on show and for sale read like a who's who of popular show-jumping sires, including the Trakehner Almox Prints (1981) Quito de Baussy (1982) Narcos I (1979) Darco (1980) Sandro (1974) Quidam de Revel (1982) Libero H (1981) Nimmerdor (1975) Voltaire (1979) and Jalisco B (1975).

There is no doubt that the Zangerheide Stud has had enormous success with its original breeding program. It will be interesting to follow the progress of the new selection format and see if the expansion now in motion will continue to produce the same high percentage of 'winners' to mares covered.

THE BELGIAN INFLUENCE

Due to its comparative youth as a breed, the demand for Belgian stock as breeding stallions and mares for other countries is not established. Because of their talents as show jumpers Darco, Saygon and the British-based Didi (1980) (at one time known as Next Didi and latterly as Henderson Didi) by Colorado X are probably the only three sires

PEDIGREE OF **DIDI** – BAY BELGIAN WARMBLOOD, 1980			
Didi WH 93 (NFWP)	Colorado X W 001249	Courlis	Royal Nostra
			Collonges
		Bellina	Le Galop
			Belle de Nuit
	Wiske W 041167 VB (NFWP)	Fantastique W 00183 (SF)	Ibrahim
			Joyeuse
		Nini W 018278 (NFWP)	Unicum v.d. Schootehoef
			Fiji W 012197

Michael Whitaker seen here winning the Kings Cup at the 1989 Royal International Horse Show on the talented stallion Didi (1980) by Colorado X.

bred in Belgium (as distinct from being imported) to have their bloodlines actively sought. Interestingly, Didi (ridden by Michael Whitaker) is available for stud use in Britain, France Germany and Belgium through transported semen, which offers a practical solution to his busy competition career. Other stallions of Belgian descent which stand in Britain: Quendel de Bornival (1978) also by Colorado X, Welf (1976) by Flügel van la Roche, the British-Sports-Horse-graded international eventer Gruenhorn du Trichon (1983) by the Westphalian Angriff and the older stallion, Wendekraus de Lauzelle (1976).

A number of other countries have purchased Belgian competition horses, which are still fairly priced in comparison to the cost of animals from more established breeds. The Reims Grand Prix was won by the mare Karina by Hedjaz (1973) by Ibrahim, ridden by Kim Rachamba for the United States. Hedjaz is also the sire of Cyris who is starting his jumping career in France with E. Navet.

Goldspring de Lauzelle is the sire of Coldspring (ridden by Jay Land), winner of the Florida Grand Prix in the United States. Maria Haugg from Luxembourg jumped 7ft 6½ins (2.3m) at the Aachen CSIO on Safir by Goldspring de Lauzelle, and Thomas Frühmann from Austria rides Butterfly. One of the best show jumpers of the 1980s was the Etretat son Big Ben, ridden by Ian Millar of Canada. Big Ben won the richest ever prize money in Calgary in 1988.

Ian Millar riding Big Ben, the Calgary 1988 top money winner.

FUTURE DEVELOPMENTS

There is no doubt that the Belgian Warmblood will continue to expand and become a more dominant force in the show jumping circuit. With the introduction of a marketing and auctioning programme in 1985, and a new brand (a circle with a stylised horse heads) to enable a horse to be easily recognised as a Belgian Warmblood, it will be much easier to follow the progress of members of the breed. Judging by the new bloodlines imported in 1990, while still well endowed with the best of show jumping lines, a number of owners are swinging towards more dressage-orientated sires. One of the very best and well-established Hannoverian sires, Pik Bube (1973) was presented for inspection in Belgium in March 1990. Winston (1987), the first Belgian-based son of the very good moving Wenzel I (1976) has also entered the stud book (this stallion is out of a Shogun XX mare). Finally, sons of Matcho X (1978), by Pancho II X, and Bolero (1975), by Black Sky XX, have also been successfully presented, so the proven dressage lines from Germany will soon have an influence on the Belgian youngsters of the 1990s.

Chapter 10

Warmblood Breeding in the United Kingdom

by

CELIA CLARKE

Section on the British Warm-Blood Society
by Debbie Wallin

FOR A COUNTRY with such a long and distinguished history in horse breeding, the British position in the heirachy of Warmblood breeding is currently rather low. Many much smaller countries with weaker traditions of horse breeding and stud books of comparatively recent foundation (such as Belgium and Denmark) have quickly established international reputations as sources for top-class warmblood competition horses, whilst Warmblood breeding in Britain has remained somewhat disorganised, despite the growing numbers of Warmblood stallions at stud, particularly in the south of England.

The reasons for this are many, but chiefly they lie in the historical and continuing importance of racing and hunting to the British equestrian public, the unsuitability of all but the most modern Warmbloods for eventing, the tradition of using Irish Draught blood to add substance to finer thoroughbreds and the reluctance of a substantial number of British stallion owners to submit their stallions to normal Warmblood grading procedures. In addition, although the increased interest in dressage and the changing demands of the top-class show-jumping circuit has led many British competition riders to seek Warmblood mounts since the mid-1970s, these same riders are often reluctant to purchase the home-grown product despite the often almost prohibitive cost of purchasing ready-made animals from Germany, France and The Netherlands. Even so, some British breeders have been trying to meet the demands of competition riders for some time, but unfortunately, because of the unregulated nature of the non-Thoroughbred breeding industry in the UK, the progress towards universal acceptance of what some still see as 'foreign' methods of grading and registration has been very slow.

In fact, although the first two studs to stand Warmblood stallions, the Louella Stud in Leicestershire and the Maple Stud in Surrey, began to stand Hannoverian stallions in the 1960s, by the late 1970s the vast majority of progeny of these matings had been lost to Warmblood breeding because of the lack of a recognised grading and registration system. It was not until 1977 that the first major organisation to register and grade Warmbloods in the UK, the British Warm-Blood Society (usually known as the BWBS) was formed by two breeders, Marie Smith and Deborah Wallin, because the stock produced at their own recently founded Warmblood studs were not eligible for registration with any existing British stud book. From its inception, it was the aim of the BWBS to follow European practices of grading and registration in so far as possible, and apart from 100-day performance tests (which it has found impossible to organise because of the financial commitment expected from stallion owners and the limited number of stallions that could be involved in what is essentially a comparative process), the policy and rules of the Society still reflect this. To help endorse the practical application of these rules, foreign judges (most notably Dr Hanfried Haring of the Germany FN) have always officiated at every BWBS grading and in-hand show along with a top British judge. Public stallion grading (a first in Britain) began in 1979, an in-hand breed show in 1979, mare grading in 1982 and branding of foals in 1990.

In recent years, however, the picture has become more complicated with an increasing number of Warmblood societies being formed, each with their own registration, grading and branding procedures. As many of these breed societies have strong links with breeding organisations in Europe (for example, the British Hannoverian Horse Society is the official representative and 'daughter' society of the Hannoverian Verband within the UK and the Trakehner Fraternity of Great Britain is the official representative of the Trakehner Verband), their pedigree papers carry considerable prestige and they are strongly supported by a growing number of breeders. At the other extreme, some Warmblood breeders have taken the decision to register their breeding stock with non-Warmblood organisations such as the National Light Horse Breeding Society, weatherbys Non-Thoroughbred Register and the recently formed British Horse Database (which is primarily a register designed to collate and centralise data on the breeding and performance records of competition horses in Britain). As Ministry of Agriculture licensing of stallions ceased in 1982, the situation could have been even worse had not a number of societies across all breeds founded the National Stallion Association (NASTA) to encourage the continuation of veterinary inspection of stallions for freedom from hereditary disease. (The BHHS, the BWBS and the TBF are all enthusiastic supporters of NASTA and its operations.) Finally, in order to cope with the increasing numbers of animals who have a small percentage of Warmbloods on their pedigree but are ineligible for BWBS papers, the BWBS itself set up the British Sports Horse Register (BSHR) in 1986. This register, conceived as a possible foundation book for the BWBS, soon increased its range to enable many previously unregistered competition stallions of any breed to come forward to Warmblood-type grading. It gained support, particularly from breeders of eventers and continues to exert a degree of influence on British competition horse breeding.

The slow start to organised Warmblood breeding in the UK meant that the stallion who is viewed as the first foundation sire of Warmblood breeding in the country was already dead by the time Warmbloods could be graded and registered in their own right. The chestnut Hannoverian **Maple Duellist** (1956), by Duellant (1946), was imported in 1960 and stood at stud very successfully from that date until his death in 1977, producing many Grand Prix dressage horses, which included the international winner Maple Zenith. However, his chestnut British Warm-Blood son **Maple Duel** (1972) became one of the earliest BWBS-graded stallions along with another Maple stallion, the liver chestnut Hannoverian **Maple Courier** (1973) by Kurier, the bay Hannoverian **Furisto** (1971) by the Selle Français Furioso II and the dark brown Danish Warmblood **Atlantus** (1975) by Galanthus. Furisto in turn was the sire of another early stallion, the chestnut British Warmblood Finale (1976), and within a few years Atlantus had also sired a number of good stallion sons including the bay Wadacre Chico (1980) – who sired several highly priced auction horses – and

PEDIGREE OF **ATLANTUS** – DARK BROWN DANISH WARMBLOOD, 1975			
Atlantus WH 2 (DV)	Galanthus DH 221 (DV)	Gunnar DH 185 (Trak)	Komet
			Gudrun 2027
		Veronica DH 1206 (Hann)	Wöhler 3880
			Lagune H 64 214
	Anet DH 1209 (DV)	Astronaut DH 141 (Hann)	Abhang 3931
			St Pr St Axtherrin H 62 469
		St Pr St Senderdrössel DH 783 (Hann)	Sellhorn 3982
			St Pr St Funkenblatt H 59 519

The imported Danish Warmblood Atlantus (1975) by Galanthus (DV), a foundation sire for the British Warm-Blood Society, producing highly graded sons and daughters as well as international competition horses.

the dark bay Alizar (1986) plus numerous highly graded mares such as the first-ever BWBS Gold Medal Mare Bramhope April Love (who went on to be a successful dressage horse under the name Aprillis) and several top show jumpers, so all these stallions went a considerable way in helping establish the value of Warmblood pedigrees in the minds of British breeders.

The late 1970s also saw the introduction of some top class Dutch Warmbloods into Britain, of whom the international dressage horse **Dutch Courage** (1969-1991) by Millerole XX was by far the most important. Dutch Courage went on to found his own sire line with several graded sons to his credit across a range of Warmblood stud books, including the international dressage horses Dutch Gold (1971) and Catherston Dazzler (1983).

Increasing numbers of stallions were imported during the following decade. These included three Hannoverians, the chestnut **Akkord** (1977), by Aperitif (who was to be the sire of the 1989 BWBS Stallion Grading Champion Stonegrove Ace), the black international dressage horse **Demonstrator** (1981) by Dynamo and the chestnut **Galvarno** (1978), by Gigant, a noted sire of winners of young competition horse and show classes. Trakehner stallions were also making their mark by then, particularly the two bays **Illuster** (1977), by Osterglanz XX and **Holme Grove Istanbul** (1972) by Flaneur. Both these stallions had already proved themselves before being imported into the UK, with Illuster's daughter Korna becoming Young Horse Champion of Germany and Istanbul leaving some good offspring, mostly in Bavaria, where he stood for many seasons.

Danish Warmbloods also featured strongly in the 1980s importations, but although the stallions concerned were attractive, modern types they often tended to concentrate more on a career under saddle than on covering mares; the four chestnuts Rabinowitz (1978) by Go On Then XX (dressage), Tapster (1978) by the Hannoverian Fleuret (dressage), Tallents Wellesley (1985) by the Hannoverian Weibfang (dressage) and Aron (1985) by the bay Holstein Rasant (show jumping) are examples of stallions whose careers took this turn. On the other hand, the bay Belgian Warmblood **Didi** (1980), by Colorado X, managed to combine stud duties in the breeding areas of Britain, The Netherlands, Belgium and Oldenburg (chiefly through extensive use of frozen semen) with an international show-jumping career to Olympic level and should make his mark as a competition horse sire.

The need to prove stallions in competition in the absence of stallion testing, and the increasing use of high technology methods in the stud world has led to an ever-growing number of conceptions by artificial insemination (and to a lesser extent embryo transplant) since the late 1980s. This has meant that British breeders have had access to an outstanding source of proven bloodlines from outside the country, and as many of the stallions from which this semen comes are based in Denmark, France, The Netherlands and Germany and have fulfilled the stringent quarantine requirements necessary for semen being imported into the UK, this has increased the choice even more for mare owners.

The quality and availability of these stallions has gone some way to counteract the potential damage that could have been done to the prestige of Warmblood breeding in the UK by the use of the many ungraded and failed stallions available (nearly 200 at the time of writing), but it has done little to improve the already complicated situation relating to the conflicting systems of registration that now exist within the numerous breed societies involved. In addition, since the introduction of the Single European Market in 1992, an increasing number of progeny conceived by artificial insemination and foaled in the UK are now being inspected, branded and registered directly with foreign breed societies using full official breeding committees, rather than any independent 'British' branch of the studbook concerned. Dansk Varmblod is an example of a foreign-based organisation that operates in this way.

GENERAL DESCRIPTION OF WARMBLOODS BRED IN THE UNITED KINGDOM

Because of the wide range of bloodlines being used in the UK today, allied to the many breeding organisations and judging criteria involved in grading and the varying quality of the stallions and mares involved, no discernible national type has yet really emerged although pure-bred Trakehner-type horses with two Hannoverian parents tend to look like Hannoverians and so on. Although it is therefore rather hard to describe what a typical Warmblood bred in the UK looks like, often in comparison with most other British-bred horses they already tend to have more athletic movement, more correct limbs and better quality of bone, whatever their weight carrying ability.

BREEDING ORGANISATIONS IN THE UNITED KINGDOM

The number of organisations registering Warmblood stallions and broodmares and their offspring in the UK are now well into double figures. Of these, several use grading procedures of their own derivation, while others use procedures laid own directly by governing bodies in mainland Europe and a still further group register Warmbloods and their progeny but do not require breeding stock to undergo any form of grading process in the recognised European sense of the word as they do not restrict themselves to Warmbloods and such an approach is therefore unacceptable to them.

In order to try to shed light on this rather confusing picture, the remainder of this section will attempt to outline how these many organisations currently conduct their various breeding policies, the bloodlines that are involved and the types of horses being produced.

THE ANGLO EUROPEAN STUDBOOK

The Anglo European Studbook (AES) grew out of the Anglo-Dutch Breeders Association, which was formed to register and grade horses of Dutch origin. It changed its name when it opened its studbooks to other European breeds and foundation stock and now claims to be the only studbook operating in England and Ireland that specifically grades its horses not only on their conformation and soundness but also on their ability to perform successfully in affiliated competition to a set level within a stipulated period of time. There is an annual grading show for stallions (who are registered, licensed or approved according to a system based on the structure of the KWPN grading in The Netherlands), a number of mare gradings are also held and a Foundation Studbook was also opened in 1993 to grade and register stallions with a good competition record but lacking complete pedigree details.

Currently most of the stallions approved by the AES were bred in The Netherlands and their bloodlines and the current emphasis on showjumpers reflect this. Amongst the most popular sires are, not surprisingly, the international showjumpers **Vital** (1979) by Fresco, **Animo** (1982) by Almé Z, **Irco Mena** (1982) by Irco Marco and **My**

The UK-based AES and KWPN-graded international show jumping stallion Animo (1982) by Almé Z, who has covered mares throughout Europe by frozen semen.

Man (1981) by Tangelo. However, an increasing number of dressage horses are also AES-graded , including the successful young Cameleon Cocktail son **Hucarlos** (1989) and the 1977 Dutch Performance test winner **Pentagon** (1974) by Erdball XX.

With such a young organisation, few registered horses have yet reached competition age, but two that have – **Its The Business** (1986) by Jasper and **Renkum Englishman** (1986) by Renkum Arturo – have already proved themselves talented performers under saddle in the toughest of company. The AES-approved stallion **JR** (1991) by

Nimmerdor also became the first-ever British-based stallion to be graded into the Zangersheide Studbook, thus proving the competition and performance bias of his pedigree. Finally, the AES-graded BWBS-registered stallion **Broadstone Chicago** (1990) by Calypso I, whose dam's Furioso II/Gotthard bloodlines also make him eligible for Hannoverian grading on completion of a 100-day performance test is also proving to have huge talent under saddle as a show jumper and is already collecting a top quality book of mares. At the present time, the AES is not a member of the National Stallion Association (NASTA).

THE BRITISH BAVARIAN WARMBLOOD ASSOCIATION

This breed society is based in Scotland and concentrates mainly on stallions bred and/or graded in Bavaria. It is the only Warmblood breed society in the UK to conduct a 100-day test, but as the number of stallions taking this comparative test rarely rises into double figures, the overall influence of the BBVA has been somewhat limited.

The bloodlines in the studbook reflect those in the Bavarian Verband, with **Duplikat** (1975) by Duell, who has sired two graded sons since being imported into Scotland, and the Jalisco Jun son **Japaloupe S** (1988) whose progeny are especially highly soughtafter at the British High Performance Horse (BHPH) sales, being probably the most important stallions to date. The BBWA is not a member of NASTA.

THE BRITISH HANNOVERIAN HORSE SOCIETY

The British Hannoverian Horse Society (BHHS) was formed under the patronage of the Hannoverian Verband by a group of British owners of horses registered in the Hannoverian Studbook. Some of these horses had been imported from Hannover, while others had been born and bred in the UK. However, wherever they were bred, all horses registered with the BHHS have satisfied the rigorous requirements laid down by the Hannoverian Studbook. The role of the BHHS is to oversee the maintenance of a studbook for Hannoverian horses in the UK and to ensure a standard of selection and testing of horses equivalent to the standard approved in Hannover. To this end, as an official 'daughter society' of the Hannoverian Verband, the BHHS works under a code of breeding laid down, and regularly updated, by the breed society in Hannover. This means that a horse licensed by the BHHS will be accepted in Hannover as equivalent in status to a horse bred in Hannover and licensed by the Hannoverian Verband.

Stallion and mare gradings and associated foal inspections and branding are held annually under official Hannoverian Verband judges and colts inspected and approved as stallions are required to attend a 100-day performance test in Germany in order to complete the licensing requirements.

Akkord (1977) by Aperitif has probably been the most successful stallion in the earliest group of BHHS and Hannoverian Verband-graded sires in the UK. His progeny includes a number of good dressage horses and graded stallions, but ironically, he has generally been most effective when used on Thoroughbred (or near-Thoroughbred) mares, of whom there are only limited numbers graded with the BHHS. His most successful competition horses to date are the mare Abrakkadabra and the stallions Son of Charm and Crown Marcasite.

Young stallions such as **Cardinar** (1986) by Cardinal XX and **Glucksfall** (1988) by Gluckstern have also proved popular, with foals in particular often selling well at the BHPH Sales, but the international dressage horse **Demonstrator** (1981) by Dynamo is probably the BHHR stallion most in demand with mare owners at the moment, particularly in view of the success of such competition horses as the dressage horse Broadstone Dixi Le Mans and the riding horse Daytona, both of which he sired. One of the few stallions to be dual-

The Hannoverian stallion Akkord (1977) by Aperitif, sire of the BWBS-graded stallion Stonegrove Ace and the late international dressage stallion Crown Marcasite.

PEDIGREE OF **AKKORD** – CHESTNUT HANNOVERIAN, 1977			
Akkord	Aperitif	Adlerfarn II	Alderschild XX
			St Pr St Anglerbad
		St Pr St Chinablume	Ceylon
			Eichmadel
	Sennerin	Sender	Senator
			St Pr St Abenkleid
		Worklage	Wohlan
			Alpenwarte

graded with both the BHHR and the BWBS, his full sister Didaktik also made her mark on British breeding when she produced the outstanding young BWBS Stallion Grading Champion Broadstone Lady's Man (1991) by Broadstone Landmark (DV) before going onto a very successful showjumping career. However, Demonstrator could be closely pursued in the popularity stakes in the future by the Olympic dressage horse **Giorgione** (1981) by Grundstein, who was graded by the BHHS at the age of fourteen in 1995, having been graded by the Oldenburg Verband in Germany eleven years previously but never used at stud. With proven dressage talent combined with outstanding pedigree rich in show jumpers he looks set to be an outstanding dual-purpose sire of the future.

The BHHS is a member of NASTA and many BHHS stallions are dual-registered with the BHD. Several are also graded with the AES, as part-bred stock is difficult to register with the BHHS for breeding purposes.

THE BRITISH WARM-BLOOD SOCIETY

The British Warm-Blood Society (BWBS) is a 'parent' society within the EEC regulations and was founded in 1977. Immediately, the BWBS set its goals along the same lines already established by the well known Warmblood organisations on the Continent, knowing full well that this would be an uphill struggle.

The problem lies in the fact that, whereas on the Continent the government has taken a hand in the breeding of horses and in some countries recognises it as an agricultural animal, here in Great Britain they do not. Over there it is required by law that a breeding animal reaches a minimal standard and goes through various testing; here, the stallion owner can still do whatever he likes.

The BWBS is lucky that so many of its breeders are seriously interested in only standing the best possible stallions at stud; pedigree passports, a recognised brand and the good prices received for youngsters means a strict grading criteria within the society is still supported.

There are some societies here that accept and continue to use Warmblood stallions which have already been failed abroad. The British Warm-Blood Society, like the Danish, Dutch, Swedish and most German societies follow a general rule that these horses are not eligible.

The BWBS has not so far given its support to the British Horse Database. The data being gathered by the BHD does not necessarily reflect a stallion's true history, as the records only commence when a horse registers. This means that many of the older and most impressive sires may show no progeny winnings over the last ten to fifteen years at stud; this in turn gives an inaccurate picture.

The BWBS also has strong reservations about the BHD's current policy of registering *all* stallions, including failed Warmblood stallions, for breeding, which the BWBS sees as a potential problem for the future quality of Warmblood breeding in the UK.

The BWBS runs its office on the Royal Showground at Kenilworth in Warwickshire. Computerised pedigrees and data as well as the BWBS passports are issued from this office. Each year in August, a large Mare Grading and In-Hand Breed Show is held on the showground with a full range of classes for broodmares, foals and youngstock. As of 1992, special awards of gold, silver and bronze medals are given to the very best of the newly graded mares, while the best pure-bred yearling receives a £500 prize. Show classes for BWBS horses are also held at the Royal Show in July of every year.

The most important event is the Stallion Grading Show which is held every year in November. The judges for all these grading shows, as well as the summer show, always come from abroad to ensure that the standard remains the same as on the continent.

BREEDING POLICY

Most imported pedigree Warmbloods carrying the original 'parent' society's papers (as well as those with BWBS pedigree passports) are eligible to be registered. Thoroughbreds, large Anglo Arabs of riding type, and some NTR mares are also eligible.

As the British Isles has no tradition of Warmblood breeding, these imports formed a vital foundation of competition bloodlines. Once accepted for registration, both mares and stallions must complete the BWBS grading process before entering the Breeding Stud Book. Foals born in Britain conceived by imported frozen semen from full-graded sires are also eligible for registration.

MARES

There are three sections to the BWBS Breeding Stud Book.

- *Select Stud Book* Mares must have two graded parents and a full pedigree for three generations. They must score very highly in the grading, and must be a 15.3hh (160cm) or above to qualify for this book. However, imported mares already entered into a foreign Select Stud Book do not need to be presented at BWBS grading and enter the BWBS Select Stud Book automatically upon registration acceptance. Only about 10% of mares enter the Select Stud Book. If not previously branded on the left side of the neck by another society, Select Stud Book mares may be branded there.

- *Main Stud Book* Mares must have at least one graded parent and a full pedigree for three generations. They must reach a suitable standard at the grading. If Warmbloods, they must be above 15hh (152.5cm) whereas non-Warmblood mares of Thoroughbred, Weatherbys Non Thoroughbred Register or Anglo-Arab origin must be at least 15.2hh (158cm). Main Stud Book mares are not eligible for the BWBS neck brand.

- *Permanent Breeding Register* Mares must have one graded parent. The other parent may be only partially known or completely blank. They must reach a suitable standard of conformation and movement. minimum height is 15hh.

All mares must arrive at the grading show with a basic certificate of health (supplied by the BWBS) completed by a veterinary surgeon stating freedom from visible signs of hereditary disease, as well as height and bone measurement. All are shown in-hand in their relevant class groups. The scores for type, conformation, correctness, elasticity and swing of movement and overall impression decide the stud book they enter into, once the pedigree details decide their eligibility.

Medals are awarded to the exceptional mares of the top groups. No medals will be awarded unless the year's standard warrants extra recognition. This ensures that only the most outstanding mares become the owners of a gold, silver or bronze medal.

All foals with two graded parents registered with the BWBS, and a fully completed pedigree in all generations, are issued with 'pink papers'. These 'pink-papered' animals are eligible to be branded on the left thigh with the BWBS brand. Each horse will also receive a three-digit number directly under the breed brand for further identification. This number is copied into the passport.

STALLIONS

The Stallion Grading Show takes place over two-days. All must be fully vetted by the BWBS's appointed veterinary surgeons. Stallions will also be 'scoped for wind problems and x-rayed, should any query arise during the vetting process. Stable managers are on overnight duty to observe any behaviour problems. British-bred colts are requested to appear at two-and-a-half years of age. They must have a full passport and be free from vice. Imported colts of the same age must carry their original breed society documents and may not have failed in their country of origin in any grading process. Older imported stallions will have their competition career and progeny quality taken into consideration.

A panel of foreign judges sees the stallions in classes of their own age group. On the morning of the first day the stallions are stood up on hard ground, walked and trotted in hand. In the afternoon they are again shown in hand, but this time indoors and then are shown loose. This enables the judges to see their natural self-balance and freedom of movement in all three paces.

On the second morning the stallions are loose jumped indoors. Each stallion has a score sheet which is completed over the two-day period. They receive detailed points for their head, neck, overline and croup, limbs, correctness and swing and elasticity, overall impression and type as well as individual marks for walk, trot and canter. Expression and masculinity also rate highly in the final decision, which is announced in the afternoon of the second day.

There is no preset percentage of stallions which will pass or fail each year. If the quality standard is high, then a number will grade; likewise a year with poorer quality will see very few or possibly none passing.

Once the stallions have passed this first stage, they are eligible for a brand on the left side of the neck. The BWBS also requires bloodtyping of each stallion at this time. If they have not already completed a performance test abroad, they can now do so in Great Britain on a simplified, shorter format. The BWBS Breeding Stallion Stud Book is divided into three groups.

• Group III is for all stallions which have passed the grading.

• Group II is for the stallions which have either completed their performance test, or are competing at medium level in any disipline or must have produced an advanced horse or passed a BWBS progeny inspection.

• Group I is for the stallions which have produced advanced horses in any disipline. They must also have passed the BWBS progeny inspection or if imported be a Premium sire in their own country. If they are not old enough to have produced advanced competition horses then they must be competing at a high level themselves.

This system seems to work very well in Britain, giving a clear indication where a stallion's talent lies. It also gives owners more freedom to plan their horses' careers whether at stud or in the competition arena.

Broadstone Lady's Man (1992), champion stallion at the British Warmblood Grading 1994 by Landmark (DV)/Dynamo (Hann).

INFLUENTIAL BLOODLINES

The BWBS has been lucky enough to have had some small studs and private breeders who have imported a number of extremely high-class mares with excellent pedigrees. The progeny of these mares are now coming to the fore, winning in-hand as youngsters, then going on to a successful career under rider.

Mention should be made of Takohama (1970), a bay Danish mare by Ackjonariusz. She has produced to Atlantus a medal mare (Meacham Arlena) now competing in dressage and winner of Semi-Finals Novice Badminton Horse Feed Championships, 1994. A full sister (Durfee Arianna) was awarded the trophy for the Best British Mare at the Goodwood Novice Championships in Dressage and was purchased by Germany.

Dulita (1966), a bay Swedish mare by Drabant, has one Select Graded daughter, Tallents Aldine, winner of the Shell Gas Medium Dressage at the Hereford Festival, 1994. She also is the dam of the Graded stallion Durfee Augite (1980). Ostrea (1971) is a bay Danish mare and a full sister to the well-known dressage sire, May Sherif. Her first son bred in Great Britain, Alizar Kignaes (1985), was the Reserve Champion at grading as well as proving himself in the dressage arena. Lydia (1976), a bay Holstein mare by Landgraf I out of a Ramiro mare, has produced two medal mares to date, with a third daughter due to appear at grading in 1995.

The BWBS has over 50 stallions graded and the older ones mentioned below have all established themselves in Britain as either performers and/or producers.

• **Atlantus** (Galanthus/Astronaut). Brown Danish stallion (1975). Imported as a foal and standing at stud privately, therefore only modestly used on outside mares. He has sired three graded sons, and is the leading sire of medal awards and select graded daughters. From over 200 hundred mares shown, fourteen Medals have been awarded to date, and eight of these have gone to Atlantus daughters. He is also the sire of Byron, winner of one of the show-jumping Grands Prix at Donauschingen. Another son, Everest Early Devil is currently being jumped by Michael Whitaker; a daughter, Clear Spring is winning with Di Lampard, and Atlantic Dancer won a Stoneways Championship Award in 1993.

Atlantic Affair earned a place on France's Junior International three-day event team, and Aprillis (Bramhope April Love), one of the first Gold medal mares, has been successfully competing at Prix St Georges in Holland.

•**Cannabis** (1977). Chestnut Trakehner stallion bred in Denmark (Donauwind/Herzbube). Imported as a foal, before Warmblood breeding became popular, and was only lightly used. He first came to public notice when his daughter Rylandes Crystal won the *Horse and Hound* Working Hunter Championship at the Royal International Show 1990. She was then sold to Ireland and was Reserve Champion Mare at the Dublin Show. Next came Annaconda, a Grade A show jumper competed in Belgium and ridden by Amanda Lanni. His stock also does well in dressage with Flagg competing at Prix St Georges, ridden by Jackie Hulmes.

•**Dallas** (1974). Chestnut Selle Français stallion. Imported as an older stallion and already a Grade A show jumper (Brillioso/Monseigneur). He has produced a number of talented show jumpers, including the youngsters Hello Feliz and Dexter IV, and the well-known Grade A, Hello Oscar ridden by Geoff Glazzard. His progeny have also been very successful in the county shows.

•**Demonstrator** (1981). Black Hannoverian stallion (Dynamo/Pik Bube). Imported after his preliminary grading in Germany he returned to Germany to complete his 100-day ridden testing. He has also been in training with Ferdi Eilberg and has won Grand Prix dressage. He has produced one graded son, Broadstone Dickens (1990). In 1992 his son, Disco Night won the Competition Horse award for the Best Dressage Horse. His daughter Demeter was the Supreme Champion Broodmare at the Royal Show.

•**Dutch Courage** (1969-1991). Brown Dutch stallion imported by

PEDIGREE OF **DEMONSTRATOR** – BLACK HANNOVERIAN, 1981			
Demonstrator	Dynamo	Don Carlos	Domonik
			Fasanenmoos
		Goldmodell	Goldfalk
			StPrSt Dormärdel
	StPrSt Pippa	Pik Bube	Pik König
			Franka
		Dakota	Derby
			Flügelheimat

Jennie Loriston-Clarke (Millerole XX/Avenir). His international dressage career was recognised worldwide. He won the individual bronze medal at the World Championships in 1978, and has founded a long line of sons and grandsons which continue to excel. His son, Dutch Gold (1976) out of the Thoroughbred mare Gold K, is the only British-bred horse to win the European League points table. He also won the Midland Bank Horse Trials and three Volvo World Cup Dressage qualifiers. In 1988 he and Jennie Loriston-Clarke competed at the Soeul Olympics. Dutch Gold is the sire of two BWBS-graded sons, Dutch Dream (1991) and Catherston Gold Storm (1991). He has produced Dutch Display (formerly Callow Hill) which qualified for the World Equestrian Games in 1994 and the well-known large riding horse winner at major shows, Leading Light.

<table>
<tr><td colspan="7">PEDIGREE OF DUTCH GOLD – BROWN
BRITISH WARMBLOOD, 1976</td></tr>
<tr><td rowspan="8">Dutch Gold
WH 29
(BWB)</td><td rowspan="4">Dutch Courage
WH 11
(WPN)</td><td rowspan="2">Millerole (XX)</td><td>Cobalt (XX)</td></tr>
<tr><td>Musicida (XX)</td></tr>
<tr><td rowspan="2">Higonia 21092
(WPN)</td><td>Avenir</td></tr>
<tr><td>Cigonia</td></tr>
<tr><td rowspan="4">Gold K (XX)</td><td rowspan="2">Golden Cloud</td><td>Golden Bridge</td></tr>
<tr><td>Rain Storm</td></tr>
<tr><td rowspan="2">Cyrella</td><td>Phideas</td></tr>
<tr><td>Royal Palette</td></tr>
</table>

• **Catherston Dazzler** (1984). Brown stallion graded with the BSHR (Dutch Courage/Welton Gameful). Another very talented homebred horse, he won the Prix St Georges Dressage Horse of the Year in 1992, having previously won the Competition Horse Finals in 1988 and 1989. In 1993 he was the winner of the Grand Prix Special at Addington.

Catherston Dazzler is very modern in type as warrants his good Thoroughbred performance blood. His progeny include Broadstone Harvest Moon now competing as an Intermediate eventer and Indica Dazzler who won fourth place at the Dutch National Championships in 1994. The newest graded sons from this line are Catherston Dance in the Dark (1989), Catherston Humbug (1990) and Catherston Zebedee (1990). This line will continue to make its mark in many future Warmblood competition horses in Britain.

The BSHR-graded international dressage stallion Catherston Dazzler (1983), ridden by Jennie Loriston-Clarke. He is one of the many sons of the BWBS-graded international dressage stallion Dutch Courage.

•**Odysseus** (1970). Dark bay Hannoverian stallion (Orbis XX/ Dorilias). Imported from Denmark and originally graded in Germany, Odysseus is a Grade A show jumper. His progeny have done exceptionally well. Limmey's Comet won the Blenheim Audi International CCI Horse Trials. Another son is Otto the Great, who was second in Chantilly, France. Havens Marco Polo, a promising show jumper ridden by Tina Cassan, and Helicon, a winner of ridden show hunter championships with Robert Oliver, show that Odysseus is a sire of great diversity.

THE SCOTTISH DUTCH WARMBLOOD ASSOCIATION

As its name indicates, the Scottish Dutch Warmblood Association is a Scots-based organisation dedicated to developing, supporting and promoting the breeding of the Dutch Warmblood horse in Scotland. As a result, the bloodlines used tend to be based strictly on those available in The Netherlands and the studbook is deliberately more closed than that of the AES and its numbers and influence tend to be limited to relatively small number of Scottish studs. Founded in September 1990, it is not currently a member of NASTA but a number

The first-ever BWBS Gold Medal mare Bramhope April Love (1985) by Atlantus, who has since become a successful dressage horse under saddle, under the name Aprillis.

of SDWA stallions compete under saddle.

THE TRAKEHNER BREEDERS' FRATERNITY

The history, grading policy and bloodlines of the TBF are fully dealt with in the section on the Trakehner influence in the UK in Chapter 1. In the context of the breed societies in the UK it is probably unique in that many of its stallions are dual-graded with the BWBS, and some are also graded with the AES. Unfortunately, however, as none of the Trakehners in the UK were graded with the Hannoverian Verband before being exported from Germany, their stock cannot be fully registered with the BHHS, and the benefits of an occasional injection of Trakehner blood is therefore denied many of the top Hannoverian mares in the country. The TBF was a founder member of NASTA, with whom it runs the annual NASTA Stallion Performance Test.

OTHER WARMBLOOD SOCIETIES

With the adoption of the Single European Market in 1992, some foreign-based breed societies decided to use the opportunity to expand their registration, grading and branding activities into the UK. Such expansion is well within both the letter and the philosophy of the current EU law and several organisations such as the Oldenberg Verband, the Rheinlander Verband and Dansk Varmblod in particular were quick to recognise this. The fact that many top foreign-based stallions had now become available to British breeders through imported frozen semen – the German National Riding Horse Champion **Induc** (1990) by Marduc, the top Danish Warmbloods **Diamond** (1982) by Allegro and **Rambo** (1986) by Racot are typical of the standard of stallions that are used in this way – allied with the fact that many foreign-graded mares had already been imported by knowledgeable breeders, has been the spur for this. A few UK breeders have been enthusiastic about the merits of the kind of quality control enforced by visiting full official breed committees working to criteria identical to those used in the breed's country of origin, while the foreign organisations themselves have seen it as an ideal opportunity to market their breed (and breeding stock) and raise its profile in the UK.

How this new development will progress, and how many other organisations that operate outside their own borders – such as the studbooks of the Selle Français, the Swedish Warmblood and the Holsteiner who all grade, inspect and register in the USA – will adopt the same procedures is a subject for speculation at the moment.

At present, the foreign-based societies are officially outside the NASTA and BHD organisations, but progeny registered abroad still have to comply with BHS regulations on BHD registration in order to compete when mature.

NON-WARMBLOOD ORGANISATIONS

Five further organisations also have an input into Warmblood breeding in the UK, although many would argue that the lack of true Warmblood grading procedures emanating from most of these bodies enforces the belief that they are to be regarded as registers, rather than studbooks. However, together they have a key role in current competition horse-breeding practice in the UK and so warrant inclusion.

The organisations concerned are:

• **British Horse Database** Launched in November 1993, the British Horse Database (BHD) is not a breed or breeding society; it aims to complement the work of the services offered by the breed societies, not to compete with them. Its stated objective is to provide accurate data on breeding and performance for horses and ponies and it is therefore an essential source of information for competition horse breeders, being open to all types and breeds of horse. As its records build up, the BHD hopes to be able to help competition horse breeders, in particular, by giving them access to a broad range of information on pedigree and performance, which will help them in the selection of their breeding stock. Through the BHD, breeders will also be able to follow the progress of animals that have been bred by them and sold on, or have been sired by their own stallion, helping them to chart the progress of their breeding programme and providing useful marketing information for subsequent stock. Because of this, and because competition horses now require BHD registration prior to competing in affiliated classes, many stallions were among the 18,000 horses registered by the BHD in its first eighteen months of operation.

In early 1995, the BHD was taken over by Weatherbys, the organisation responsible for the studbook side of the racing and Thoroughbred industry in the UK. The computerised resources and expertise of Weatherbys are unparalleled by any other British horse breeding organisation but as the BHD covers all horses in Britain it does not specialise or focus on Warmblood bloodlines. The BHD is affiliated to NASTA.

•**British Sports Horse Register** The British Sports Horse Register (BSHR) is the performance-oriented arm of the BWBS, where breeding stock and/or its progeny that have successful competition results are given due recognition. In 1993, for instance, **Catherston Dazzler** won the Maple trophy for the most outstanding competition results amongst the BSHR-graded stallions. Breeding stock is graded at the Stallion Show in November and the Mare Grading Show in August, and stock with performance credentials for themselves or their progeny are encouraged to enter, with these records playing a major part on the judges' assessments. The BSHR is a foundation register for British horses that cannot fulfil the entry requirements for BWBS grading because of missing generations or lack of graded Warmblood stock in the pedigree (for example, Catherston Dazzler himself qualified as a BSHR graded stallion because his dam's dam was unregistered, which made him ineligible for BWBS stallion grading). The BSHR is a separate registry from the BWBS. It does use the same veterinary inspection for soundness and hereditary diseases, and its horses have to complete the same grading format using the BWBS judges at the shows.

As of 1995 the new BSHR passport will be issued by the BWBS office in Kenilworth and the registry will be put on their computer. This new passport will fulfil the requirements within the EEC and be the same format as that of the BWBS. This passport should stay with the horse for life.

•**National Light Horse Breeding Society (HIS)** The National Light Horse Breeding Society (NLHBS) was founded in 1884 under the name of the Hunters Improvement Society to encourage the breeding in the UK of a sufficient number of horses to meet the demands of the army and counteract the expenditure of the many millions of pounds which were being spent annually on importing horses from abroad. Financed by the War Office and the Ministry of Agriculture, the scheme entailed the selection of good sound Thoroughbred stallions, which travelled set routes throughout the country on foot, covering the many agricultural and vanner type mares that were being used at that time at pre-arranged stopping places on the way. With the decline in the demand for cavalry horses, the emphasis nowadays is on the production of competition horses. Fifty or so Thoroughbred stallions are selected to stand throughout the country each year after winning 'Premiums' at the annual stallion show held at Newmarket in March. Many of these stallions cover Warmblood mares, both graded and ungraded, and these Thoroughbred X Warmbloods are often highly sought after by British competition riders. A number of Warmblood stallions are also accepted as Grade I and Grade II Approved stallions following inspection by a panel of NLHBS judges and veterinary surgeons. Stallions such as the BWBS-graded Selle Français **Dallas** (1974) by Brillioso and the BWBS Grading Champion **Stonegrove Ace** (1986) by Akkord have been accepted onto this list, as have a number of horses by HIS Premium sires out of Warmblood mares, such as **Blitzen** (1987) by Bohemond out of a Hannoverian mare. Stallions of other breeds, such as those of Cleveland Bay and Irish Draught origin are also currently on the NLHBS Grade I and Grade II lists. The NLHBS was a founder member of NASTA.

•**National Stallion Association** The National Stallion Association (NASTA) was created by a number of breed societies when the Ministry of Agriculture decided to withdraw from stallion licensing. Led by the NLHBS and a small number of other founder members including the BWBS and the TBF, it was charged with maintaining the standards necessary for a stallion at stud. As such it drew up a set of veterinary standards relating to the approval of stallions based on the original Ministry standards and has continued to up-date them slightly to meet current requirements as necessary. NASTA has also taken on the responsibility for performance testing its approved stallions and therefore now also runs an annual non-compulsory Stallion Performance Test in collaboration with the TBF. This is becoming increasingly popular with a wide range of owners of Cleveland Bay and Arab stallions in particular, but non-Trakehner Warmblood stallions tend not to come forward because it does not usually count towards the generally more stringent competition or performance test regulations that their individual breed societies require them to meet. NASTA comprises a Council made up of nominated delegates from a representative section of British breed societies. Many other breed societies are also now affiliates of NASTA – although Warmblood affiliated societies are comparatively few on the ground for historical reasons – and most breed societies in the UK now abide by NASTA veterinary regulations, whether members or not. Although NASTA did occasionally register stallions in its own right at the beginning, this is no longer the case as the NLHBS has taken over this part of its functions.

• **Weatherbys Non-Thoroughbred Register** Weatherbys is the organisation that runs the General Stud Book, the internationally recognised stud book of the Thoroughbred breed. Its Non-Thoroughbred Register was originally intended to be a register for mares and geldings by Thoroughbred stallions out of non-Thoroughbred mares and horses with Weatherbys NTR papers were usually destined for National Hunt or point-to-point careers. However, until the mid-1980s colts and stallions bred in this way were expressly excluded from registration but it was then recognised that there was a danger that if all steeplechasers were bred from mares with an increasingly high percentage of Thoroughbred blood, the stamina and bone required of them could be sacrificed in the quest for speed. Weatherbys therefore opened a stallion section of the Non-Thoroughbred Register and stallions so registered were given the suffix VII to their names. As a result, the progeny of these stallions were then also eligible for Weatherbys NTR papers through their sires in the normal way. This stallion section of the NTR book proved immediately popular with owners of Warmblood stallions with a high percentage of Thoroughbred blood, as can be shown by the fact that one of the first stallions to be included was the BWBS registered and graded international dressage horse **Dutch Gold** who was in fact 75 per cent Thoroughbred in his own right, being by the Millerole XX son Dutch Courage and out of a Thoroughbred mare.

FUTURE DEVELOPMENTS

Despite the proportionally very large number of Warmblood stallions currently at stud in the UK (about 350 at the moment) and the multiplicity of organisations competing to grade them and register their offspring, Warmblood breeding in Britain is really only just out of its infancy. Predictions for the future are therefore very difficult to make, as they depend on the rise or fall of the popularity of correctly conducted Warmblood breeding in the next few years, the willingness of British breeders to learn from, and adapt 'foreign' methods to their own specific needs and the vagaries of the Single European Market. Great steps have already been taken, but until all British breeders and riders realise the importance of correct grading and registration procedures, the continual upgrading of stock will be a long hard struggle. Hopefully, the growing impact of the high quality of stallions based in mainland Europe that have been increasingly easily available to UK breeders since 1992 will help to reduce the impact of some of the less successful and unproven stallions currently in use and provide an object lesson in how to develop an up-to-date, authentic and successful approach to Warmblood breeding.

The superbly bred Broadstone Chicago (1990) by Calypso I, approved with the AES and hopefully destined to combine the careers of show jumper and breeding stallion in future years.

Chapter 11

The Eastern European Warmbloods

by

JANE KIDD

HORSES ABOUND IN MANY of the countries of Eastern Europe, particularly Poland, Hungary and Czechoslovakia. In the USSR there were in the region of 7.5 million horses and they produced Olympic medal winners, but in other Eastern Europe countries, despite the large numbers bred, there have been few international winners. Hungarian horses have had the greatest successes, but in FEI Carriage Driving which is not an Olympic discipline. The Polish horse Volt, from East Prussian lines and whose sire was Polarstern, won the individual title in the 1965 European Three-day Event Championship, but the post-Second World War horses of Eastern Europe have tended to be rather utilitarian, with a very large percentage being produced for work rather than sport. This is likely to change as Warmbloods become one of their viable exports. The countries of Eastern Europe have plenty of the necessary assets, many of them having a long history of horsemanship and special skills in equestrian breeding, and there are a good number of large state studs. But as they have as yet underdeveloped Warmblood markets and access has been restricted for so many years this chapter cannot be so detailed as for other Warmbloods.

POLAND

Poland is thought to have one of the largest equine populations in Europe with forty-two major government studs, but this includes the heavier breeds and ponies which are used for work not sport.

The two main breeds for riding are the Malopolski in the south-east of Poland, and the Wielkopolski in the north, although there is also, in a country famous for Arabs, quite a big population of Anglo Arabs.

The Malopolski is a little smaller than the Wielkopolski and is a general-purpose horse used for driving and riding. The foundations are the local horses that were crossed with Arabs and Thoroughbreds, but then the Hungarian Shagya, Furioso and Gidran have had an influence, as well as the Lipizzaner and some Wielkopolski. There are about 300 Malopolski stallions in state studs, and about a further 800 that stand privately. In the past they were rather small, but today they are being bred larger with increasingly successful results in competitions.

It is the Wielkopolski which has been used more extensively in sport, and being close to Thoroughbred in type has been most successful in eventing. Polish event teams have done well internationally, and the Wielkopolskis sent to Britain are making a name for themselves in horse trials.

Thoroughbreds, Oriental stock, Trakehners and East Prussians are the foundations of this breed which was divided into the Poznan and the Masuren, but as these became increasingly similar it was logical to merge and establish the Wielkopolski. The East Prussians, today usually referred to as Trakehners, have had the biggest influence on the development of the Polish Warmbloods. That famous stud where this

Centyfor by the French Anglo Arab Kwartet, a good example of the coloured (tobiano/pinto) Warmbloods that have been bred in Poland for many years.

Arak (1976) by Parysow, who traces back to one of Poland's best Thoroughbred stallions, Perkoz XX.

great Warmblood was developed and bred for nearly two hundred years now lies just inside the Russian borders, and very close to Poland. Thousands of East Prussians were bred in the area in the inter-war years and those left behind when the few made that famous trek to West Germany at the end of the war, have been used mainly in the former Soviet Union and in the development of the Wielkopolski.

Foremost amongst the Thoroughbreds are **Aquirio** (who produced the successful stallion **Colombo**), **Perkoz** and his son **Sopran**, and **Parysow** whose best son was **Arak**.

Recently Hannoverian blood has been used. At the end of the Second World War Hannoverian mares in particular were used with great success when put to the Trakehner and Thoroughbred, but stallions have also been important. Two of the most influential Hannoverians were **Fling**, who produced such important sons as **Falkner II** and **Feiertraum**, and **Fahnenetrager** who, when crossed with the Trakehner mare by Folliant, produced **Templer**. Two recent Hannoverian purchases are **David** by Darwin and **Grand As I** by Gardeulan II.

Of the Trakehners, probably the most influential was **Celsius** by Hirtensang (great grandsire of Donauwind), who traces back to Parsival, and he produced such outstanding sons as **Dyrektoriat** and **Brankard**. Then there was **Traum** (not to be confused with the stallion of the same name who appears in the Trakehner chapter), a son of

Pilger, who produced many successful broodmares and such important stallions as **Eliop** and Poprad who was exported to the USA after producing, amongst others, the high class stallion **Aspirant**. **Astor** was another important Trakehner sire who had two important sons, **Capriui** and **Polarstern** (again, not the same stallion as the Polarstern discussed in Chapter 1), the latter producing Flotenspieler (out of a Hannoverian), Froysen and that event champion Volt. French Anglo-Arab blood has also been introduced recently, chiefly in the form of the Arlequin son Kwartet and this is producing some useful jumpers.

The breeding policy is highly selective with stallions first being examined as foals. Later they are tested for their conformation, gaits and jumping in liberty. Those that pass go into training for one year before performance testing. The most talented then compete in the disciplines and score points for each prize won. They are registered as sports horses of high quality if they earn more than 100 points.

Polish breeding stock has been exported to such countries as Germany, Britain and the USA, but Denmark is the country in which they have made the most impact on the breeding. Eight stallions went there between 1968 and 1971 and foremost amongst them was Ackjonariusz. Born in 1953 at Statsstutteret Lisk, he was by Sandor and out of a Polarstern mare. Ackjonariusz came to Den mark in 1968 and became the leading sire of DH mares from a number of coverings. One of his daughters, Takohama, was exported to Britain and produced such winning stock as Durfee Appelle and Durfee Arianna. Gotyk was imported one year later and he was by Kafar and out of a mare by the Trakehner Traum. He was made champion of the Danish stallion grading in 1969 and produced such good mares as Amigo, dam of graded stallions Rastell and Ramir. Censor was performance-tested in Poland and graded in Denmark in 1971. He went on to become a Grade A show jumper and produced the graded stallion Nevada. He was by Jodko and, like Gotyk, out of a Traum mare.

Two of the best stallions to go to the USA were Narrator, taken there by Robert Hall (founder of the Fulmer School of Equitation) and made a champion at the Devon Dressage show in 1981, and Poprad by Traum. The latter jumped in two Olympics – Mexico and Munich – before at twenty going to the USA. His best son in Poland was Aspirant. It is Germany, however, who imported the best known of the Polish stallions, namely Ramzes X, who was by the Thoroughbred Rittersporn and out of an Anglo-Arab mare by 523 Schagya X-3. He founded an R-line both for the Westphalians and the Holsteins. Germany has also benefitted from the most successful Polish horse in the early 1990s Cyprus by Senior who Gina Capellman-Lutkemeier has been riding with considerable success.

Finally, Poland is now becoming internationally famous as a source of coloured (skewbald and piebald) Warmbloods. These have been bred there for generations but are now becoming popular far outside Poland as they combine Trakehner quality with spectacular colour. the stallion Markiz is the most notable sire of recent years and several horses with his bloodlines are now at stud in the UK.

HUNGARY

The most famous Hungarian cross-bred is the one produced at the Kecskemet stud, where the Lipizzaner mares are crossed with Trotter stallions to produce the world-famous driving horses. Imre Abonyi, Sandor Fulop and Gyorgy Bardos are some of the Hungarian champions who have driven these horses with enormous success. Many have been exported to Britain.

It is Mezöhegyes, however, that is the stud that has been officially assigned to be the major producer of sports horses and the animals produced there carry the same name. These Mezöhegyes are strong Hungarian cross-breds used for sport and are based on the older Hungarian breeds, the Gidran, and the Furioso and North Star, breeds originally founded by two Thoroughbred stallions imported from Britain with these names. In the 1960s established Warmblood breeds, the Hannoverian and Holstein, were used to help turn the Mezöhegyes into leisure and sports horses.

The other major stud is Kisber, named after the Hungarian winner of the 1876 British Derby. The strain is lighter than the Mezöhegyes having more Thoroughbred in it, and two relatively recent imports were Guy's Choice XX and Supreme Court XX, both Thoroughbreds from Britain. Holsteins and Mecklenburgs have been used in the past, but the Thoroughbred has been the most influential.

CZECHOSLOVAKIA

The Kladruber, the stronger, bigger version of the Lipizzaner and famous as a carriage horse, has been the best known of the Czechoslovakian breeds, but at the government studs they are breeding Warmbloods for riding and sport in increasing numbers. The most famous of these government studs is Albertovec in Silesia.

Various well-known Warmbloods have been imported to develop the Czechoslovakian sports horse and these have included Oldenburgs, Selle Français and Hannoverians. They have also used the Furioso from Hungary, some Polish horses, the Trakehner, of whom the most influential was **Quorium**, and their own Kladruber. The Thoroughbred has played an important part, Czechoslovakia long being well known for her racehorses, particularly steeplechasers. The Pardubice, with its fearsome obstacles attracts runners from all over the world and is held annually just outside Prague.

A very big emphasis has been placed on temperament in the development of the Czechoslovakian sports horse, and even the males have to go through stringent performance tests. Between three and four years of age they have to take driving, dressage, jumping and cross-country tests. Czechoslovakian horses have been exported to Germany, Italy, Austria and Britain but this relatively new Warmblood has yet to make a mark in international competitions.

COUNTRIES OF THE FORMER SOVIET UNION

Horses of the USSR won many Olympic honours, and their greatest successes were in dressage. Absent, one of the best modern representatives of that ancient breed, the Akhal Teke, won the Individual Olympic gold in 1960 but more recently it has been the Ukranian Saddle Horse, a new breed of Warmblood, which has been earning most of the honours.

The USSR covered a huge area and there are various breeds from the Tersk (based on Arab-type breeds), through the Latvian Riding Horse, to the Russian Riding Horse (based mainly on Thoroughbred, Arab, Turkmen, Karabakh and some Donblood), that are bred selectively and used for general riding and sport. The Trakehner has also been important, with the original stud of Trakehnen now lying within Russia. In the early 1990s the three most successful modern Russian Trakehners were Dikson, who was second in the 1991 Dressage World Cup, Edinburg by Elever whom Kyra Kyrklund rode into fourth place at the World Equestrian Games and Biotop by Blesk whom Dr Reiner Klimke competes. Most of the successful horses are born Ukrainian Saddle Horses and these include the dressage winners Ikhor, 1968 Olympic Gold medal, Plot, Shkval and Igrok, who won the 1980 Olympic team gold medal, and Rukh, who won the team bronze at the 1985 European Championships.

The development of the Ukrainian Riding Horse started after World War Two when bloodlines from the Hannoverian, East Prussian, Furioso, Gidran and Thoroughbred were imported. The most influential foundation stallions were **Typhoon**, an East Prussian, and **Shtorm** and **Khrustal** who were both Hannoverians. Later more

The Russian Trakehner Dikson, a top performer in international dressage.

Thoroughbred blood was introduced.

FUTURE DEVELOPMENTS

The opening up of Eastern Europe has lead to considerable changes on the international Warmblood scene. With horses being a good source of hard currency large numbers have been exported, and especially in Russia and the Ukraine their breeding stock has been seriously depleted. It is to be hoped that with their other assets of government studs, relatively cheap overheads and traditional knowledge they will realise their potential as major international Warmblood breeders.

Chapter 12

Warmbloods in North America

by

CELIA CLARKE

THE DEVELOPMENT OF Warmblood breeding in North America has been characterised by the importation of high quality stock, including some of the most outstanding stallions in recent Warmblood breeding history, and the foundation of numerous, sometimes conflicting, registries and stud books. This confused picture has been compounded on the one hand by a strong resistance amongst some breeders to accept the quality control and standards required to sustain and develop the modern Warmblood competition horse, and on the other by a tendency for certain factions within the industry to breed only from animals coming from one particular breeding area in Europe, regardless of type. This practice is based on belief in the prestige earned by, for example, American-born Hannoverians being able to be registered, branded and marketed as such. This attitude is firmly entrenched in North America and actively encouraged by European breed societies who cross the Atlantic to inspect, brand, register and grade stock in association with the American appendices to their stud books.

North America has been a lucrative market for European Warmblood breeders since the early 1960s when better air transport meant that riders from the United States and Canada could more easily travel the world and compete with horses based in Europe. Tougher competitions created a need for improved competition horse power and the dollar became increasingly important at the Verden riding horse auctions and similar events during the 1960s and 1970s. However, apart from a few notable examples, it was not until the late 1970s that serious importations of breeding stock began, and it was the 1980s that saw the real explosion of interest. The huge financial investments made by some American breeders were encouraged by lucrative tax shelters, which in turn led to one or two very highly priced transactions ($100,000 was paid for one colt foal in 1983) and to stud fees over three times those paid in Europe, all of which served to discourage the small breeder. It is these small breeders who form the backbone of Warmblood organisations in Europe, where their knowledge and vision often serves as a counterweight to the financial interests of the bigger studs. Such small breeders frequently have an altruistic view regarding the need to abide by stringent standards of bloodlines, grading, registration and performance testing, even though the rules involved sometimes cause them short-term financial loss. However, they realise that the long-term improvement of the horses in their own breeding area will benefit them ultimately, and so they tend to take the longer view. This 'longer view' is not so common in North America, where some owners of unregisterable stock have founded stud books to register them in, and failed and ungraded stallions do still stand at stud, often used by mare owners unaware of the intricacies and regulations of Warmblood breeding.

On the positive side, the amount of money invested in Warmblood breeding in North America has led to the availability of some superb imported stallions, including the Trakehner Donauwind (1965) by Pregel, who was imported from West Germany in the early 1980s after standing in both West Germany and Denmark; the Selle Français Galoubet by Almé (also known as Almé Z); the Hannoverian stallion Dirk (1968) by Duft II, champion at the German National Agricultural Show; the highly rated Dutch Warmblood Calimero by Legaat and Best of Luck by Lucky Boy; the Swedish Warmblood Grand Prix dressage horse Elektron (1968) by Gaspari; the Oldenburg international show jumper Golan (by Goya) and the Westphalian-born Dutch-graded Roemer, by Pilatus, who was the leading producer of dressage horses in the Netherlands in the 1980s. The rising young Danish Warmblood stallion Rambo (by Racot) has also recently been bought for the USA. As yet it is too early to be able to assess the long-term success of these stallions in their new homes, although a number of their progeny have already done well in classes designed to identify young potential competition horses, such as those held during the Dressage at the Devon Show.

In the last few years, some Warmblood breeds have become more popular in North America whilst others have waned in support. Warmblood breeders throughout the world are a little prone to be 'dedicated followers of fashion' with everyone rushing to use the new top young stallion in his first year, but in America (despite the tendency to put Hannoverian to Hannoverian, Dutch Warmblood to Dutch Warmblood, Selle Français to Selle Français etc.) whole breeds have been subject to the vagaries of fashion. The stallion advertisements in the stallion issues of such American magazines as *The Chronicle of The Horse* and *Practical Horseman* are probably the best indicators of these trends, and these show that although the numbers of Thoroughbred and Holstein stallions advertised in the past few years have remained fairly constant, those of the Dutch Warmbloods and Hannoverians have risen dramatically, whilst those for Trakehners have slumped dramatically. Although there is an increasingly wide range of stallions also available through imported frozen semen, such a volatile market cannot help either stallion or mare owners in the long run. Some stallions, such as the Holstein Fleming (1983) by Farnese and the Selle Français I Love You (by Almé) have tended to stay at stud in the USA only a short while and have therefore had a rather more limited impact than their bloodlines merit.

BREEDING POLICIES

Over recent years a large number of breed societies have operated in the USA and Canada, some of them with conflicting aims, and all of them with their own specific rules for registration and grading. The societies concerned include the American Warmblood Registry, the Belgian Warmblood Breeding Association (North American District), the American Association of Breeders of Holsteiner Inc., the American Holsteiner Horse Association, the American Hannoverian Society, the Pure-bred Hannoverian Association, the American Trakehner Association, the North American Trakehner Association, the Dutch Warmblood Association (NA/KWPN), the Swedish Warmblood Association, the North American Selle Français Horse Association Inc., the International Sport Horse Registry and Oldenburg Verband, the Hungarian Horse Association and more generally – as they are open to some non-Warmbloods – the Canadian Hunter Improvement Society, the Northwest Sport Horse Breeders' Association and the Canadian Sport Horse Breeders' Association. A number of these organisations work closely with European societies, most notably the American Hannoverian Society (which has links with the Verband Hannoverscher Warmblutzüchter eV, or Hannoverian Verband), the American Trakehner Association (recognised by the Verband der Züchter und Freunde des Ostpreussischen Warmblutpferdes Trakehner Abstammung eV, or Trakehner Verband, as the only official registry for Trakehner horses in North America), the North American Selle Français Horse Association, the Dutch Warmblood Association and the Swedish Warmblood Association (whose standards and procedures are both very closely controlled by their parent organisations in the Netherlands and Sweden respectively). However, other organisations seem to have rather more flexible rules of registration and grading, with bloodline requirements and performance criteria of a correspondingly more open standard.

With this mix of organisations, it is impossible to deduce an overall breeding policy for Warmbloods in North America. Not only do the organisations concerned each have their own set of rules, the rules applied by foreign-linked breed societies operating within America cannot be identical with those of the parent society abroad for a variety of reasons. These mainly relate to compatibility of performance-test results inside and outside Europe, when the numbers of animals tested might be around 50-100 in Europe and 5 in North America; the limited numbers of different graded bloodlines available in the United States and Canada and the consequent need to broaden the broodmare base with non-Warmblood mares; and the resistance of European societies to accept American-bred stock with European papers for grading in the European country of origin. Indeed, the Trakehner Verband specifically forbids this, presumably in order to protect its own markets. In these circumstances parity cannot be enforced, and comparisons between, say, on the one hand, American-bred horses with Hannoverian bloodlines and two German-bred parents in the American Hannoverian Register (the organisation working most closely with the Hannoverian Verband in the United States), and their contemporaries and relatives born in the Hannoverian breeding district on the other, for the most part is likely to be subjective as they are unlikely to meet in performance test conditions in sufficient numbers.

Despite the efforts of the American Warmblood Registry, which does concentrate on correlating breeding and performance records, the lack of comprehensive breeding statistics (such as those compiled by the FN in West Germany) have already had an effect on the marketing of American-bred Warmbloods. A number of futurity competitions have been launched for young jumpers and hunters as well as one specifically for Trakehner stock. Taking their model from futurity stakes for Thoroughbred race horses, stallions are registered for a set period of years with one or more of the relevant futurity schemes (the International Hunter Futurity, the International Jumper Futurity and the American Trakehner Association Futurity) so that their progeny conceived during those years can compete in the qualifying rounds and finals (which are usually held when the progeny are four- five- and six-year-olds). Offspring of stallions who are not nominated cannot compete, and prize money and breeder premiums are often very high – an average of just over $140,000 per annum for one scheme – as are the numbers of stallions competing (sometimes in the region of 150 nominated sires per season). These futurity prizes therefore provide a lucrative incentive programme for breeders and owners and valuable feedback on competition records for nominated stallions whose progeny compete. However, they do not solve the problem created by the difficulty of keeping grading records of progeny when so many conflicting breed organisations exist, and strong sire and broodmare lines still cannot be identified with any accuracy or ease. In this context, it is difficult to predict future developments, except to say that as has been the case with Warmblood breeding throughout its history, market forces will surely play their part in encouraging the development of higher overall standards and a more cohesive approach to the selection of stock, although the fluctuating exchange rate of the dollar must surely be a moderating influence.

GENERAL DESCRIPTION OF THE NORTH-AMERICAN WARMBLOOD

With a Warmblood breeding industry organised in the way it is in North America, it is difficult to draw up a 'general description' of the animal produced on the North American continent. Obviously, those animals produced from two parents originally graded in the same European stud book do look like the European versions of those animals (provided, of course that they are fed and raised correctly), but it is not easy to generalise any further. The only noticeably different thing about Warmbloods based in America to European eyes is that many American horses are often shown with full tails, in contrast to the pulled, trimmed and cut treatment they receive in Europe. Europeans feel that full tails detract from the powerful impression given by the overline of the quarters in Warmbloods and are, therefore, hinder assessing conformation – a small point, but an interesting one.

IMPORTANT BLOODLINES

Most of the major Warmblood breeds have found their way to North America since the 1970s, and through them most of the important bloodlines.

Probably the first breed to make an impact on the continent was the Trakehner. The only pure-bred Warmblood, this light weight, middle-sized horse with a fairly hot temperament immediately found favour because it combined the looks and elegance of the Thoroughbred with the paces and athleticism of the heavier, stronger types of Warmblood such as the Hannoverian. The Trakehner breed formed an ideal bridge for breeders and riders unused to Warmbloods but enthusiastic to improve their competition horses along European lines, but in recent

Donauwind's (Trak) most successful son Abdullah (1970), gold medallist at the Los Angeles Olympics and a successful sire in his own right.

years some criticism has been voiced by American riders as to the temperament of notable numbers of the stock being produced. Although a Warmblood with a kind and generous nature, the Trakehner is also frequently a flighty tempered horse, and this combination can prove taxing, even to riders used to explosive Thoroughbreds. The numbers of Trakehners at stud in North America has fallen, as have the numbers of breeders of pure Trakehners, but with the increasing numbers of other Warmblood breeds being imported, many Trakehner stallions have begun to take on the role that they have in much of Europe – as an outcross and improver for heavier, more old-fashioned stock. Many of the Trakehner stallions who have stood in North America have been of world-wide importance. The most notable ones are:

- **Ameigo** by Handel. Grey Trakehner (1974). A Pan-Am Games bronze medallist in eventing, his grey colour comes from his dam Abiza (by Maharadscha), who was also the dam of Abdullah – an outstanding record for any broodmare.

- **Azurit** by My Lunaria XX. Chestnut Trakhner. An outstanding dressage horse, winner of over 20 international classes and second in the World Championships in 1982, he combined stud duties and a top-class competiton career, being shortlisted for 1986 World Championships and the 1988 Olympic games and winning progeny awards from the Trakehner Verband and the American Trakehner Association at the same time.

- **Donauwind** by Pregel. Bay Trakehner (1965). The sire of over twenty graded sons in Europe and one hundred graded broodmares, he was outstandingly successful as a stallion in both West Germany and Denmark before ending his days in Texas. His grey graded son Abdullah (who is also approved by the American Hannoverian Register for use on graded Hannoverian mares) was imported *in utero* and was a gold medal winner at the 1984 Olympics in show jumping, as well as being the sire of a number of AHSA Horses of the Year in his own right. Donauwind's son Unkenruf, the sire of the well-known dressage horse Rubelit von Unkenruf, was also imported into the United States as a mature stallion.

- **Donauschimmer** by Valentin. Grey Trakehner (1969). He was the champion of the West German stallion performance test for his year and competed successfully in dressage. As a sire he produced highly regarded horses who were winners both in-hand and under saddle, including Casar, a grand champion in dressage at Devon who has since become an ATA stallion, as has another of his sons Lenzsturm.

- **Eligius** by Mackensen. Grey Trakehner (1980). He was reserve champion at the 1982 stallion grading at Neumünster and a highly placed horse under saddle at his performance test. He is a noted sire of outstanding movers.

- **Enrico Caruso** by Elchniederung. Black/brown Trakehner (1978). Reserve champion of his 100-day test, he was rated the top producer of jumpers in his age group in Germany in 1991 and in the top ten as a producer of dressage horses. He is also the sire of Kostlany, champion at the 1987 Trakehner stallion grading and several other good competition horses.

- **Morgenglanz** by Abglanz. Chestnut Trakehner (1965). This horse has founded a strong sire line in North America, as befits a son of Abglanz (1942, by Poseidon), who founded his own line when graded into the Hannoverian stud book. One of the first Trakehners imported into the United States, he sired many top performance horses in both Europe and America, and was responsible for the ATA-graded stallion Traum as well as the dam of the ATA graded stallion Troy (by Ameigo).

- **Tannenberg** by Sterndeuter. Bay Trakehner (1966). A sire of twelve graded stallions, including the short-lived 1976 West German stallion grading champion Schiwago, he was imported in 1975 and was a leading sire of ATA-registered stock in the 1980s.

- **Zauberklang** by Prince Condé. Chestnut Trakehner (1974). Zauberklang is a stallion with a notable record in West Germany, being Reserve Champion at his performance test, DLG show champion in 1980 and sire of the champion West German performance test stallion Markzauber and the premium stallion Turnus. He completed successfully in dressage in the United States and soon made his mark as a sire in his adopted land. His son, the grey Oldenburg Boy Oh Boy is new also a successful stallion in his own right in the USA.

Another significant group of sires in North America are the Hannoverians. Although there are still considerable numbers of ungraded and failed Hannoverian stallions at stud in the United States and Canada, sufficient numbers of high-quality animals are now available to mare owners to ensure the influence of inferior breeding stock will continue to decline. All major lines are found amongst the graded stallions in North America, and amongst the particularly noteworthy stallions to have stud in North America are:

- **Adios II** and **Adios III** (full brothers by Arsenik). Chestnut Hannoverians. Both these stallions have proved popular with mare owners, and foals sired by Adios III have been particularly praised at foal inspections.

- **Aktuell** by Absatz (Hann). Dark bay Hannoverian (1974). Imported into the United States during the late 1980s with an outstanding record as a sire, his services had already been available to American breeders through transported semen. A regular producer of highly sought-after riding horses at the Verden auctions, his record as a dressage sire is very impressive. He eventually returned to Europe, and

PEDIGREE OF **AKTUELL** – DARK BAY HANNOVERIAN, 1973			
Aktuell 314700273 (Hann)	Absatz 310405260	Abglanz (Trak) 310353442	Termit
			Abendluft
		Landmoor (Hann) H 315356	Landeck
			St Pr St Schlinka
	Violine H 316996366 (Hann)	Valentino (XX) 310394750	Nuvolari
			Valencia
		Wotansliebe (Hann) H 316215557	Wotan
			Jodlerrebe

The Hannoverian Aktuell (1974) by Absatz, a stallion of international repute, graded into a number of German stud books and imported to stand at stud in the United States at fifteen years old.

stood in Denmark for a short while.

• **Bordeaux** by Bolero. Chestnut Hannoverian (1984). A German bred stallion who completed his performance test successfully in the United States, this representative of the 'Bolero boom' has quickly

The Hannoverian DLG champion and ex-Celle stallion Dirk (1968) by Duft II, another proven sire based in North America during his latter years.

established himself at stud. Other representatives of the outstanding, but sadly short-lived Bolero (1975), by Black Sky XX, to stand in North America include Banter, Bruderhertz and Baryshnikov.

•**Dirk** by Duft II. Dark brown Hannoverian (1968). A Celle stallion until 1986, this DLG champion left behind twelve graded sons when he crossed the Atlantic. He is one of the three important sons of Duft II to stand in North America, the others being Demosthenes and Dederick, who sired some successful competition horses in West Germany.

•**Goldschlager** by Gotthard. Grey Hannoverian (1977). The only graded son of Gotthard at stud in America in the 1980s, he won his performance test in West Germany. He is very prepotent as to colour and has become equally popular with both show jumpers and dressage breeders alike. His Belgian-born Hannoverian-registered son Goldhard Z was graded in Britain in 1990.

•**Granduell** by Grande. Chestnut Hannoverian (1976). A strong horse with good movement, he is one of the few graded stallions with

PEDIGREE OF **DIRK** – DARK BROWN HANNOVERIAN, 1968			
Dirk 310417768 (Hann)	Duft II 4029	Duellant 3586	Dolman
			Forstweihe
		Gotensange H 53590	Gote
			Flügelmücke
	Semester H 62276	Senator 3898 (Hann)	Semper Idem (Trak)
			St Pr St Allerweitskleid (Hann)
		St Pr St Firnmeise H 58292	Firnis
			Abendschätzchen

both Grande and Duellant bloodlines. He proved the value of these bloodlines when coming second in his performance test and then siring competition horses.

• **Grundstein** by Graphit. Chestnut Hannoverlan (1975). He was already the top sire of dressage horses of his year in West Germany and the sire of thirteen graded sons before finding his way to America. As befits such a noted sire of dressage horses he has also worked at Grand Prix level himself, and some of his progeny have also found success as jumping horses, although used on American based mares his progeny have sometimes had a tendency to be slightly over-sized.

• **Manitu** by Matador. Bay Hannoverian (1974). This stallion was noted for his superb jumping during his performance test, but he has also produced dressage horses as well as jumpers. He has the distinction of siring both Medallion (the first American-bred stallion graded by the AHS) and Manola (the first American-bred broodmare accepted in to the AHS stud book), which could well be a unique record for a stallion.

• **Wertherson** by Werther. Chestnut Hannoverian (1983). A proven FEI-level dressage horse, whose sire produced 25 licensed sons and 40 StPrSt daughters, this stallion has already produced a number of good offspring including a top-graded mare Wall Street, who was winning in the dressage arena only seven months after being broken.

• **Wolkenflug** by Woermann. Chestnut Hannoverian (1977). An all-

The Hannoverian dressage stallion Grundstein (1975) by Graphit, noted not only for his graded sons and dressage horses but also for his show jumping progeny.

round stallion attracting mare owners breeding for a wide variety of disciplines, this Canadian-based horse has been noted for his excellent movement and potential as a show horse and hunter sire as well as a producer of dressage horses and show jumpers.

• **Wodka** by Wolfsburg. Hannoverian (1972). This stallion is the sire of Concorde, one of the first Canadian-bred Hannoverians to compete internationally. Concorde, who is out of a Thoroughbred mare, was highly placed in the 1989 show jumping World Cup final in Tampa, Florida. Wodka is from the same sire line as Wohler and competed himself in show jumping very successfully only being retired when he sustained a serious leg injury at the Los Angeles Grand Prix in 1983. Wodka stands at Spruce Meadows, in Canada, which is one of the largest Hannoverian studs outside Celle. In addition to Wodka, three further licensed breeding stallions stand there, Elute (1985) by Eiger I, the Celle stallion Goodwill (1974) by Good Match XX, and uniquely the Hannoverian-graded Thoroughbred Anforan XX (1972) by Four and Twenty. Spruce Meadows is the location of the Spruce Meadows Grand Prix and is one of the most regular purchasers of stock at Verden. It also regularly performs its own dressage quadrille with the Hannoverian stock based there.

The other breeding districts of West Germany are also well represented by stallions. For instance, Oldenburg has Frohwind Furst, Fabriano, and Furian Heisman – the five sons of the Selle Français Furioso II (1965) by Furioso XX – and the Furioso II grandson Korbel by Koeningstreur as well as Ideal by Inschallah, Le Champion by Landadel and the graphit son Grand Canyon. Westphalia is represented not only by the Olympic show jumper Starman (1979) by Carrera, but also by the much travelled Roemer by Pilatus (who is discussed more fully later on), and by Chrysos (1984), whose sire, the Trakehner Condus, was also imported into the USA, and Pelion (1980) by Pelikon.

However, the most powerful district for its size is undoubtedly that of Holstein. Unfortunately, the early days of Holstein breeding in North America was marred by a number of legal disputes and inter-society conflicts, (resolved in 1984 when the American Holstein Horse Society took over the American Association of Breeders of Holstein Horses to become the official breeding organisation), but the value of Holstein blood was such that the breeders continued in their efforts throughout some of the very difficult circumstances Considerable numbers of good young stallions have been imported since the early 1980s and these include:

- •**Cabaret** by Cor de la Bryère. Bay Holstein (1980). The only full brother of the Olympic and international champion dressage horse Corlandus, this stallion is not only a Grand Prix dressage horse but also a winner in show jumping and combined training competitions as well. His foals are very highly rated at inspections and he has already produced a graded son and several champion mares despite his heavy competition commitments.

- •**Calmé** by Calypso II. Black Holstein (1980). The sire of the graded stallion Con Brio, he is one of the many North American representatives of the bloodlines of the Holstein-graded Selle Français Cor de la Bryère (1968), by Rantzau XX, who sired twenty seven graded stallions. Calmé is closely related to the American based stallions

Columbus (1980), also by Calypso II, Constitution (1981) by Caletto I and the Cor de la Bryère son Condino (1979) amongst others.

• **Cottage Boy** by Corporal. Black Holstein (1982). This stallion is one of the rare representatives of the male line of Cottage Son XX (1944), by Young Lover, through his sire, who was one of the last of Cottage Son's fourteen graded sons.

• **Fasolt** by Farnese. Bay Holstein (1969). An early Holstein import, in West Germany he sired Flamingo (exported to Denmark as a graded stallion) and is also the sire of the American-based graded stallion Franat (1979).

• **Laredo** by Ladykiller XX. Bay Holstein (1974). Another early import, he is the senior representative of the male line of Ladykiller XX (1961), by Sailing Light. Other American-based stallions of this line have included the Spruce Meadows winner Lemgo (1981) by Landgraf I and Lordsville (1979) by Lord.

• **Manchester** by Marlon XX. Bay Holstein (1969). This horse was also graded in the Netherlands under the name Kommandeur, where he was the third-highest leading dressage sire of all time, and he produced graded sons in both countries and a total of over one hundred competition horses.

• **Racket Star** by Rapallo. Dark bay Holstein (1980). A successful competition horse, he is already proving to be a sire of note. Other American stallions of this line include Rapport (1979) by Ricardo and Rantares (1979) by Ronald.

All the major Holstein bloodlines can therefore be found in North America, but the limited number of stallions at stud, and the great distances involved for mare owners mean that much of the marketing of these stallions is done by video and shipped semen for artificial insemination is widely used. The broodmare band is also being expanded by the judicious inclusion of some American Thoroughbred mares into the stud book, the Holstein X Thorough bred being a particularly sought-after competition horse.

Dutch Warmbloods are one of the rising breeds of North America, having come on the American scene a little later than most of the German breeds. The first important stallion to be imported was Telstar (1977) by Nimmerdor, who arrived after spending three years at stud in the Netherlands and was very popular during the 1980s. Other stallions of note (apart from Kommandeur mentioned above) are:

• **Anriejetto** by Afrikaner XX. Grey Dutch warmblood. The only stallion to have been champion at dressage at Devon Breeding Show four times in a row, and a favourite with many of the top international judges in Warmblood breeding.

• **Ommen** by Abgar. Black Dutch Warmblood. A Grand Prix show jumper, whose stock are already proving to be talented performers over fences themselves.

• **Argus** by Pion. Bay Dutch Warmblood (1982). He was in the top three of his grading year in the Netherlands and he has combined a highly successful jumping career with a full book of mares since the age of five.

• **Octrooi** by Lucky Boy XX. Dutch Warmblood. Known as Best of Luck in the United States, he is a proven sire of competition horses, particularly Puissance and Grand Prix jumpers.

• **Roemer** by Pilatus. Chestnut Westphalian (1969). Although by birth a Westphalian, this stallion is generally known for his Dutch connections, because of his graded status and his record as the leading sire of dressage horses there. He is also the sire of the American-based graded stallion Winston, winner of a US Dressage Federation performance award.

The Swedish Warmblood is most strongly represented in the Grand Prix dressage Gaspari sons Elektron (1968) and Gassendi, the Iran son Three Crowns, the good-moving Imperium (1982) by Ganesco, the Indus son Spartacus (1979) and Concarneau (1972) by Caracas, who spent some time at the Piber Stud in Austria before crossing the Atlantic. Gauguin de Lully has also been widely used through imported frozen semen.

All these stallions are primarily dressage horses, and their ability to pass on movement is highly prized by American riders.

Finally, the Selle Français has also made an impact, but this time chiefly in show jumping, as might be exspected. The two Almé sons Galoubet and I Love You are mainly responsible for this, as both these world-class stallions found their way to the United States, where their nominations and youngstock often make fabulous prices. Luckily for French breeders, however, a plentiful supply of frozen semen from these stallions was built up in France before they were exported and made available for selected mares after their departure. In fact, home demand for these bloodlines proved so strong that I Love You eventually returned to stud in France, but his frozen semen remained available in North America where his stock are registered with the American Warmblood Registry.

Almé's (SF) two sons I Love You (1974), shown here, and Galoubet (1972) have both proved popular in North America, although I Love You returned to France after a short while, due to demand for his progeny at home, and has only been available through frozen semen in recent years.

FUTURE DEVELOPMENTS

It is the ability of North American owners to invest in high-quality bloodstock that is the great merit of the approach of these breeders. With the superb stallions that have been imported, the future should be bright for Warmbloods in America, but this opportunity can only be realised with tight control of standards, a developing broodmare band of equal quality and a knowledgeable market. This is where progress has to be made, but looking at the size of the industry as it is now, and its meteoric rise since 1975, the problems must be surmountable.

Chapter 13

The Australian Warmblood

by

JANE KIDD

A USTRALIA JOINED the international trend of using Warmbloods to inject rideability, elasticity and good temperament into
the country's riding horses when in 1968 Mr and Mrs Don Paul bought
Flaneur. It was the German Olympic show jumper Fritz Thiedemann
who recommended they buy the strong 17.3hh (180cm) Holsteiner
stallion as the right type to cross with Australia's tough Thoroughbred-
type mares. He arrived in 1969 and created much interest.

Further imports were made, with Holsteiners, Hannoverians (and
later Trakehners, and some Oldenburgers) being the most numerous.
Only small numbers were imported from other Warmblood breeding
countries, Swedish, Dutch and French horses having no influence in
the early years and only the Danish Warmblood offering any competition to the German breeds in the initial development of the Australian
Warmblood.

The early interest in Warmbloods was followed by a suspicious phase
as the Australians found it difficult to ride the traditional strong and
rather phlegmatic Warmbloods. There was also a lack of consistency
amongst the progeny as they were crossing the extremes of a big,
heavy-type stallion with light, spirited Thoroughbreds. Later imports
were of the more modern Warmblood with a refined head, lighter
action and more forward-going style. The greater harmony between
sires and dams led to a more predictable type of offspring.

The Australians, too, learnt more about the techniques of riding
Warmbloods, which are very different from those used on the
Thoroughbred. The latter are so sensitive that they need little more
than rein aids, but the Warmbloods usually need to have more of their
impulsion created, and this entails greater use of the seat and the legs.
A well-timed influx of European trainers and riders helped the

Australians learn about this method of riding, leading to an increased popularity in Warmbloods, further importations, and establishment of societies to set breeding standards.

The Australians have some pretty strong advantages when it comes to breeding horses. They already have a thriving industry in bloodstock breeding based mainly where the environment is most suitable, in Victoria and the south-western areas. There the temperate climate and mineral-rich soils are ideal for rearing horses. There is also a good supply of native foundation mares of Thoroughbred and Anglo-Arab origins, which are highly suitable for crossing with the Warmblood stallions.

The results of Australia's Warmblood breeding have been good with the current Australian Warmblood being of a high enough standard to be bought by Americans, Japanese and even Germans. More and more exports are going to those countries.

DEVELOPMENT OF THE AUSTRALIAN WARMBLOOD

There are no central authorities, the government does not have authority over horse breeding and it has been left to individual initiative. The Holstein Association was the first to be established in Victoria in 1972. This was renamed the German Warmblood Horse association but its title became a misnomer with the native Australian stock making a big contribution towards the development of a performance horse. Once again, the name was changed and it remains today the Australian Warmblood Horse Association (AWHA). It is, however, still orientated towards and based upon German and Dutch approaches for the breeding of performance horses.

This is the major Warmblood society in Australia with branches in each state, and twenty-two years after it started, there are horses throughout Australia that have been assessed and branded with the 'W' and there are 70 approved and licensed stallions. Standards are high, with stallions first being tested at three years, and those that pass receiving an annual licence. A full licence is only granted to stallions who go through further performance tests.

The other major general society, the Australian Warmblood and Sporthorse Association (AWSHA) was founded in 1977. It does not impose tests, but encourages breeding stock to prove itself in competitions. Annual performance awards are given in all disciplines with premium awards to breeding stock who, over a number of years, have been outstanding performers or producers of performers.

There are also Hannoverian, Holsteiner and Trakehner societies and many breeders are members of two or more. Without the central influence of government or a long tradition of breeding Warmbloods, there has been a multiplication of societies in Australia in a similar way to that in North America and Britain.

Many of these Australian breed societies keep in close contact with those in the country of origin of their breed, and the Hannoverian Verband sends a representative on an annual classification trip when mares with eligible pedigrees, including Thoroughbreds, may, if they come up to standard in conformation and action, be branded with the Hannoverian brand.

Until the mid-1980s most of the top stallions were imported, but after this some Australian Warmbloods began to come to the fore. The most outstanding of these is Stirling Luther by Ludendorf, and he is owned by Dirk Dijkstra, the president of the Victoria branch of the AWHA. He stands at one of the most active centres for Australian Warmblood breeding, the Australian Equestrian Academy and Stud and he has produced amongst others the 1994 Medium Dressage Champion Apprack Talisman. Northern Congress is another Australian Warmblood stallion and he had the highest score at the Victoria Warmblood performance test for jumping when free and under saddle. He has Holstein blood on both sides being by the imported Contact (Holst), and out of a Flaneur (Holst) mare. His son Northern Classic is a dressage winner and stands at the River Range Warmblood Stud.

BREEDING POLICY

In the early years of Warmblood breeding it has been difficult to formulate a clear breeding policy as there is no strong central authority. Two different approaches have been developed with the AWHA imposing, as the Europeans do, stringent tests for all breeding stock, with a pass or fail system, and the AWSHA allowing the stock to prove themselves in competitions and recording their results.

Most of the stallions imported into Australia have not confined their activities to breeding but have been used in the competition arena, mainly dressage and show jumping. The trend in Australia Warmblood breeding appears to be similar to Thoroughbred practices, i.e. proof of the breeding stock by their own and their stocks' performance. This is a healthy situation although it does take a longer time to achieve results in competitions than in racing.

The Australian Warmblood Horse Association organises a Warmblood Stallion Gala Day when three-year-old colts are judged for conformation, movement and jumping ability when free. At four years of age those stallions who have passed this classification have to pass a performance test before they can hold a permanent licence. Only progeny by a licensed stallion can be registered with the AWHA.

To be given an AWHA birth certificate the foal must have registered parents, and the dam need not be a Warmblood as Thoroughbred and Anglo-Arab mares with a pedigree of three generations can, if classified, be foundation stock. The foal is then branded, and at three years old can apply for classification.

From 1990 onwards the AWHA has rewarded performance with High Point Performance awards for the Warmblood with the most Equestrian Federation of Australia points in dressage, show jumping, eventing and showing.

This is also the approach of the Australian Warmblood Sport horse Association which awards annual premiums for outstanding Warmblood sport horses. It issues annual stallion breeding permits, as does the Holsteiner Horse Association of Australia. The Trakehner Society of Australasia does too, but because it is recognised under contract and licensed by the Trakehner Verband in Germany, only stallions which have passed the German selection test are eligible.

There is also an Australian Trakehner Association which covers a further group of Trakehners, and the Hannoverian Society of Australia.

The Holsteins are represented by the Holsteiner Horse Association of Australia Ltd. The imports for the Western Australia branch include the performance-tested stallions Talisman and Wildfleur; for Queensland, Monopol by Moltek I, Falkland by Farnese and Lander by Lorenz; and for Victoria, Romedio by Rigoletto.

IMPORTANT BLOODLINES

With few Warmbloods in Australia until the late 1970s, the rather disjointed development due to the size of the country, and the multiplication and overlapping of breed societies, it is not yet possible to establish a clear picture about important bloodlines, but some of the most influential stallions are mentioned below.

It was **Flaneur**, born in 1964, who started Warmblood breeding in Australia. He was a Holsteiner by Fax whose dam was an Anglo Arab. A big strong horse, he produced good middleweight horses then crossed with the Australian Thoroughbred, Anglo-Arab and other light foundation mares. Many of his sons became stallions including Canellor, Grand Flaneur, Pfrinzen and Arctic Vision.

The other important Holsteiner to come to Australia was **Contact**, who was by the great Cor de la Bryère. He has an excellent jumping pedigree and produced stock with good jumps, including the classified stallion Northern Congress who now stands with his father at the Northern Warmblood stud.

Of the Trakehners it is probably **Kassiber** by Ibikus who has had most influence. His progeny include Neversfelde Kensington the 1994 Grand Prix Special Dressage Champion. Kassiber a bay Trakehner stallion had an excellent performance record himself, having been in the German eventing team at the European Championships, and becoming the 1983 One day Event Champion of Australia. He died in 1990, but his line is being carried on by his son Solo II who won the 1994 Australian Medium and Advanced Medium Championships and is standing at the stud of Mary Hanna the Australian Grand Prix champion.

The bay Trakehner stallion Kassiber, a former international event horse whose progeny are proving successful in all disciplines.

Another son is Foxground Klimke, who was the only three-year-old to be classified in New South Wales in his year.

The first important Hannoverian was **Domherr** by Dominic, out of a Wulf mare; he died in 1989. This rather old-fashioned type was performance-tested in Germany,was a good cross with Australia's Thoroughbred mares and produced the 1992 Olympic gold medallist

Kibah-Tic-Toc who was out of the Thoroughbred mare Sandrift. Donherr has sons standing at stud in Heyde Donnezaar and the 1994 Intermediaire I Dressage Champion Time after Time. Then there is **Daktylus** (1979) by Diskus, the sire of the great show jumper The Natural. Daktylus passed his performance test in Germany. **Winterkoenig** (1979) by Woermann, is a Hannoverian who traces back to Abglanz and should produce dressage horses. He has also been performance tested in Germany.

Then there is **Duellschutz**, a Hannoverian who made his name when based at Hanlueg Stud owned by Mr R. Crosby. He was performance-tested in Germany and has produced such good stock as the 1988 Olympic show jumper Schnapps and the Grand Prix dressage horse Duell Diablo. A more recent Hannoverian import is **Moselfischer** (1979) by Mozart who was brought to Australia by Theo Wagner of the Treehaven Equestrian Centre. Moselfischer had already passed his performance test in Germany. Since coming to Australia he has won advanced dressage tests and been placed in Prix St Georges and has sons who are approved stallions.

Ludendorf is by Luciano, out of the state premium mare Elfit. He

The Hannoverian Moselfischer (1979) by Mozart, a Prix St Georges dressage horse and proving to be a successful sire of competition horses.

threw two licensed stallions out of his first and only crop of six foals in Germany. After arriving in Australia he won the national novice two-day event title, the elementary and medium dressage championships, and has competed in Grand Prix. His son Stirling Luther was champion stallion at Melbourne in 1988, and two of his sons have been exported, one to stand at stud in Columbia and another in Indonesia.

Kilof McOhl by Kilof, is a Danish Warmblood and has himself won one-day events before converting into a top dressage horse and coming second twice in the Haig Cup. His progeny, which includes Kormoran McOhl and Abdullah McOhl, are winning at Prix St Georges level.

Dutchman by Le Mexico, a Dutch Warmblood is full brother to the licensed stallion Zelham and one of his sons has won the Perth Royal Champion stallion. Although Dutchman scored well in the performance test in the Netherlands, because he did not get as high marks as his brother, he was free to be exported.

Leonardo by Lungau was performance-tested in Germany and

Aachen by Argentinus, an Oldenburg stallion who was performance-tested in Germany and now stands at stud in Australia.

graded into both the Oldenburg and Hannoverian societies. In Australia he has been the national elementary champion, the High Point stallion and the ACT medium champion. Other Oldenburg stallions who were also performance-tested in Germany before arriving in Australia include Valeur by Volturno and Aachen by Argentinus.

The Danish Warmblood **Valuta** by Dominent, out of an Alf mare, was the champion stallion at the Melbourne Royal in 1982, 1983, and 1985. He is a Grand Prix and Grand Prix Special dressage winner.

THE AUSTRALIAN INFLUENCE

The quality of the imports, the excellent Australian foundation stock, the conducive environment in the south west of the country and the enthusiasm of the breeders has resulted in some high-class stock being produced. In Australia the Warmblood can be given a certain toughness and stamina from the mares and the climate, which is difficult to acquire in Europe. Certainly Kibah-Tic-Toc's gold medal gave Warmbloods in general and Australia's in particular a great boost especially as he won the ultimate prize in three-day eventing under such demanding conditions. The Australians had produced a very tough Warmblood with considerable power of endurance and disproved the critics who claimed Warmbloods lacked stamina. As yet exports have been limited but New Zealand has been a beneficiary with one of its graded stallions, Sacramento, being a grandson of the original Warmblood sire, Flaneur.

Vancouver II by Happy Day is an exciting import as he stood at Sweden's Flyinge stud and when ridden by Kyra Kyrklund was successful in international dressage.

Two further important imports have been made by the Val d'Argent Stud. These are Biathlon by Bolero who was the 1994 Champion Warmblood Stallion at Sydney Royal Show and the Dutch Warmblood Gullit by Ulf who won the 1993 Australian Novice dressage championship.

Thanks to the more extensive and successful use of AI, Australians are now not having to rely on imported stock. Such top stallions as Wellington, Flemmingh, Olympic Ahorn and Waltzertakt have Australian-born produce.

Chapter 14

The New Zealand Warmblood
by
JANE KIDD

NEW ZEALAND HAS some of the most favourable conditions in the world for breeding horses. The climate is temperate and the grass grows year round, both of which make the rearing relatively cheap. The results are more horses per head of population than anywhere else in the world.

New Zealand's Thoroughbreds are famous internationally, as are her polo ponies and eventers, for which there are two major sources, retired racehorses and sheep and cattle station produce reared to tend the animals in rugged country. The latter are close to Thoroughbred but with a touch of Clydesdale or Cleveland Bay and they are bred free, the stallion running loose with his mares.

The main native New Zealand stock which is, or is close to, Thoroughbred is much tougher than the northern hemisphere counterparts because of an out-of-doors upbringing. Even the most valuable Thoroughbreds spend little of their time in stables. This stock does, however, have the typical Thoroughbred action of long, sweeping strides and lacks the elasticity and spring looked for by so many show jumpers and dressage riders. The desire for these attributes led to importations of Warmblood stallions in the mid 1970s. The tough Thoroughbred-type native mares are ideal for cross-breeding with Warmbloods into whom they can inject stamina and 'class'.

Various societies sprang up to cover the development of the New Zealand Warmblood: the New Zealand Sports Horse Association, which, like its Australian counterpart, places emphasis on performance information; and the New Zealand Warmblood Breeders' Association, which has been gradually introducing grading standards for the breeding stock. There were close ties too with the Hannoverian Verband, and the Hannoverian Society of New Zealand was the first

Antipodean society licensed to produce Hannoverians. This permission was then granted to Australia, which means that in both countries Thoroughbred mares can be branded if passed by inspectors. Their stock then has the right to be branded and registered, but for substantial fees, which is reducing the demand.

DEVELOPMENT OF THE NEW ZEALAND WARMBLOOD

The first stallions to be brought in were from Britain and Australia, and although by Hannoverians, had not gone through the grading system in Germany. It was Bob Berkhan of Ngaruawahia who had the initiative to take this first step in Warmblood breeding and he still stands Mount Everest by Ferdi, one of these original imports. Wöhler II by Wöhler who died in 1948 and was another of his imports. This stallion has moved around the country spending some seasons in South Island before going to Auckland with John Smith.

The first registered Hannoverians were brought in by a syndicate under the leadership of Nick Williams, the Olympic dressage judge, Mrs Tiny White, an international dressage rider and judge, and Eric Ropiha. They imported stock which had passed all its tests in Germany and their first, **Winnebago** (1972) by Winnetou, produced some high-class horses including Mark Todd's Olympic show jumper Bago and Andrew Nicholson's eventer Tempo. Sadly he had fertility problems, so was only a short time at stud.

Witzbold, also by Winnetou, was another stallion brought in by this syndicate and he produced Grand prix dressage horses Oliver, Witzstein and Mosaic. The example they set led to further syndicates being formed: Rupert and Anne Vallance headed one which brought in **Distelfink** by Diskus; and Te Peka Stud was another who in 1987 imported the three-year-old **Genius** by Garibaldi I and out of the Diskus mare Dreamy. Kevin Cholmondeley-Smith imported **Allermund** by Absatz and although only at stud for two seasons produced international jumpers.

Importations were also made from Holland, the first being **Ramzes II** by Rigoletto, and later **The Immigrant** by Formateur, Polaris by Luxus, **Urban** by Makelaar and **Oldenburg** by Inschallah X.

Two veterinarians, Brian Pyke and Sylvia McLean headed syndicates which chose the Trakehner breed. The first to come in on loan from Australia for five seasons was the Grade A show jumper **Polarschnee** by Gazal by Gazal VII, and his dam was Polarrose, the youngest daughter of one of the best Trakehner mares to reach West

Germany, Polarfahrt. One of his first New Zealand-born sons Jaegermeister II was ridden by Andrew Nicholson at the World Equestrian Games. But he was soon followed by the attractive son of the Danish Trakehner Chopstick, **Falkansee**, who is there to stay.

The one Holstein amongst the original imports was Sacramento, who is a second-generation Australian Holstein as his grandparents Flaneur and Romedio were imported. His sire is Siegfried.

Jaguar, a Belgian Warmblood, is proving himself as a competitor being successful in dressage and show jumping.

With the expense of the journey from Europe and the abundance of high-class Thoroughbreds available for breeding, very few broodmares were imported. The tough native New Zealand mares, usually Thoroughbred but occasionally Arab or Anglo-Arab, are playing an important part in the development of the New Zealand Warmblood. A sire who is likely to attract New Zealand-bred warmblood mares is Sambruk a Thoroughbred by Kris whose first stock won in hand classes. Another exciting import is the Selle Francais stallion Valliant by Galoubet who competed successfully in the USA.

BREEDING POLICY

The first to impose standards in New Zealand was the Hannoverian Breeders' Association of Australia and New Zealand which organised annual inspections by representatives of the Hannoverian Verband in Germany. They considered only Thoroughbred mares over $15.3^1/_2$hh (160cms). Those with good paces and conformation were branded and their progeny registerable in both Germany and New Zealand. This resulted in a good standard of broodmare being bred to the Hannoverians in those early years of Warmblood breeding in New Zealand, and consequently a good class of progeny.

The New Zealand Warmblood Breeders' Association has been growing and works with two further societies for Trakehners and Holsteins. The Warmblood Association started by running an annual show and it has now introduced a policy to encourage the higher standards of breeding.

The breeding goal is a noble, correctly built Warmblood horse capable of superior performance, a horse with natural impulsion and space-gaining elastic movements, a horse which, because of temperament, character and willingness is suited as an all-round riding horse.

Their stallions are eligible for the stud book if they have been licensed, successfully performance-tested in Europe, and inspected upon arrival in New Zealand. Imported stallions that are licensed, but not performance-tested, are eligible for the appendix. New Zealand-bred stallions are eligible for this appendix if they are registered, out of a mare with four generations of traceable pedigree, have passed a veterinary inspection and one for conformation and paces.

Stallions in the appendix are eligible for the stud book if before seven years of age they finish a novice one-day horse trial in the top 50% of the competitors and gain at least 55% of the marks in the dressage. Older stallions may qualify by winning five times at elementary level dressage, being placed in the first three five times in Grade B show jumping or intermediate horse trials.

This appears to be a very practical solution to the performance testing, a sensible adaption of Continental practices for a country lacking the trained riders found in Europe, who are essential if all stallions are to be given an equal chance in the specifically designed stallion performance test. For the stallions that qualify through the novice horse trials there is also a rideability test as this has been found to be one of the most important indicators of the stallion's potential as a successful sire. An expert rides the horse and reports on his willingness to work. This report is published together with the results of the performance test but the rules have proved rather stringent and only two stallions

Winnebago by Winnetou, the first graded Hannoverian stallion to be imported into New Zealand.

passed in the first three years.

A stallion can be upgraded from the appendix through the successes of his progeny. If they perform well in dressage, show jumping and/or horse trials the committee can put the sire in the stud book.

Mares are subject to similar grading and are accepted for the appendix if they have pedigrees tracing through four generations or more and after passing an inspection for conformation and paces and a veterinary examination. To be listed in the stud book mares must pass that performance test at a novice horse trial or have performed well in dressage, show jumping and/or horse trials. Again successful progeny is another means of entry into the stud book.

The highest grade is the Elite mare, a title which is awarded to those whose progeny or themselves have performed with distinction.

New Zealand is gradually developing the standards which will help her to ensure the best stock is used for the breeding of the Warmblood. Traditions have not helped this development as haphazard economical breeding has been quite effective. Large numbers of horses have been produced running free on the stations. The ordinary ones were needed as station hacks; the occasional exceptional one could be directed into the more demanding market for performance horses.

Today such large numbers are not being produced, as the farmer uses the motorbike more and more to herd his animals. At the same time some expensive Warmbloods have been imported that should not rely on being put to large numbers of mares to produce the odd good foal. The more selective methods became important and farmers are adjusting to the more disciplined approach to breeding that this requires.

The Sports Horse Promotion Board receives some government funds and registers all non racing stock. It has no grading requirements for breeding stock but uses data to prove stallions, mares and their progeny through their results in competitions. Stock has been branded with a kiwi symbol but future plans are simply to use NZ.

THE NEW ZEALAND INFLUENCE

There is no doubt that New Zealand has the right basics, with its climate, grass and agrarian-orientated economy, to produce top class horses. There are as yet too few New Zealand Warmbloods to assess their influence, but Bago by Winnebago showed his jumping ability by getting into the second round of the individual contest at the Seoul Olympics, Monopoly by Witzbold won the 1989 Horse of the Year Show Jumper with Jon Cottle before being sold to the USA, and Willoughby by Wöhler II is competing with success in Prix St Georges in the USA.

Winnebago also produced the first New Zealand born Warmblood stallion, Hahndorf, to pass the performance test and go into the stud book by virtue of being an elementary dressage horse and intermediate eventer. His stock include Medium Dressage horses Charlton Commander and Charlton Clem. Polarshnee, the Trakehner, has a son, Loewennerz, who has been passed for the appendix, as has Polaris, the Dutch Warmblood whose son Trick or Treat passed those same inspections and has sired the 1994 Champion Sport Horse colt Fleetson. Perhaps the most interesting young stallion to be licensed is Uraeus, as he is the first generation of New Zealand Warmblood on both sides being by Polaris and out of Karika, who was by Ramzes II and her dam was by Mount Everest. His daughter Bitte Schön as a four-year-old won the Wellington Dressage Preliminary Championships.

Bibliography

BOOKS

BARMINZEV, J.N., *Russlands Pferde*, Albert Müller Verlag, Zurich, 1978.

CHRISTENSEN, I.C., *Kronen & Bolgen*, Dansk Varmblod, Aarhus, 1987.

DOLENC, M., *Lipica*, Mladinska Knija, Ljubljana, Yugoslavia, 1980.

DOSSENBACH, M., DOSSENBACH, H. D. and KÖHLER, H.J. (trans Loman, D.), *Great Stud Farms of the World*, Thames and Hudson, London, England, 1977.

FRIEDHOFF, F., MARAHENS, F. and SCHETTLER, R. (eds), *Pferdezucht im Wandel: Festschrift für Gerd Lehmann 25 Jahr Landstallmeister in Warendorf*, Landwirtschaftsverlag GmBH, Munster-Hiltrup, 1991

GRAUMANN, G. and STEIN, H-H., *Das Holsteiner Sportpferde*, W. Keller & Co., Stuttgart, 1980.

HARTLEY EDWARDS, E. (ed), *A Standard Guide to Horse and Pony Breeds*, Macmillan, Basingstoke, England, 1980.

KIDD, J., *Horsemanship in Europe*, J. A. Allen, London, England, 1977.

KÖHLER, H.J., *Hannoversche Pferde: Geschichte, Zucht, Erfolge*, Reich Verlag AG, Lucerne, Switzerland, 1978.

LIDNER, N-O and FREDRICSON, I., *Flyinge 1661-1986*, Stiftelsen Svergises Avels och Hastsportscentrum, Flyinge, Sweden, 1986.

MACHIN GOODALL, D., *The Flight of the East Prussian Horses*, David and Charles, Newton Abbot, England, 1973.

ROSSOW, D. (trans Smarslik, K. N.), *Stallion Book of the Holsteiner Warmblood Breed 1952-1986*, Holsteiner Federation of West Germany/American Holsteiner Horse Association Inc.

SCHAFER, M., (trans Dent, A.), *An Eye for a Horse*, J.A. Allen, London, England, 1980.

SCHILKE, F., *Das Ostpreussische Warmblutferde*, BLV Verlagsgesellschaft, Munich, Germany, 1974 (originally published in 1938).

SCHILKE, F., (trans Gibble, H.K.), *Trakehner Horses: Then and Now*; American Trakehner Association, Norman OA, USA, 1974.

SCHLIE, A., *Der Hannoveraner*, BLV Verlags Gesellschaft, Munich, 1977.

VON STENGLIN, GRAF C. (trans Belton, C.), *The Hannoverian*, J. A. Allen, London, England, 1990.

STRICKLAND, C. *The Warmblood Guidebook*, Half Halt Press, Maryland, 1992.

SYMANCYZK, K., *Des Westfälische Pferd: Zucht und Sport*, BLV Verlagschellschaft, Munich, 1987.

244

VON THUN-HOHENSTEIN, GRAF R., *Das Holsteiner Pferd*, L. B. Ahnert Verlag, Friedberg, Germany, 1977.

VON VELSEN-ZERWECK, E. and SCHULTE, E. (trans Belton, C.) *The Trakehner*, J.A. Allen, London, England, 1990.

ANNUAL PUBLICATIONS

American Horses in Sport, The Chronicle of the Horse, Middleburg VA, USA.

AMMANN, M. E. (ed), *L'Année Hippique/Das Internationale Pferdesportjahr/The International Equestrian Year*, L'Année Hippique, Best, The Netherlands.

Directory of Approved Stallions, National Stallion Association, Knutsford, England.

EYLERS, B., *Ausgewählte Hengste Deutschlands: Ein Jahrbuch der Hengste*, Bernd Eylers, Hude, Germany.

Hingstar i Enskild Ago Verksamma inom Svensk Halvblodsavel, Tidningen Ridsport, Trosa, Sweden.

Hingstar vid Stiftelsen Sveriges Avels och Hastsportoentrum, Flyinge, Tidningen Ridsport, Trosa, Sweden.

HOOGEN, M. VAN DEN (ed), *Europees Hengstenboek*, Uitgeverij Hippocreen, Mariaheide, The Netherlands.

Jahrbuch Zucht: Leistungen und daten der Deutschen Pferdezucht, FN Verlag, Warendorf, Germany.

MANZONI, G. and PELLEGRINI, A. (eds), *Gli Stalloni in Italia*, Il Mio Cavallo, Milan, Italy.

MELISSEN, J., *The Leading Stallions of The Netherlands*, Jacob Melissen BV, Pesse, The Netherlands.

MONNERON, F-H. (ed), *Annuaire de L'étalon Sport Français*, Haras de River Editions, Irvy-la-Bataille, France.

SCHION, D. (ed), *Trakehner Almanach*, Edition S, Wentorf, Germany.

JOURNALS AND PERIODICALS

BWBS News Published bi-annually by the British Warm-Blood Society, 4th Street, National Agricultural Centre, Kenilworth Park, Warks CV8 2LG England.

Der Hannoveraner and *Hannoversches Pferde* Both published bi-monthly by Peragon Verlag, Verden, Germany.

Dressage Magazine and *Showjumping Magazine* Both published monthly by Cecile Park Publishing, 55-63 Goswell Road, London EC1V 7EN

Het Belgisch Warmbloedpaard Published bi-monthly by Het Belgisch

Warmbloedpaard, Postbus 111, 3000 Leuven, Belgium.

Hippologisk Published monthly by Nørhaven Bogtrykkeri, Copenhagen, Denmark.

Horse and Hound Published weekly by IPC Magazines Ltd, London, England (first and second Show issues and Competition Horse issue, all published in March, particularly important).

L'Eperon Published by L'Eperon, 10 rue Guynemer, 92130 Issy-les-Moulineaux, France.

Oldenburger Sportferd Published bi-monthly by Verland der Züchter des Oldenburger Pferdes eV, 26093 Oldenburg, Postfach 4908, 26123 Oldenburg, Germany.

Pferde und Sport in Schleswig-Holstein und Hamburg Published by Verlag Pferde und Sport, Hamburg, Germany.

Reiter Pferde in Westfalen: Magazin für Pferdezucht and Reitsport Published monthly by Landwirtschaftsverlag GmbH, Hulsebrockstraße 2, 48165 Münster, Germany.

Rheinlands Reiter Pferde Published monthly by the Verband der Reit und Fahtvereine Rheinland eV, Germany.

Ridehesten Published monthly by Forlaget Wiegaarden, 9500 Hobro, Denmark.

Ridsport Published monthly by Tidningen Ridsport, Trosa, Sweden.

The Chronicle of the Horse Published weekly by The Chronicle of the Horse, PO Box 46, Middleburg VA 22117, USA (mid-December stallion issue particularly important).

Trakehner Hefte Published monthly by Symposion-Verlag, Wagnerstrasse 12, 73728 Esslingen, Germany.

Visa Z Magazine Published quarterly by Cooperation Studbook Zangersheide, Domein Zangersheide, 3620 Lanaken, Belgium.

Warmblood News Published bi-monthly by Warmblood News, PO Box 15167, Tallahassee, FL 32317-5167, USA

Brands

AUSTRALIAN WARMBLOOD   NEW ZEALAND WARMBLOOD

BELGIAN WARMBLOOD

ZANGERSHEIDE STUD

BELGIAN SPORT HORSE

DANISH WARMBLOOD

DUTCH WARMBLOOD

SWEDISH WARMBLOOD

SELLE FRANÇAIS

ANGLO ARAB

BRITISH WARMBLOOD

BAVARIAN
WARMBLOOD

BADEN-WÜRTEMBURG

GERMAN RIDING
HORSE

BERLIN-BRANDENBURG

HANNOVERIAN

HESSEN

HOLSTEIN

MECKLENBURG-
VORPOMMERN

OLDENBURG

RHEINLAND

RHEINLAND-PFALZ-
SAAR (ZWEIBRÜCKEN)

SACHSEN

SACHSEN-ANHALT

TRAKEHNER

THÜRINGEN

WESTPHALIAN

Useful Addresses

American Hannoverian Society, 4059 Iron Works Pike, Lexington, KY 40511, USA

American Holstein Horse Association, 222 East Main Street, 1 Georgetown, KY 40324, USA

American Trakehner Association, 1520 West Church Street, Newark, OH 43055, USA

American Warmblood Registry Inc, PO Box 15167, Talahassee, FL 32317-5167, USA

American Warmblood Society, 6801 Wromley, Phoenix, AZ 85043, USA

Anglo-European Warmblood Studbook, PO Box 61, Tonbridge Wells, Kent, TN3 9AJ, England

Association de Éléveurs du Cheval Normand (ADNECO), BP 360, 50010 St Lô, Cedex, France

Australian Warmblood Horse Association (Victoria), RMB 4000, Mt Wallace 3342, Victoria, Australia

Avelsföreningen för Svenska Varmblodiga Hasten, 240 32 Flyinge, Sweden

Belgische Warmbloedpaard VZW, Minderbroedersstraat 8, P. B. 11, B-3000 Leuven, Belgium

British Bavarian Warmblood Association, Sittyton, Straloch, Newmacher, Aberdeen, AB2 0KP, Scotland

British Hannoverian Horse Society, Midwinter Lodge, Manshill, Bossingham, Canterbury, Kent, CT4 6ED, England

British Horse Database, 52-60 Sanders Road, Wellingborough, Northants, NN88 4BX, England

British Sports Horse Register, 4th Street, National Agricultural Centre, Stoneleigh, Warks, CV8 2LG, England

British Warm-Blood Society, 4th Street, National Agricultural Centre, Stoneleigh, Warks, CV8 2LG, England

Dansk Varmblod, Landskontoret for Heste, udkaersvej 15, Skejby 8200, Aarhus N, Denmark

Deutsche Reiterliche Vereiningung eV (FN), 4410 Warendorf 1, Germany

International Hunter Futurity, PO Box 13244, Lexington, KY 40583-8244, USA

International Jumper Futurity, PO Box 2830, Roseville, CA 95746, USA

Koninklijke Vereniging Warmbloed Paardenstamboek in Nederland, Postbus 382, 3700 AJ Zeist, The Netherlands

International Sporthorse Registry and Oldenburg Verband NA, PO Box 849, Streamwodd, IL 60107, USA

Landesferdzüchtverband Berlin-Brandenburg eV, Hauptgestut 10, 16845 Neustadt/Dosse, Germany

Landesverband Bayerischer Pferdzüchter eV, Landeshamer Strasse 11, 81929 München, Germany

National Light Horse Breeding Society (HIS), 96 High Street, Edenbridge, Kent, TN8 5AR, England

National Stallion Association, School Farm, School Lane, Pickmere, Knutsford, Cheshire, WA16 0JF, England

New Zealand Warmblood Breeders' Association, RD1, Te Kuiti, New Zealand

North American Department of the Royal Dutch Warmblood Studbook (NA/KWPN), PO Box 828, Winchester, OR 97495-0828, USA

North American District of the Belgian Warmblood Breeding Association, 5749 General Hunton Road, Broad Run, VA 22014, USA

North American Selle Français Horse Association Inc, PO Box 646, Winchester, VA 22604-0646, USA

North American Trakehner Association, 1660 Collier Road, Akron, OH 44320, USA

Pferdezüchtverband Baden-Württemburg eV, Heinrich-Baumann Strasse 1-3, 71090 Stuttgart, Germany.

Pferdezüchtverband Rheinland-Pfalz-Saar eV, Pferdezentrum, 67816 Standenbühl, Germany.

Pferdeszuchtverband Sachsen eV, Winterberg Strasse 98, 01237 Dresden, Germany

Pferdezüchtverband Sachsen-Anhalt eV, Frommhagen Strasse 55, 39576 Stendal, Germany

Rheinisches Pferdestammbuch eV, Endenicher Allee 60, 53115 Bonn, Germany.

The Scottish Dutch Warmblood Association, Sherifhall Mains, Millerhall, Nr Dalkeith, Midlothian EH22 1RX, Scotland.

Service de Haras et d'Equitation, 14 Avenue de la Grand Armée, 75017 Paris, France.

SIRE, 19230 Arnac, Pomadour, France.

Studbook Zangersheide, Domein Zangersheide, 3620 Lanaken, Belgium.

Swedish Warmblood Association of North America, PO Box 1587, Coupeville, WA 98239, USA

Swiss National Stud, 1580 Avenches, Switzerland.

L'Union Nationale Interprofessionelle du Cheval (UNIC), 51 Rue Dumont d'Urville, 75116 Paris, France.

Verband Hannoverscher Warmblutzuchter eV, Lindhooper Strasse 92, 2810, Verden, Germany.

Verband Hessicher Pferdezüchter eV, Thomee Strasse 3, 34117 Kassel, Germany.

Verband der Pferdezucheter Mecklenburg-Vorpommern eV, Speicher Strasse 11, 18273 Güshow, Germany.

Verband Thüringer Pferdezüchter eV, Liszt Strasse 4, 99423, Weimar, Germany.

Verband der Zuchter des Holsteiner Pferdes eV, Steenbekerweg 151, 24106 Kiel, Germany.

Verband der Zuchter des Oldenburg Pferdes, Donnerschweer Strasse 72-80, 26123 Oldenburg, Germany.

Verband der Zuchter und Freunde des Ostpreussichen Warmblutferdes Trakehner Abstammung eV, Max-Eyth Strasse 10, 24537, Neumunster, Germany.

Weatherbys Stud Book, Sanders Road, Wellingborough, Northants NN8 4BX, England.

Westfalen Warmblood Association of America, 18432 Biladeau Lane, Penn Valley, CA 95946, USA.

Westfalisches Pferdestambuch eV, Sudmuhlenstrasse 33, 48157

Munster-Handorf, Germany.

World Breeding Championship for Sport Horses, PO Box 245, 5680 AE Best, The Netherlands.

Zuchtverband für Deutsch Pferde eV, Johanniswall 2, 27283 Verden, Germany.

Acknowledgements

THE AUTHORS would like to thank the following people for their valuable help and advice in preparing this book: Dr Eberhard Senckenberg, Verband der Züchter und Freunde des Ostpreussischen Warmblutpferdes Trakehner Abstammung eV; Dr Ludwig Christmann, Verband Hannoverscher Warmblutzüchter eV; Verband der Züchter des Oldenburger Pferdes eV; Dr Hanno Dohn, Rheinisches Pferdestammbuch eV; P. and E. Millot and T. Carbanne, Élévage de la Guyardière; Count Joja Lewenhaupt; Mrs Tøve Højergaard, Dansk Varmblod; Per Høst Madsen; Hans Kingmans, KWPN; Hank Mindermann, Anglo-Dutch Breeders Association; Professor Ewald Sasimow-ski, Institute of Animal Breeding and Production Technology, Poland; Magyar Totenyesztes; Dr Pal Janox; Dr Varady Jeno; Mrs John Parker; Vivienne Burdon; Margaret Hansen; Sonja Karschau-Lowenfish, Warmblood News; Theo Wagner; Kalman de Jurenak, formerly Verband Hannoverscher Warmblutzüchter eV; Libby Sauer; Belinda Klatte; Nick Williams; Sara Williams; Herr Wilhelm Ayecke; Lady Victoria von Wachter; Natalie Kilpatrick; Graham Davies; John Rose.

PICTURE CREDITS

Deutsches Reiterliche Vereinigung eV 24; H. Sting 43, 45; Werner Ernst 48, 55, 59, 61, 63, 64, 65, 66, 67, 81, 82, 83, 85, 87, 90, 98, 101, 103, 107, 213, 219, 222, 223, 225, 234, 235, 236; Helmar Mutschler 95; Y. de la Fosse-David 118, 123; Rik van Lent 131, 137, 138; Jan Gyllensten 133, 139; Jens Peter Aggesen 145; Jørgen Bak Rasmussen 146, 152; Sven Fogh 149; Ib Nicolajsen 154; Jochmann Disco 158; John Birt 160; Jacob Melissen 161, 189; Ellen van Leeuwen 164; Bob Langrish 180, 200, 206; Sally Anne Thompson 186; Hamish Mitchell 196; Photo Delcourt 229.

Index

This index is a selective one, due to restrictions of space, and concentrates on citing the more significant and internationally important horses mentioned in the book. References to illustrations are in *italic*, and to tables of bloodlines in **bold**.